"*One Year to Better Pre*
preaching not just in one
seek to follow Daniel Overdorf's insightful advice."
—*Scott M. Gibson, Haddon W. Robinson Professor of Preaching and
Director of the Center for Preaching,
Gordon-Conwell Theological Seminary*

"The only thing worse than listening to a dry, tasteless, colorless sermon is preaching one! That is why I am so glad that an effective communicator like Daniel Overdorf has taken the time to identify some creative ways to sharpen the tools we preachers turn to in our study each week. Thanks for the book, Daniel, and I'm sure my congregation will thank you as well!"
—*Gary Brandenburg, Lead Pastor,
Fellowship Bible Church, Dallas, Texas*

"If you are a growing preacher, then you should be better at your craft a year from now than you are today. Here are some exercises you can do each week that will help you grow stronger as a communicator of God's truth."
—*Haddon W. Robinson, Harold John Ockenga Distinguished Professor
of Preaching and Senior Director of Doctor of Ministry Program,
Gordon-Conwell Theological Seminary*

"The gospel is ever fresh and renewing, but many preachers fall into ruts when speaking about it. Even preachers who make a conscientious effort to keep up with new developments in preaching are not always able to find the newest insights or to keep up with recent approaches to preaching. Daniel Overdorf's *One Year to Better Preaching* puts into one volume many of the most exciting themes to emerge in the preaching ministry in the last generation. Each week this bright new voice in preaching introduces the preacher to a new perspective on the sermon, offers practical exercises for putting that perspective into practice, and adds a bibliography for further reading. Subjects range from how we interact with Scripture to paying attention to listener tendencies to bringing children into the process of sermon preparation. Preachers who follow this plan will not only find that their sermons will become more vital witnesses to the gospel, but that their own worlds will enlarge and they will have a lot of fun in the process."
—*Ronald J. Allen, Professor of Preaching and Gospels and Letters,
Christian Theological Seminary*

"Daniel Overdorf is creative, thorough, and practical—a great combination! These insightful exercises, combined with the books, articles, and websites he mentions, will greatly impact anyone's preaching."
—*Donald R. Sunukjian, Professor of Christian
Ministry and Leadership, Homiletics Chair,
Talbot School of Theology, Biola University*

"Put these exercises into practice and you will not, you cannot, fail to improve in your preaching. These steps are practical and within reach of anyone ready to apply themselves. Daniel Overdorf, one of evangelicals' leading young homileticians, has given a gift to those who take seriously Paul's admonition to let 'our progress be seen by all.'"

—Jeff C. Magruder, Associate Professor of Bible and Church Ministries, Southwestern Assemblies of God University

"Daniel Overdorf has written a practically simple, one-year guide that will strengthen every preacher. Whether you have preached for over twenty-five years, or you are just beginning, you'll need a coach to guide you from time to time. This book includes a year's worth of spiritual workouts that will help keep all preachers at their sermonic best."

—Mike Baker, Senior Pastor, Eastview Christian Church, Normal, Illinois

"Veterans and beginners in the art of preaching will benefit from Daniel Overdorf's creative and unique approach to improving communication skills. His experience in both the church and the academy give Dr. Overdorf an especially helpful perspective, and it will be well worth your while to spend a year with him. The exercises are so fascinating that you will be tempted to move even faster."

—Mike Shannon, Professor of Preaching, Cincinnati Christian University

"Every growing preacher senses the need, in Stephen Covey's words, to sharpen the saw. Rust happens, and both pulpit and pew join voices in calling for a resource that encourages growth in preaching and the preacher. Daniel Overdorf has done us all a great service in supplying such a resource. Sensitivity to the preacher's person, skills, and context sets this book apart from the rest. Daniel knows his craft and has given both the seasoned preacher and the anxious novice a helpful tool to sharpen their preaching ministries. Highly recommended!"

—Blayne Banting, Pastor, Caronport Community Church, Caronport, Saskatchewan, Adjunct Professor, Briercrest College and Seminary

"Preaching is both an art and a skill. Many preachers, teachers, and other communicators, young and old, lack a clear understanding of the basic techniques of oral communication. Daniel Overdorf is both a gifted preacher and teacher and has a deep well of knowledge to offer his readers concerning the craft of preaching. Without a doubt, *One Year to Better Preaching* is a must read for anyone who wants to hone their skills as a preacher."

—David Martin, Regional Director, Young Life Europe

ONE YEAR TO

Better Preaching

52 *Exercises to Hone Your Skills*

Daniel Overdorf

Kregel
Ministry

One Year to Better Preaching: Fifty-Two Exercises to Hone Your Skills
© 2013 by Daniel Overdorf

Published by Kregel Publications, a division of Kregel, Inc., P.O. Box 2607, Grand Rapids, MI 49501.

All Scripture quotations, unless otherwise indicated, are from the *Holy Bible, New International Version*®. Copyright © 1973, 1978, 1984 by International Bible Society. Used by permission of Zondervan. All rights reserved.

Library of Congress Cataloging-in-Publication Data
Overdorf, Daniel, 1972-
    One year to better preaching : fifty-two exercises to hone your skills / Daniel Overdorf.
     pages cm
  Includes bibliographical references.
  ISBN 978-0-8254-3910-0
  1. Preaching—Textbooks. I. Title.
  BV4211.3.O94 2013
  251—dc23
                                                    2012049582
  ISBN 978-0-8254-3910-0

Printed in the United States of America
14 15 16 17 / 5 4 3 2

To my homiletics professors:
David Enyart,
David Reece,
Wayne Shaw,
Mark Scott,
Haddon Robinson,
Duane Litfin,
Don Sunukjian,
and Sid Buzzell.

Contents

Acknowledgements

I want to thank Kregel Publications for the opportunity to write this book; the fifty preachers who tried the exercises in the book and provided comments and suggestions about their experiences; Ken Overdorf, Debbie Miller, Matt Zingraf, and Austin Greco for assistance in proofreading the manuscript; and my family—Carrie, Peyton, Tyler, and Claire—for their love, support, and encouragement.

Introduction

Left unsharpened, tools grow dull. So do preachers. Like a lumberjack who heaves a blunt blade against a stubborn oak, preachers across the world heave murky, anemic sermons across the rims of their pulpits toward listeners who are about as eager as the stubborn tree. When tools lose their edge, progress stalls, effectiveness wanes, and frustration escalates. If only the lumberjack (and the preachers) would periodically pause from the strain to sharpen their tools.

Many preachers graduated from Bible college or seminary with honed and gleaming homiletical skills. They could exegete with brilliance, introduce with intrigue, move with suspense, apply with conviction, illustrate with vividness, transition with ease, and conclude with passion. Their homiletical toolboxes brimmed with numerous options—deductive and inductive techniques, storytelling prowess, artistry, humor, logic, and an astute awareness of both the ancient and contemporary worlds. Our studies pulsated and our sermons soared.

Granted, our memories might exaggerate the reality, but at least in our better moments we proclaimed God's Word with passion and some effectiveness.

But that was ten years ago. Or twenty-five. Or forty. As the years passed, most of our homiletical tools sank to the rusty depths of our toolboxes, and they haven't seen the light of the sanctuary since. The one or two tools we use weekly lost their edge months ago (or was it years?).

We need to rediscover and sharpen our homiletical tools. The book in your hands will help. The following pages contain exercises designed to sharpen preaching skills. Most of the exercises require an hour or two of effort. This time investment may sound costly—I know few preachers who have an "extra" hour a week. But consider that lumberjack. If he would cease

9

battering the oak with his dull ax just long enough to sharpen his blade, the remainder of his work would grow less grueling and more effective. Rather than interrupting or delaying the work, the time spent sharpening the ax enhances it, turning monotonous strain into fruitful labor.

HOW TO USE THIS BOOK

Readers can use this book in at least four different ways:

1. Weekly Exercises for a Year

One Year to Better Preaching contains fifty-two exercises designed to sharpen various homiletical skills. The book assumes you will complete the first exercise the first week, the second exercise the second week, and continue in this manner for a year. The process can begin at any time of the calendar year—no exercise is tied to a holiday or particular season.

Different exercises hone different skills. Readers who complete the exercises in order, therefore, will enjoy a process similar to cross-training. One exercise might sharpen your exegetical proficiency, the next might help you understand your listeners, the following week might lead you into more strategic prayer for your sermons.

2. Focus on Your Particular Weaknesses

The exercises in the book address eight categories of homiletical skills:

1. Prayer and Preaching
2. Bible Interpretation
3. Understanding Listeners
4. Sermon Construction
5. Illustration and Application
6. Word Crafting
7. The Preaching Event
8. Sermon Evaluation

Rather than completing all fifty-two exercises in order, some preachers may want to skip to those exercises which focus on their particular weaknesses. The chart on page 13 identifies what particular exercises address what particular skills.

3. One or Two Exercises Per Month

If tackling an exercise every week proves too burdensome, consider completing one or two per month. You might glance through the fifty-two exercises, choose the twelve or twenty-four that will most benefit your preaching, and complete them in the upcoming year.

4. Collaborate With Others

You may find it beneficial to pursue *One Year to Better Preaching* with a few preaching friends. Feel free to organize the group however you feel will best serve the preachers involved. You might consider these two possibilities:

- Gather a small group of preachers who each commit to the weekly exercises for one year. Communicate with each other—and hold one another accountable—through weekly phone calls or electronic communication, and/or meet together face-to-face once a month.
- Assemble a group of four preachers. The first month, have each preacher complete a different exercise chosen from the book's first four chapters. For example, during the first month Bob completes exercise 1, Joe completes exercise 2, Frank completes exercise 3, and Terry completes exercise 4. When the group meets at the end of the month, each preacher discusses his or her experience. The second month, each preacher completes a different exercise chosen from the book's fifth through eighth chapters, then the group discusses them at the next meeting. The process continues such that each preacher completes one exercise per month, but gains exposure to three additional exercises through discussion with the other group members.

WEB LINKS

Each chapter lists suggested resources for additional study. Many of these resources are found on the Internet. Though you can manually type each web address into your Internet browser, you will find it easier to visit and bookmark www.kregel.com/BetterPreaching, where you can simply click on each link.

ADDITIONAL SUGGESTIONS

Three additional suggestions deserve mention:

- You will find it beneficial to read a chapter on whatever day you typically begin work on your next sermon (Monday for most). This will allow time to plan how and when to complete that week's exercise.
- Some exercises might require you to plan a week or two ahead, perhaps to arrange a conversation or a focus group. In these cases, you might make these needed arrangements for the following week, then proceed to the next exercise so that you will not get behind.
- Following the fifty-two weekly exercises, the book includes seven bonus exercises. These will help if, for whatever reason, one of the weekly exercises would be impossible for you to complete. In these cases, choose a bonus exercise instead.

I pray that after completing this year of growth together, you will preach more biblically, relevantly, passionately, and fruitfully. May God bless and empower you as you proclaim His Word for the advancement of His kingdom.

	Prayer & Preaching	Bible Interpretation	Understanding Listeners	Sermon Construction	Illustration & Application	Word Crafting	The Preaching Event	Sermon Evaluation
1. Commission a Sermon Prayer Group	♦							
2. Balance Your Biblical Diet		♦						
3. Speak to Three Listening Styles			♦					
4. Remember the Fundamentals				♦				
5. Seek Illustrations at Home					♦			
6. Show, Don't Tell						♦		
7. Read the Text Well							♦	
8. Have Listeners Evaluate You								♦
9. Listen to a Storyteller					♦			
10. Tell a Story					♦			
11. People Watch			♦					
12. Polish Your Thesis				♦				
13. Utilize the Five Senses						♦		
14. Exegete Before Sermonizing		♦						
15. Develop Need in the Introduction				♦				
16. Assemble a Feed-Forward Group			♦					
17. Write in E-Prime						♦		
18. Plan for Effective Delivery							♦	
19. Collaborate With Other Preachers				♦				
20. Apply Specifically					♦			
21. Preach With Women in Mind			♦					
22. Pray for Your Listeners	♦							
23. Assemble a Feedback Group								♦
24. Minimize Notes							♦	
25. Talk to an Artist					♦			
26. Try a Different Sermon Form				♦				
27. Explore the Original Context		♦						
28. Hang the Sermon on an Image					♦			
29. Expand Your Multicultural Awareness			♦					
30. Design Careful Transitions				♦				
31. Encourage Texting During Your Sermon							♦	

	Prayer & Preaching	Bible Interpretation	Understanding Listeners	Sermon Construction	Illustration & Application	Word Crafting	The Preaching Event	Sermon Evaluation
32.Assign Biographies to Children					♦			
33.Craft Evocative Words						♦		
34.Consider the Text's Literary Form		♦						
35.Include Immediate Application					♦			
36.Teach Preaching to High Schoolers				♦				
37.Analyze a Movie			♦					
38.Swap Pulpits							♦	
39.Illustrate With Video					♦			
40.Conduct E-Interviews				♦				
41.Go to Work With a Church Member			♦					
42.Employ Purposeful Humor					♦			
43.Preach in Dialogue							♦	
44.Pray Through Your Sermon	♦							
45.Make a Bee-Line to the Cross		♦						
46.Illustrate Specifically					♦			
47.Land Smoothly in the Conclusion				♦				
48.Interweave Preaching and Worship							♦	
49.Write for the Ear						♦		
50.Preach With Men in Mind			♦					
51.Read Fiction					♦			
52.Critique a Video of Yourself								♦
BONUS:								
· Incorporate Testimony					♦			
· Fashion Compelling Titles				♦				
· Think Apologetically			♦					
· Seek Illustrations Outside					♦			
· Show Websites							♦	
· Read Classic Preachers				♦				
· Peruse the Newspaper					♦			

Commission a Sermon Prayer Group

Some weeks I listen to fifteen or more student sermons. Most of them follow the fundamental principles I teach in class, with introductions, outlines, illustrations, transitions, and conclusions arranged well on paper and in presentation. Following a number of these messages, however—not all of them, but a fair number—I offer positive feedback and assign a respectable grade, then return to my office shaking my head. The sermon missed something.

As the student spent weeks preparing the sermon, it digressed into an academic exercise. The biblical text evolved into an object to study; the sermon into an edifice to build. The empowerment of God's Spirit and the magnitude of God's truth fluttered to the wayside somewhere between the commentaries and the pulpit.

We might excuse this misstep in students who are still stumbling through the homiletical maze, but I admit that I falter in the same way. I prepare my sermons—at least some of them—like I'd prepare an academic paper. I research, organize, outline, type, and edit. Then I'm done.

Such sermons fall short because they miss the divine. In truth, a sermon devoid of the divine isn't a sermon—it's a speech, and probably not a good one. Apart from God's guidance and empowerment, our messages dwindle into mere human presentations, lacking the spiritual vitality to effect lasting change.

In contrast, sermons sparked by the Spirit carry the supernatural potential to inflame hearts and lives in Christ Jesus. These messages surpass human potential and invite divine possibility. They concede the pulpit to God, and allow Him to perform His eternal work in listeners.

Effective preachers, therefore, never cease praying for their sermons and for the preaching event. They invite others to pray. They submit every aspect of the preaching process to God's wisdom and empowerment.

To lead us toward divinely empowered messages—sermons that grow beyond academic essays to Spirit-filled proclamations—this book includes three exercises that help preachers immerse their sermons in prayer (Exercises 1, 22, and 44). The first, described in this chapter, involves commissioning a sermon prayer group.

THE EXERCISE

1. Assemble at least five people who will pray for you and your sermon every day for one week.
2. Each day, email group members specific guidance for their prayers. See suggestions on the next few pages for what they might pray each day.
3. On the day you preach, invite group members to pray with you beforehand. Also, ask at least three to pray while you preach.

DAILY PRAYER SUGGESTIONS

Ask your group to pray each day in a way that best relates to your particular sermon, study habits, and preaching needs. The ideas on the next few pages offer some guidance, but feel free to adjust them to fit your own circumstances.

You might ask group members to pray for:

Monday
- Peace concerning yesterday's sermon.
- Passion to begin a new study of God's Word.
- Persistence to stay disciplined in study all week.

Tuesday
- Strength from the Spirit to complete the difficult but rewarding task of Bible interpretation.
- Guidance from the Spirit toward study resources that will provide the most help.

- Enlightenment from the Spirit to understand the Scripture passage.

Wednesday

- The devotional insight to see God's glory erupting from the text.
- The intellectual insight to connect the sermon text with God's larger story of redemption through Christ.
- The pastoral insight to connect the text with the needs of the congregation.

Thursday

- Clarity in how to structure the sermon.
- Courage to include in the sermon whatever necessary to correct, rebuke, and encourage listeners.
- Conviction to live the truth of the text before preaching it.

Friday

- The development of illustrations that shed light on the truth of the text.
- The development of applications that help listeners understand the difference the truth should make in their lives.
- The development of an introduction that invites listeners into the message, and a conclusion that motivates them to live that message.

Saturday

- A mind settled and clear about the sermon.
- A heart at peace with the message and the task.
- A body enabled to rest in preparation for preaching.

Sunday

- Boldness to proclaim Truth zealously.
- Precision to proclaim Truth clearly.
- Transparency to proclaim Truth authentically.
- Humility to lose self entirely.
- Yearning to exalt Christ eminently.
- Effectiveness to bear fruit immediately.

ADDITIONAL SUGGESTIONS

- Send the daily suggestions to your group members the prior night (send Monday's requests on Sunday evening, for example).
- The article listed on page 19 from Joe McKeever's on-line blog, "How to Pray For Your Pastor on a Saturday," contains several insightful thoughts. Group members may benefit from reading it.
- Tell your prayer team what particular hours you plan to study each day—perhaps they can pray at those times.
- If Sunday School classes or other groups meet prior to your preaching, ask them to pray something specific for the sermon. Depending on the topic of your message, they might pray, "Use today's sermon to grant peace to those who still feel burdened by previously forgiven sins;" or, "Empower our preacher to explain the mystery of grace clearly and in a manner that inspires awe."
- Those who pray during your sermon might: (1) gather in a separate room where they can pray aloud together; (2) disperse themselves throughout the congregation and intentionally pray for those seated around them; or (3) gather behind you on stage, in a visible but discreet location, giving the congregation a visual reminder of the prayers that undergird the sermon.

"I TRIED IT"

"I loved inviting others into the sermon writing process. Their prayers and encouragement throughout my preparation brought me confidence and excitement. As the week went on, I felt less pressure and more peace—I couldn't wait until Sunday. And, when I stood to preach, I knew that those who had prayed were all the more eager to hear what God had laid on my heart."

Benjamin Abbott, Prince Edward Island, Canada

"I asked several people to pray for the sermon and sent them daily updates. At first I didn't think anything was different. After the sermon, though—one I felt was just okay—several people told me that the sermon spoke directly to something they were going through. Their comments were more than the usual 'nice sermon' I get every week. Apparently, the Spirit worked in response to the prayers of His people."

Jason Warden, Knoxville, Tennessee

"One of the men who prayed for my sermon had been struggling in his marriage for some time. Though his wife attended church, she was not a believer. His prayers focused primarily on how the sermon would influence her. After the service on Sunday, she asked her husband to baptize her! The prayers definitely had an eternal impact."

Doug Krauss, Greenville, Ohio

RESOURCES FOR FURTHER STUDY

- *Praying for Sunday: You, Your Pastor, and the Next Sermon*, by Dr. Michael Fabarez (Michael Fabarez, 2007).
- "How to Pray For Your Pastor on a Saturday," by Joe McKeever. Access at www.joemckeever.com/mt/archives /001270.html.
- "Praying for God's 'Sacred Anointing' on your Preaching," by Glenn Wagner. Access at www.crosswalk .com/pastors/11608786.

Balance Your Biblical Diet

I ate pizza for five meals last week—twice for supper, and three times as leftovers for lunch. Yesterday I had pasta at noon. And, pasta for supper. Despite the temptation to fabricate an Italian heritage (which would prove difficult with "Overdorf" as a last name), I have no defense other than to promise my stomach and my diminishing supply of Tums that I'll do better. Tomorrow, I will balance my diet.

The congregations to whom we preach may experience similar nausea from the unbalanced biblical diet we offer in our preaching: "Another series on Philippians? Didn't we just do that six months ago? Or was that Ephesians? I'm sure it was one of Paul's epistles—we haven't left those since that preacher got here eight years ago." Some preachers spend most of their time in prophecy; others never seem to leave the book of Acts.

We all have certain portions of Scripture—or particular literary forms—to which we feel most drawn. Our tendencies may grow from our personalities, learning styles, or even our own lack of experience with the rich diversity of the biblical canon. Whatever the reason, left unchecked this lopsided diet will result in sickly congregations made up of frail believers with limited perspectives and poor spiritual health.

Healthy bodies—including healthy church bodies—require a balanced diet. God included two testaments and various genres of literature in Scripture. We neglect our listeners' spiritual health if we neglect this robust diet He offers. When did I last expose my listeners to the wisdom literature? To biblical poetry, or prophecy? Have I recently explored the awe-inspiring depths of (gulp) apocalyptic literature?

"But," some may contend, "shouldn't we design our preaching schedule around our listeners' needs?" Our pastoral instinct should, certainly, influence our preaching program. These two ideals—balancing the biblical diet and meeting the needs of our congregation—are not mutually exclusive.

When obvious needs exist among our listeners, we can seek portions of Scripture that best address them. If your congregation has lost its awe of God, for example, you might preach Revelation. If worship has deteriorated into only an argument, preach Psalms. If listeners have grown too comfortable in their faith, the Abraham narratives in Genesis will help. If the congregation takes a casual attitude toward sin, turn to the Old Testament prophets. God's Word addresses whatever needs might arise.

This suggestion aside, a preaching schedule driven by the Bible rather than by perceived needs will, over the long haul, stimulate greater maturity in a church. Substantial, long-term growth requires a steady diet of the Word. Rather than beginning with our people's needs, therefore, the majority of our preaching schedule should balance the biblical diet we offer our listeners. Then, as we submit to the Word and the Spirit, giving these priority over our hobby horses, creativity, and even our desire to meet people's felt needs, God will permeate our preaching and perform whatever work He needs to perform in listeners' hearts and lives.

God's Word bursts with greater power than our pastoral instinct. He will address our listeners' needs as we provide them a balanced diet of Scripture.

THE EXERCISE

1. Glance over your sermons from the last three to five years. Observe from what portions of the Bible you have preached. For sermons that were more topical in nature, consider which text(s) you used most prominently.
2. Chart your findings using a table like the one on page 23. Mark the appropriate box for each sermon you preached from a particular portion of Scripture.
3. Evaluate the results. From what portions of Scripture have you preached the most? What portions have you neglected? Did the results confirm what you would have guessed, or did they surprise you?

4. Schedule at least two sermon series from the portions of
    Scripture you have most neglected.

Pentateuch (Gen. – Deut.)	OT History (Josh. – Est.)	Wisdom Literature (Job – Song.)	Prophets (Isa. – Mal.)
Gospels & Acts (Matt. – Acts)	Pauline Epistles (Rom. – Phil.)	General Epistles & Revelation (Heb. – Rev.)	

AN EXAMPLE

I charted the texts from my last 175 sermons:

Pentateuch (Gen. – Deut.)	OT History (Josh. – Esther)	Wisdom Literature (Job – S. of Sol.)	Prophets (Isa. – Mal.)
11111 11111 11111 1	11111 11111 11111 111	11111 11111 11111 111	11111 111
= 16	= 18	= 18	= 8

Gospels & Acts (Matt. – Acts)	Pauline Epistles (Rom. – Phil.)	General Epistles & Revelation (Heb. – Rev.)
11111 11111 11111 11111 11111 11111 11111 11111 11111 11111 11111 11111 11111 11111 111	11111 11111 11111 11111 11111 11111 1	11111 11111 1
= 73	= 31	= 11

Observations:

- By far, I preached the most sermons out of the Gospels and Acts—more than twice as many (seventy-three) from this portion of Scripture than from any other. A closer look revealed that ten of these sermons were from Acts; sixty-three were from the Gospels. I have always felt drawn to the Gospels—particularly Jesus' parables and the Sermon on the Mount. I did not realize, however, that my preaching had slanted so much in this direction.
- I preached the least number of sermons from the Old Testament prophets—eight. This, I admit, did not surprise me. I was surprised to discover, however, that I preached only eleven sermons from the General Epistles and Revelation.

- Almost twice as many sermons grew from the New Testament (115) than from the Old Testament (60). I try to balance my Old Testament and New Testament preaching—apparently I have not been as balanced as I thought.
- I need to plan a series from the Prophets and another series from the General Epistles or Revelation. I should also spend more time in other portions of the Old Testament.

ADDITIONAL SUGGESTIONS

- If you are new to the pulpit and have not yet preached for three years, go ahead and chart the sermons you have preached. Or, if these are so few that the exercise would not prove helpful, skip this exercise and complete one of the Bonus Exercises at the end of this book.
- You might also chart what topics or themes you have discussed. Preachers often resort to our personal soap boxes and preferred matters of doctrine more often than we realize. The chart might include themes such as holiness, discipleship, faith, grace, worship, evangelism, Jesus' second coming, the family, and stewardship.
- Additionally, you may consider charting your recent illustrations. What aspects of life have you used most to illustrate biblical truth? How many illustrations have come from the world of sports? From your family? How many stories have you told from the Civil War, or from popular movies? How often have you quoted Tozer, Bonhoeffer, or your favorite contemporary authors?

"I TRIED IT"

"In reviewing my sermons, I was amazed at how quickly I'd forgotten what I'd preached (imagine how quickly my listeners must forget!). It humbled me and reminded me to trust God's promise that His Word never returns void. The exercise showed that, over the last five years, I've preached from the New Testament 3½ times more than the Old Testament. Also, I've avoided shorter books, especially the Minor

Prophets. So, I'm planning a series called 'Small Books With Big Messages.'"

Burt Brock, Morgantown, Indiana

"My choice of sermon texts and topics is first driven by prayer-fully assessing the needs of the culture and congregation, then filtering this through biblical balance, which is essential because it demonstrates that *all* Scripture is God breathed and suitable. This exercise helped me make sure biblical balance gets strong attention in my sermon planning. It showed that my preaching balance has been tipped by my own passion for certain genres (Gospels and Old Testament Narrative and Prophets)."

Steve Cuss, Broomfield, Colorado

"I have always sought a well balanced sermon plan—this exercise put my habits to the test! Generally, I was pleased by the results, though I did have a few surprises. We pride ourselves in being an 'Acts church' but I have spent relatively little time in Acts. Also, I have preached almost nothing from two of my favorite genres in scripture, Revelation and the prophets. Next year's preaching schedule will address these areas. I enjoyed this exercise, and found it helpful."

Greg Robbins, Heath, Ohio

RESOURCES FOR FURTHER STUDY

- *Planning Your Preaching: A Step-by-Step Guide for Developing a One-Year Preaching Calendar*, by Stephen Nelson Rummage (Kregel Publishers, 2002).
- *Preaching With Balance: Achieving and Maintaining Biblical Priorities in Preaching*, by Donald Hamilton (Christian Focus Publications, 2007).
- "The Preacher's Balancing Act," by Harold Vanderwell. Access at http://www.preaching.com/resources/articles/11567144/page-1.
- "The Rationale and Methodology of Planned Preaching," by James T. Meadows. Access at http://www.preaching.com/resources/articles/11563474.

Speak to Three Listening Styles

The PGA of America honored Harvey Penick as their Teacher of the Year in 1989, recognizing his work with golf greats like Tom Kite and Ben Crenshaw. In 1992, three years before his death, Penick authored a small book of golf instruction titled *Harvey Penick's Little Red Book*. Propelled by Penick's amusing anecdotes and simple, easily understood instructions, the book remains the highest selling golf instruction book ever published. Penick often said that the most important advice he could offer golfers was to "take dead aim." A golfer might swing the club with all the proper techniques—perfect balance, weight transfer, and flawless rotation of hips, shoulders, and arms—and hit the ball long and straight, but without proper aim the ball might fly long and straight into a lake.

Effective execution requires careful aim.

Few preachers consider where to aim their sermons. As a result, their messages soar into the rafters above, but never reach the listeners below. How can we best consider our listeners in the midst of our sermon preparation? How can we "take dead aim" with our messages?

LOGOS, ETHOS, AND PATHOS LISTENERS

Eight scholars recently embarked on a research project to discover how listeners hear sermons.[1] They conducted personal interviews

---

1. The Lily Endowment sponsored this study through Christian Theological Seminary. The project resulted in four books: *Listening to Listeners: Homiletical Case Studies*, by John S. McClure and others (St. Louis: Chalice Press, 2004); *Hearing the Sermon: Relationship, Content, and Feeling*, by Ronald J. Allen (St. Louis:

with more than 260 people who attend church regularly. The study revealed that multiple people can listen to the same sermon, but hear it differently. Though they sit in the same room at the same time and listen to the same words from the same preacher, each listener perceives the sermon in a unique manner.

People tend to hear sermons in one of three ways—ways that correspond with Aristotle's classic elements of rhetoric:

- Ethos listeners hear based on their relationships with the preacher and their perceptions of his character.
- Logos listeners hear based on the logical presentation of ideas.
- Pathos listeners hear based on the feelings the sermon stirs inside of them.

Most people reflect elements of all three categories, but have a primary tendency toward one of the three. Effective sermons, therefore, include particular elements aimed at each listening style.

Listener Type	Listens To	Key Words	Typical Listener Responses[2]	How To Preach To
Ethos	The person preaching	Relationship, Connection	"The preacher seemed like one of us." "The sermon was sincere." "The preacher was warm and authentic."	Use "we" instead of "you." Share personal stories, struggles, and praises. Discuss how the sermon's Scripture text and concepts have influenced you. Use illustrations that arise from the church and community. Use self-deprecating humor. Teach about relationships with God and other people.

Chalice Press, 2004); *Believing in Preaching: What Listeners Hear in Sermons*, by Diane Turner-Sharazz and others (St. Louis: Chalice Press, 2005); and *Make the Word Come Alive: Lessons from Laity*, by Mary Alice Mulligan and Ronald J. Allen (St. Louis: Chalice Press, 2006). The material in this chapter most reflects *Hearing the Sermon*, by Ronald J. Allen.

Listener Type	Listens To	Key Words	Typical Listener Responses[2]	How To Preach To
Logos	The ideas presented	Logic, Information	"The sermon gave me something to ponder." "I learned a lot from the sermon." "The preacher explains his points clearly."	Teach biblical truth in a logical, orderly manner. Recommend books, articles, or other resources for further study. Offer reasons your listeners should believe and act on what you're preaching. Explain historical, cultural, contextual, or linguistic issues surrounding your sermon text. Provide statistics and other factual information to explain and/or apply the text. Ask difficult questions that stimulate listeners to think.
Pathos	The emotions evoked	Feelings, Passions	"The preacher is passionate." "The sermon moved me." "The preacher speaks from the heart."	Tell stirring stories that relate to real-life questions and difficulties. Discuss listeners' concerns and needs. Demonstrate your own concern about the issue being discussed. Use poetry, music, photographs, paintings, and other artistic means to help communicate the message. Help listeners take inventory of their own lives in relation to the biblical truth being discussed. Challenge listeners to respond to the message in concrete ways.

2. Modified from Appendix C of Allen, *Hearing the Sermon* (140–142).

THE EXERCISE

Like listeners, preachers have tendencies toward ethos, logos, or pathos learning, and our sermons reflect our tendencies. If you have a leaning toward the logos learning style, for example, your sermons may contain a disproportionate amount of material aimed at logos listeners. The following exercise will help you identify which listening style you speak to most, then develop strategies to speak to all three.

1. Retrieve the notes, outlines, or manuscripts from your last three sermons.
2. Use three different colored highlighters to mark the portions of each sermon that best communicated to ethos, logos, and pathos listeners. The preceding chart should help you distinguish which portions of each sermon spoke to each listening style.
3. Evaluate the results of #2. What recurring patterns did you see? Which of the three listening styles do you speak to most? Which do you speak to least? Because of their texts and topics, not every sermon will balance equally between the three—some will require more material that relates to a particular listening style. Every sermon should, however, account for all three to some degree.
4. Once you have studied your text and discerned the central truth of your upcoming sermon, divide a sheet of paper into three equal sections. Label the sections "ethos," "logos," and "pathos." Then, brainstorm about how you might best relate the central truth of your upcoming sermon to listeners of each style. The preceding chart should spur some ideas. Record your ideas in each section of the paper.
5. Include as many of these ideas as possible in your upcoming sermon.

"I TRIED IT"

"The exercise was great! I had no doubt that my preaching was lopsided, speaking primarily to logos listeners. The exercise helped me make immediate and concrete changes to my next sermon, resulting in more effective communication to the other listening styles. I was amazed, both at the changes necessary to my sermon and by the positive responses to the message. I purchased one of the books listed in the Resources for Further Study (*Hearing the Sermon*, by Allen) and read it along with the chapter—it was quite helpful."

Jeff Brunsman, Mount Gilead, Ohio

"This exercise was a wonderful reminder to me. It helped me to communicate with my entire congregation—people who have all three listening styles. I used the exercise on my Christmas message, and it made a tremendous difference. I received a wide range of positive comments, from all three types of listeners, so I could tell that the adjustments I made helped."

Randall Sidwell, Byrdstown, Tennessee

"This exercise was both reassuring and convicting. I was reassured that given proper amounts of preparation, I tend to speak to all three types of listeners in a fairly balanced way. While I did not have proper terms for this (and now I do), I was intuitively engaging the congregation in this way. However, it was also convicting. I noticed a strong tendency to overly rely on 'Ethos' and 'Pathos' when my preparation time ran short—essentially, attempting to compensate for a lack of strong content with emotion and personality. Thank you for the reality check!"

Brian Walton, Winchester, Kentucky

RESOURCES FOR FURTHER STUDY

* *Hearing the Sermon: Relationship, Content, Feeling*, by Ronald J. Allen (Chalice Press, 2004).
* *Connecting With the Congregation: Rhetoric and the Art of Preaching*, by Lucy Lind Hogan and Robert S. Reid (Abingdon Press, 1999).
* "The Anatomy of Exposition," by Kent Hughes. Access at http://www.sbts.edu/media/publications/sbjt/sbjt_1999summer5.pdf.

Remember the Fundamentals

I coached my five-year-old son's basketball team. I use the term "coach" loosely, regarding both my ability and their receptivity. Over the course of the season, however, they learned far more than I anticipated.

During one of our last practices, I taught the boys how to block out when someone shoots the basketball—to position themselves between their opponent and the basket so that they can rebound any misses. I explained the concept, they practiced it for a few minutes, and by the end of practice they blocked out as well as any five-year-olds could. During the next game, in fact, my son blocked someone out all the way to the wall!

The evening after that practice, I watched the men from The University of Tennessee—our hometown team—play basketball against Auburn University. In the final seconds of the game, Tennessee led by one point. An Auburn player stood at the free throw line. If he made the free throw, he could tie the game, then shoot another free throw for a possible win. If he missed, Tennessee could simply retrieve the rebound, hold onto the ball until the final buzzer sounded, and win the game.

The Auburn player missed the free throw. The Tennessee players, however, forgot a fundamental of basketball—they neglected to block out. Consequently, an Auburn player grabbed the rebound, put the ball in the basket, and Tennessee lost. "Are you kidding me?" I barked, resisting the temptation to throw my shoe at the television screen. "My five-year-olds can do this, and you All-Americans can't even remember to block out?!"

Games are won and lost on the fundamentals.

A similar principle holds true in preaching. I've preached

regularly for seventeen years—long enough, regrettably, to have forgotten the fundamental principles I learned as a student. The further I stray from the fundamentals, I discover, the less effective my preaching.

THE EXERCISE

This exercise will lead you through five fundamentals of sermon preparation—fundamentals often taught in basic preaching courses, then later lost in the hustle of weekly preparation. To complete the exercise, prepare your upcoming sermon by walking through these five steps.[1]

1. *Study the Text:* Explore the Scripture text(s) you will preach *before* deciding what the sermon will say. Examine the passage's context—how does your text fit within the original author's overall flow of thought? Use commentaries and other tools to research its cultural and historical backgrounds. Compare translations to identify any linguistic issues. If you have original language skills, use them. Too often, we decide what truth we will preach before we study the text. Reverse this, and allow the text to drive your thoughts and the sermon's direction.
2. *Define the Thesis:* Effective sermons revolve around a single idea, stated as succinctly and memorably as possible. To define this idea for your particular sermon, reflect on the research you completed in step one, then state the timeless truth presented in the passage in a clear, declarative sentence. Resist the temptation to state only a broad theme with a single word, such as "evangelism." Instead, shape a full sentence that encapsulates the particular truth taught in your passage. To continue the previous example, perhaps your thesis states, "God's Spirit empowers God's people to evangelize."
3. *Choose a Sermon Form:* Though the sermon revolves around a single idea, that idea needs developed. Sermons develop, essentially, in one of two ways—deductively or inductively. The difference lies in the placement of the thesis. In a deductive sermon, the preacher states the thesis in the

---

1. Later exercises will further develop each of these five steps.

introduction. In an inductive sermon, the preacher saves the thesis until the end. To decide which form will best serve your upcoming sermon, consider your particular text and thesis, and your particular listeners, then ask yourself, "Can I best communicate this truth by stating it outright, then supporting it with points? Or, can I best communicate this truth by first presenting the problem it will solve, then working through the text to a solution?"

Sermon Form	Essential Elements	Suggestions
Deductive	1. Introduction: Thesis 2. Body: Points drawn from the text that explain, prove, and/or apply the thesis 3. Conclusion: Restate thesis and points	After stating the thesis in the introduction, use a transition statement that tells listeners how the upcoming points will develop the thesis. Will you give three evidences to support the thesis? Four reasons we know it's true? Two implications? Five characteristics?
Inductive	1. Introduction: Problem 2. Body: Movements drawn from the text that help solve the problem 3. Conclusion: Solution (thesis)	Make certain the movements (which function similar to the points of a deductive sermon) lead listeners clearly and progressively from problem to solution. Also, before you state the thesis in the conclusion, review the problem from the introduction that the thesis resolves.

4. *Develop Illustrations and Applications:* Illustrations help listeners understand truth; applications help listeners see how that truth should affect their lives. Both stand critical to effective communication. Once you define the sermon's thesis and structure, consider what stories, quotes, statistics, suggestions, or real-to-life scenarios you can include during each portion of the sermon to help listeners understand and apply what the text teaches.

5. *Prepare Introduction and Conclusion:* Finally, with the sermon mapped out, you can define more specifically how the sermon will begin and end.

- The introduction should (1) capture attention with a story, quote, or perhaps a probing question; (2) develop a sense of need by describing the human inadequacy or struggle that the text and sermon will address; and (3) give listeners a sense of the sermon's direction—for a deductive sermon this includes the thesis and a transition statement discussed in the preceding chart; for an inductive sermon it involves an affirmation that the text will resolve the problem raised.

- The conclusion should (1) highlight the thesis—in a deductive sermon restate the thesis given previously; in an inductive sermon state and emphasize the thesis for the first time, bringing the sermon to its climax; (2) provide listeners a final picture of the thesis with an illustration; (3) challenge listeners to respond to the truth taught in the sermon.

EXAMPLE OUTLINES

Deductive Sermon From Romans 14 – 15:13

Introduction

- Capture Attention: Story of church that split over differing opinions.
- Develop Need: We often divide over matters the Bible doesn't address.
- Direction of Sermon:
  - » Thesis: Love is the balance on the tightrope of disputable matters.
  - » Transition: Romans 14 – 15:13 offers five instructions about loving one another through disputable matters.

Body

1. Recognize what matters are disputable (14:1–5).
2. Act with proper motivation (14:6–9).
3. Refrain from judging (14:10–12).
4. Consider your brother (14:13–16; 15:1–13).
5. Maintain perspective (14:17–23).

Conclusion

- Restate Thesis: Love is the balance on the tightrope of disputable matters.
- Final Illustration: Story of tightrope walker using a balance bar.
- Challenge: Go now and love beyond disputes, opinions, and disagreements.

Inductive Sermon From Matthew 6:25-34

Introduction

- Capture Attention: Statistics about the prominence of worry.
- Develop Need: How do we overcome worry?
- Direction of Sermon:
  - » Jesus offers a solution to our problem in Matthew 6:25–34.

Body

1. A Problem to Recognize: Worry (6:25–32).
2. A Perspective to Cultivate: God Provides (6:25–32).
3. A Priority to Establish: Seek Him First (6:33–34).

Conclusion

- **Thesis:** (How do we overcome worry?) **Let go and pursue God.**
- Final Illustration: Story of man who lost job and pursued ministry.
- Challenge: Instead of worrying about your circumstances, pursue God in the midst of them.

"I TRIED IT"

"This exercise really helped me in two ways. First, it helped in the preparation of my sermon by giving it direction. Instead of having to deal with writer's block, I simply followed the steps and the sermon almost wrote itself. Second, it helped to bring clarity to the sermon. My listeners especially appreciated this, as they could follow it better than some of my other sermons."

Joseph Schmidt, Kewanee, Illinois

"It was refreshing for me to go back to the basics. I needed that reminder that a sermon doesn't always have to be complicated or even fancy to effectively communicate God's message. Sometimes simpler really is better. This exercise also helped me to streamline my message. Often we preachers think we have to make things overly eloquent, which may lead us to confuse or talk around our listeners. An exercise on remembering the fundamentals was just what I needed."

Randy Overdorf, Elizabethton, Tennessee

"What a refreshing review of the fundamentals! The reality of ministering to multiple needs while overseeing numerous programs consumes many hours each week. Time devoted to sermon preparation is easily sacrificed. Homiletics become mechanical. Tried and true formulas rise to the surface. Websites abound with ready-made sermons by others who already sweat and toiled over the exegesis of a biblical text. But when one prays and prepares, the message becomes a sermon that flows out of the Word of God, and from the burning heart of the preacher."

Tom Cash, Sault Ste. Marie, Michigan

RESOURCES FOR FURTHER STUDY
- *Invitation to Biblical Preaching: Proclaiming Truth With Clarity and Relevance*, by Donald R. Sunukjian (Kregel, 2007).
- *Preaching: The Art of Narrative Exposition*, by Calvin Miller (Baker, 2006).
- "2009 Celebration of Biblical Preaching," lecture given by Haddon Robinson at Luther Seminary. Access video at http://www.youtube.com/watch?v=2LU0r8XY-ks.
- "Birthing a Sermon: A Step-by-Step Guide to Bringing the Text Alive," by John Ortberg. Access at http://www.christianitytoday.com/le/2007/summer/12.38.html?start=1.

Seek Illustrations at Home

A recent country music song pictures a woman returning to the house where she grew up. She recalls burying her favorite dog beneath the live oak, learning guitar and doing homework in the back bedroom, and putting her handprints in the concrete on the front steps.[1] The song resonates with listeners because it invites them to reflect on their own experiences, and their own homes.

I now live in the same town where I lived as a small boy. I occasionally drive by my old house. As I sit in my car on the side of the road, I can almost see myself as a little boy—white-blond hair, skinny arms and legs, and teeth a little too big for my mouth—clambering up the tree in the front yard, tossing a football in the back yard, and playing hide-and-seek with my neighborhood friends. I recall the Christmas I received my first bicycle, the summer my father dug out the basement to create a downstairs play room, and the night I sat in the living room watching my parents weep when they received news of my grandmother's death.

Similar thoughts arise when I walk through the house where I live today—my daughter's first steps on the living room rug, my son's determination to heave the basketball through the hoop in the driveway, and the sparkle in my other son's eye when he showed me the moon through the new telescope he saved his allowance to buy.

Memories are stories—stories that typify life, relationships,

---

1. "The House That Built Me," written by Tom Douglas and Alan Shamblin, performed by Miranda Lambert (2009 Sony Music Entertainment).

and faith. They provide anchors when life feels unstable, warmth when life grows cold, and compasses when life gets confusing.

For the preacher, these memories provide bridges that connect biblical truth to contemporary life. Listeners best understand truth when they see its relationship to their own experience. Effective communicators build such bridges with stories. But where might we find these stories? How can we spur our imaginations to recall those memories that typify life and faith? One way to recall stories involves taking a walk through our houses.

THE EXERCISE

1. Spend at least one hour walking around your house—inside and out.
2. Take a voice recorder or a pen and paper to record your thoughts.
3. Allow memories to bubble up in your imagination. What comes to mind when you see the photographs on the walls? The back deck? The marks on the doorframes? The vase on the coffee table? The tree house in the yard? The family Bible?
4. After recording your memories, consider what truths about God or human nature they illustrate. Note these insights.
5. File the stories and the truths they illustrate so that you can use them in upcoming sermons.

TO SPARK IDEAS

- Just last week as we ate around the table, my wife described ...
- The scuffs in the wood floor came when ...
- We usually put the Christmas tree in that corner, except the one year when ...
- That's my grandfather in the picture; he always said ...
- One night that telephone rang at 2 A.M ...
- We sat on this couch when my daughter told me ...
- I bought the new suit in the closet for ...
- These softball cleats remind me of when ...
- That wall had a hole in it after ...
- Up in the attic I keep a box ...
- We stood here in a circle and prayed the night when ...

- When the faucet started leaking, I thought I could fix it ...
- The wallpaper in the kitchen reminds me of when ...
- When the baseball crashed into this window ...
- The lawnmower in the shed reminds me of when ...
- Once, when I went to that mailbox ...
- One evening as we sat in the porch swing ...
- This back yard has seen many games of ...
- I'll never forget the morning when she pulled out of this driveway ...
- The neighbors across the street once invited us to ...

ADDITIONAL SUGGESTIONS

- In addition to walking through your present house, mentally stroll through the house in which you lived as a child.
- You might walk through your church building and allow it to spur memories from the life of your church family.
- Stories like those elicited by this exercise require special care when used in sermons. A few suggestions about the use of personal illustrations:
  - » Don't overuse personal material. One or two personal stories per sermon is plenty.
  - » Don't make yourself the hero of your personal stories—keep the focus on Christ.
  - » Don't betray confidences. Get permission before telling stories that involve others (including your family!).
  - » Do feel comfortable enough to laugh at yourself.
  - » Do speak of everyday events. Listeners will identify with these most easily.
  - » Do talk about what you have seen and experienced more than talking about yourself. If the story were a movie, you should stay behind the camera, not in front of it.

"I TRIED IT"

"I walk through our home every day, but seldom stop to consider what I see. Pictures of my grandparents and aunt reminded me of their legacy of faith that endured sacrifices, cancer, and the loss of a child. My father's medals from World War II demonstrate his devotion and humility (I didn't know the medals existed until after he died). It felt as though every picture and piece of furniture reminded me that my family, during good times and bad, has remained faithful to Christ and in service to His church."

Bill Worrell, Knightstown, Indiana

"A funny thing happened on the way to doing this exercise. I found an illustration for which I was not looking. I asked my wife (her memory is much better than mine) to walk me through our six room house identifying items people had given to us. She identified no less than 61 such items! This does not include those stored in drawers, closets, and the basement. My point: God's people are loving, thoughtful, and generous. You just can't stop the saints!"

Ken Overdorf, Beckley, West Virginia

RESOURCES FOR FURTHER STUDY

- *Using Illustrations to Preach With Power*, by Bryan Chapell (Crossway Books, 2001).
- "The House That Built Me," performed by Miranda Lambert. View music video at http://www.cmt.com/videos/miranda-lambert/500805/the-house-that-built-me.jhtml.
- "Find the Perfect Sermon Illustration From Your Own Experience," audio discussion by Sherman Haywood Cox II. Access at http://www.soulpreaching.com/perfect illustrationaudio.
- "Self-Disclosure in Preaching: An Interview With Bob Russell, John Claypool, Barry Black, and Dieter Zander," by James Barnette. Access at http://www.preaching.com/resources/articles/11549465/.

Show, Don't Tell

Effective communicators picture truth for their listeners ("show") rather than just explaining it ("tell"). When a movie director portrays a character's fear, for example, he does not place a subtitle at the bottom of the screen with the words, "The little girl is frightened." Instead, the director shows viewers what fear looks like through the actor's facial expressions and movements. Perhaps, as she lies in bed at night, her eyes grow wide, her shoulders tense, and she pulls the blanket over her head.

Successful writers craft their stories in a similar manner. Seldom will a novelist write something like, "The man was nervous about his speech." Instead, the author describes what this nervousness looks like: "As he walked to the podium, a bead of sweat appeared above his lip, his legs grew numb, and his heart pounded. The thousand faces that sat before him became a blur. His hand trembled as he removed his notes from his satchel." Rather than *telling* their listeners that a character is afraid or nervous, film directors and novelists *show* their listeners what fear or nervousness looks like.

Jesus often employed this principle in His teaching. He sometimes told of the kingdom, the Father, and discipleship. Usually, however, He taught by showing. When asked, "Who is my neighbor?" Jesus did not respond as you and I might, with a definition pulled from Webster's. Instead, He showed His listeners: "A man was going down from Jerusalem to Jericho ..." (Luke 10:30). When confronted about His association with sinners, He could have simply explained, "It's the sinners who really need me." Instead He pictured, "It is not the healthy who need a doctor, but the sick" (Luke 5:31). Elsewhere, in response to the same question, He described a woman who celebrated when she found a lost coin, a shepherd who rejoiced when he found a lost sheep, and a father who threw a banquet when his rebellious son returned home (Luke 15). Jesus taught in pictures.

Preachers can enhance their effectiveness by implementing the same principle into their sermons—show, don't tell. We typically ask ourselves, "How can I best explain this?" Instead, we should ask ourselves, "How can I best picture it?"

EXAMPLES

When you hope to draw attention to a particular scene or teaching, you might use a full paragraph or more to picture it. The first two examples demonstrate this extended approach. In other cases, you might use just a sentence or two of description to give the sermon more texture. The third and fourth examples demonstrate this brief approach.

Example 1 (extended scene):

- TELL: When he went to college, things that seemed important in high school didn't matter much anymore.
- SHOW: Mom and Dad said their good-byes and headed home. He dropped his suitcase in the middle of the floor of his dorm room. Thankfully, his roommate wouldn't arrive until the next day—he needed time to adjust. He put his socks in the drawer and his toothbrush on the dresser. He arranged his shirts on hangers and placed them in the cold closet. Then, he pulled his high-school letterman's jacket from the suitcase—the school colors, the varsity letter. He'd only had it for nine months, but already the ends of the sleeves were ragged. He slept in it the first night after Coach handed them out, then wore it every day to school. Now, though … now he hangs it in the back of the closet, behind the new sweaters he doesn't like and Dad's old overcoat that he'll never wear.

Example 2 (extended scene):

- TELL: Some men place too much emphasis on their careers and wealth, and ruin their marriages.
- SHOW: A man hurries out of his office building downtown. He pulls his coat's collar tight to fend off the nighttime chill. He waves to the parking attendant, finds his Lexus, and settles behind the wheel. Before he ignites the engine, however, his phone rings. His wife's voice streams from his Bluetooth. She and their daughter had vacationed on Cape Cod for the weekend—he backed out at the last minute because of some issues that arose at work. "We're not coming home," she said. "You're staying an extra day?" he asked. "No," came her curt reply, "that's not what I mean. I mean, we're not coming home ... ever."

Example 3 (brief word change):

- TELL: She had great difficulty forgiving her father.
- SHOW: After stammering through another brief phone conversation—fraught with awkward pauses—she returned the phone to its cradle and pulled some stationary from the cabinet. She scratched on the paper what she couldn't say aloud, "Father, I forgive you."

Example 4 (brief word change):

- TELL: Jesus suffered on the cross.
- SHOW: With every blow of the soldier's hammer, Jesus' body shuddered and curdling screams erupted through His bloody, clenched teeth.

THE EXERCISE

1. Use the exercises in the chart below to practice the "show, don't tell" principle.

Instead of telling:	How might I show it?
I felt intimidated when I walked into her office.	
He was worried about the family budget.	
She grew passionate in her faith.	
Parents and their teenage children do not understand each other.	
Gossip hurts friendships.	

2. After preparing this week's sermon, read back through it and find at least five places where you *told* something that you could more effectively *show*.
3. Rewrite the five portions that you noted in #2 so that you are showing rather than telling.

"I TRIED IT"

"I used this method when teaching one of my Bible classes, and found it very helpful. I find that when I just explain something, it seldom hits home. For me, this has always been one of the most difficult parts of preaching and teaching. This chapter gave me an advantage by teaching me to effectively create word pictures. I believe we should 'show' just as much as we 'tell' to most effectively present the Gospel."

Keith Ratamess, Columbia, South Carolina

"The 'show, don't tell' exercise gave my sermon more points of contact with the congregation. After I reviewed the completed sermon, it was obvious which areas needed more depth to produce a clearer picture in the listeners' minds. As a result of the changes I made, after the sermon several people shared personal stories which came to their minds while they listened to the modified sermons. I believe the 'show, don't tell' preaching exercise helped me to connect God's Word to listeners' experiences and predispositions."

Joe Heins, Auburn, Indiana

"Using more descriptive imagery gave my sermon a different tone. Overall, that tone was a more serious one, but that was likely because the places in the sermon where I used this exercise were more serious. I believe that showing, not telling, helped me to better connect and create empathy with people. I would warn, however, to plan carefully with regards to sermon length, as using more descriptive language can add several minutes."

Nathan Crowe, Galax, Virginia

RESOURCES FOR FURTHER STUDY

- *The Write Stuff: Crafting Sermons That Capture and Convince*, by Sondra Willobee (Westminster John Knox, 2009).
- *Preaching That Connects: Using the Techniques of Journalists to Add Impact to Your Sermons* by Mark Galli (Zondervan, 1994).
- "How to 'Show Don't Tell,'" by Dawn Copeman. Access at http://www.writing-world.com/dawn/dawn02.shtml.
- "On Writing: Show, Don't Tell," by Robert J. Sawyer. Access at http://www.sfwriter.com/ow04.htm.

Read the Text Well

The most important part of the preaching event often receives the least attention. We carefully craft our sermons, fashioning each transition, illustration, and explanation. Once we complete the message, we practice it aloud—even three or four times. Amid these preparations, however, we barely consider how we will read the Scripture text from which the sermon will grow. As a result, we stumble over words, mispronounce names, and bulldoze past punctuation. Our actions betray an unspoken assumption: the Scripture text is but a necessary step to reach what is most important—our own thoughts about the text.

The opposite held true in the first-century church. Few people owned Bibles, so believers' only exposure to the Bible came from hearing it read. The public reading of Scripture, therefore, held high priority. In his epistles, Paul repeatedly instructed churches to read Scriptures aloud: "Until I come, devote yourself to the public reading of Scripture" (1 Tim. 4:13); "I charge you before the Lord to have this letter read to all the brothers" (1 Thess. 5:27); and, "After this letter has been read to you, see that it is also read in the church of the Laodiceans" (Col. 4:16).

Today, many people own Bibles—even multiple copies (I count fourteen within eyesight as I type). We cannot assume, however, that all of our listeners consistently read them. Like first-century believers, many of our listeners receive their only exposure to the Bible when they hear it read on Sunday morning.

The text's divine authority and our listeners' needs beckon us—let us read the text well.

EFFECTIVE SCRIPTURE READING

Effective public Scripture reading includes at least five elements:

- *Familiarity:* We read the text well when we know the text well. This familiarity comes by reading the text aloud multiple times, noting the rhythm and structure of words, phrases, sentences, and paragraphs, and the punctuation that ties them together. Any terms in the text that are difficult to pronounce—names or places, perhaps—require additional practice.
- *Understanding:* As we read a text aloud, we make interpretive decisions about the text. These decisions include what words to emphasize, what phrases merit raised volume or pitch, and what concepts warrant a quieter voice or lower pitch. Pauses and pace variance give listeners clues about the text's main and subordinate ideas. Reading the text well, therefore, requires prior and careful exegesis of the text, assuring that we understand the text's various ideas and how they relate to one another.
- *Emotion:* Biblical texts brim with emotion—Abraham's heartache when God instructed him to sacrifice Isaac, Jesus' anguish on the cross, John's exuberance when picturing Heaven's worship in Revelation, or his fright when describing God's judgment in the same book. If we read such texts with flat voices and stiff faces, we betray their meanings and intentions.
- *Verbal Communication Skills:*
  - » Based on the rhythms of the text, the preacher's voice should provide variety in both pitch and pace. A lower pitch and slower pace signifies something to contemplate: "Father, into your hands I commit my Spirit" (Luke 23:46). A higher pitch and quicker pace signifies enthusiasm: "He is not here. He has risen!" (Luke 24:6).
  - » Pauses before and after main ideas set them apart: "Therefore, there is now [pause] no condemnation [pause] for those who are in Christ Jesus" (Rom. 8:1). Furthermore, pauses allow listeners time to digest vital truths or to consider difficult questions.
  - » Every sentence contains words or phrases that serve as the focal point of the sentence's message. We can

verbally emphasize these particular words or phrases to reflect the text's emphasis.

- *Nonverbal Communication Skills:*
  - » Effective Bible readers maintain a degree of eye contact with their listeners, even while reading. When readers know their texts well, their eyes can alternate every few seconds between the text and their listeners.
  - » Physical movement while reading can reinforce (1) actual movement occurring in the text, such as a character traveling from one city to another; and, (2) a text's transition from one idea to another.
  - » While a preacher holds a Bible in one hand, the other hand remains free to gesture.
- *Conversational Tone:* The previous elements should not exaggerate the reading such that it becomes an inflated theatrical performance. Imagine a lively conversation between two friends. Each friend speaks with variance in pitch and pace. They emphasize particular words, and their voices and body language reflect emotions appropriate to the conversation. Those who read Scripture well speak in a similar manner.

THE EXERCISE

1. Print your upcoming sermon's primary Scripture text on a piece of paper that is small enough to fit in your Bible, but has margins and spacing sufficient for notes.
2. Answer these questions and follow these instructions, based on your careful interpretation of the text:
   - What emotions does the text display? What expression do you imagine on the biblical writer's face while he wrote each paragraph? Label these emotions in the margins next to the paragraphs (maybe: excited, frustrated, concerned, heartbroken, joyful, awestruck, or confused).
   - What portions of the text should you read more quickly and with a higher pitch? Mark them with an arrow pointing up. What portions should you read more slowly and with lower pitch? Mark them with arrows pointing down. Some portions of the text, of course, should be read at a normal, conversational pace and pitch. Leave these portions unmarked.

- What junctures in the text call for physical movement—either because of movement described in the text (such as a character traveling), or because of a transition in the author's thought? Mark with arrows pointing left or right, corresponding to the most appropriate movement.
- If the original author spoke the text aloud, what words or phrases would he emphasize in each sentence? Underline them.
- Where should you pause to set apart the text's main ideas, to let listeners digest a particular concept, or to indicate the transition to a new idea? Mark these places in the text with two vertical lines.
3. Utilizing the reading aids prepared in step 1, practice reading the text aloud at least five times in the days before you preach. Read while standing so that you can move and gesture. The final two times you read, attempt to make some eye contact with an imaginary audience.
4. Tuck the text that you prepared into your Bible to use the day you preach.

ADDITIONAL SUGGESTIONS

- Either video or audio record yourself reading the text a few days before you preach. Critique the video in relation to the principles discussed earlier in this chapter.
- Memorize the Scripture text so that you can recite it to the congregation, rather than reading it. This will allow unbroken eye contact and unrestricted movement and gestures.
- Briefly introduce the passage before you read it. At minimum, state the book, chapter, and verses. A sentence or two of background may also prove helpful: "Acts 2:42–47, as Luke describes the fellowship of the church in its earliest days ..."
- Have someone else read the sermon text immediately before you preach. This will isolate the reading of Scripture from other elements of the worship service, giving it more emphasis. Make sure the person knows how to read well publicly, grasps the gravity of the task, and practices sufficiently.
- Organize a team of Scripture readers who read sermon texts and other appropriate passages during worship

services. A local speech or drama teacher might help you train the team.

"I TRIED IT"

"I didn't think this exercise would help me, even though I have always struggled reading aloud (and am a little self-conscience about it). I did the exercise in preparation for three Sundays this month. After doing the exercise, I felt far more confident when I read my sermon text from the stage. Using the arrows for emotions and lines for pausing were particularly helpful, as was giving extra practice to difficult names. I plan to continue doing this exercise."

Jason Warden, Knoxville, Tennessee

"I was surprised by the results. For two messages I inserted all the Scriptures I used in my notes. For two other messages I picked up and read my Scriptures from the Bible itself. I then asked a large sampling of people for their input. An overwhelming number of people commented that my actual physical holding of the Bible added both significance and power to the reading of God's word and my message. It is a lesson in nonverbal communication I won't forget."

Jeff Whitlock, Memphis, Tennessee

"I used this exercise while preaching a series from Jesus' parables. I memorized the passage each week, and presented it in a dramatic way, relating Jesus' emotions as best as I could. This helped the congregation get in touch with the text better than they had in previous weeks. Also, we added three additional Scripture readings each service that related to the sermon text. In the end, the congregation had a better sense of the authority of God's Word over the sermon and service."

Matthew Sullivan, Shoals, Indiana

RESOURCES FOR FURTHER STUDY

- *Devote Yourself to the Public Reading of Scripture: The Transforming Power of the Well-Spoken Word,* by Jeffrey Arthurs (Kregel, 2012).

- *Unleashing the Word: Rediscovering the Public Reading of Scripture*, by Max McLean and Warren Bird (Zondervan, 2009).
- "Mark's Gospel," video of Max McLean reciting Mark. Access at http://www.listenersbible.com/performance.
- "Giving Voice to the Bible: Expository Scripture Reading," by Wayne McDill. Access at www.preaching.com/resources /articles/11581093.
- "Reading Scripture Aloud," by Richard F. Ward. Access at www.religion-online.org/showarticle.asp?title=342.

Have Listeners Evaluate You

Great athletes depend on coaching even after they achieve success. Michael Jordan had Phil Jackson. Rocky Marciano had Charley Goldman. And Jack Nicklaus, Jack Grout. These legends knew that another set of eyes—someone with thorough knowledge of the sport and intimate familiarity with their particular games—could provide invaluable feedback.

Preaching students receive similar feedback when they study in Bible college or seminary. They deliver sermons in front of professors and other students. They critique one another, offering encouragement, insight, and suggestions. Once they graduate, however, few preachers seek deliberate, thoughtful feedback about their sermons. As a result, they receive only sporadic and unreliable evaluation. An elderly lady may rave at the door that it was the best sermon she's ever heard. She said the same thing last week, though, and will say it again next week. Someone else may offer an occasional complaint based on a particular pet peeve, or challenge a point of doctrine. Substantive feedback, though, seldom occurs.

A preacher who never seeks intentional, systematic evaluation after leaving the classroom is like a baseball player who learned to hit in little league, but never receives coaching in the years that follow. He thinks his body aligns correctly, that his hips and shoulders rotate in harmony, and that the bat stays on the proper plane. It takes another set of eyes, however, to see the reality—a reality which may look more like Bugs Bunny than Babe Ruth.

Other preachers can help provide such evaluation, as can a simple video camera that enables us to view ourselves (future exercises address both of these). Our own listeners, however, may provide the best insight. Those who listen to our preaching on a weekly basis, who know our quirks and passions, can—if prodded and guided—provide multiple sets of eyes to evaluate whether or not our sermons communicate in the manner that we perceive and intend.

THE EXERCISE

1. Develop a questionnaire that you will distribute to a select group of your listeners after an upcoming sermon.
   - Feel free to include whatever questions you believe will provide the most valuable feedback.
   - Include portions related to content, delivery, and relevance.
   - Include questions that ask participants to rate aspects of the sermon on a scale, and open-ended questions that invite them to provide comments.
   - The questions should give specific, concrete data concerning that day's sermon (not, "Do you think I'm a good preacher?").
   - The survey should require five to ten minutes to complete.
   - See an example questionnaire on the next page. Also, Calvin Seminary provides an excellent evaluation tool online: http://cep.calvinseminary.edu/engageCongregation /sermonEvaluation/sermonEvaluationForm.pdf.
2. Invite at least fifteen people who will be in attendance the next time you preach to complete the questionnaire immediately following the service. The more surveys you receive, the more reliable and helpful the results.
3. Collect and tabulate the results.
4. Evaluate the results. What did the surveys indicate were the sermon's strengths and weaknesses? What recurring themes appeared in the participants' comments? Did anything surprise you? As you prepare your next sermon, how can you better capitalize on your strengths and work to overcome your weaknesses?

EXAMPLE QUESTIONNAIRE

I need your help! As I continually try to grow in my preaching, I would appreciate your feedback about today's sermon. Your responses will remain anonymous.

Gender (circle one):   male   female

Age (circle one):   under 20   20 – 39   40 – 59   60 +

For questions 1 – 12, use the following scale to indicate the degree to which you agree or disagree with each statement about today's sermon:

*1=strongly disagree 2=somewhat disagree 3=unsure
4=somewhat agree 5=strongly agree*

CONTENT

1. The introduction made me want to listen to the rest of the sermon.   1 2 3 4 5
2. The sermon had a logical flow; it was easy to follow.   1 2 3 4 5
3. The sermon clearly explained the meaning of the Scripture text.   1 2 3 4 5
4. The conclusion brought the sermon to a challenging climax.   1 2 3 4 5

RELEVANCE

5. The sermon addressed themes that are important to my life.   1 2 3 4 5
6. The stories and examples helped me connect with the sermon.   1 2 3 4 5
7. The sermon motivated me to live more faithfully to Christ.   1 2 3 4 5
8. The sermon equipped me to live more faithfully to Christ.   1 2 3 4 5

DELIVERY

9. The preacher's style of speaking helped make the sermon interesting.   1 2 3 4 5
10. The preacher's vocabulary was appropriate to the sermon and setting. 1 2 3 4 5
11. I felt as if the preacher was talking *with* me (as opposed to *at* me).   1 2 3 4 5
12. I felt as if the preacher believed what he was saying.   1 2 3 4 5

For questions 13–17, circle the numbers that best reflect your perceptions of today's sermon.

13.	cold	1	2	3	4	5	warm
14.	obscure	1	2	3	4	5	clear
15.	dull	1	2	3	4	5	interesting
16.	impractical	1	2	3	4	5	relevant
17.	formal	1	2	3	4	5	conversational

18. As well as you can remember, please write the main point of the sermon in one sentence.

19. What did you most appreciate about today's sermon?

20. What suggestion(s) would you make to improve today's sermon?

21. Did you feel today's sermon was more or less effective than usual? Why?

Thanks for your help!

ADDITIONAL SUGGESTIONS

- In addition to gender and age, collect more demographic information. You might ask how long the participant has attended this church, or how long he or she has been a Christian. Such information will help gauge how your sermons reach listeners of various demographic groups.
- For smooth logistics, ask participants to meet in a classroom immediately after the service, and have a friend administer the survey.
- If you administer the same survey two or three times over the span of a year, you can compare them to see recurring patterns and to check your progress in particular areas.
- When evaluating the results, check your ego. Often, we respond to criticism with defensiveness, or by rationalizing away suggestions. Instead, evaluate with humility and a genuine desire to grow and improve.

"I TRIED IT"

"It's easy to fall into the trap of measuring success by how I 'feel' the sermon went. The real question is, 'What did people hear?' We can't know unless we ask them. Inviting evaluation is a win-win. If your preaching is effective, people have the opportunity to encourage and affirm you. If you're missing the mark, they can help you improve. In asking for evaluation, we check our egos at the door to do whatever it takes to most effectively spread the gospel!"

Paul Wingfield, St. Louis, Missouri

"In addition to a written evaluation, I asked our videographer to tape the service. This evaluation was an excellent opportunity for me to get specific feedback on my preaching, something I have never had before. We included people of all ages, both long term members and newcomers. It was especially helpful to see how the sermon was received by the different generations. I will do this again."

Rodger Thompson, Wichita, Kansas

"When I did this exercise, I asked for some demographic

information—this helped me see who I was connecting with and who I might have been missing with my sermons. The evaluations also helped by showing areas of my preaching style that may not be as effective as I thought. This is definitely a practice that can benefit my ministry and preaching."

Tim Grasham, Frankfort, Indiana

RESOURCES FOR FURTHER STUDY

- *Make the Word Come Alive: Lessons From Laity*, by Mary Alice Mulligan and Ronald J. Allen (Chalice Press, 2006).
- "Sermon Evaluation Form," provided by Calvin Theological Seminary. Access at http://cep.calvinseminary.edu/engageCongregation/sermonEvaluation/sermonEvaluationForm.pdf.
- "Sermon Evaluation," by Paul Lamey. Access at http://expositorythoughts.wordpress.com/2007/02/11/sermon-evaluation.
- "Sermon Evaluation," a free tool provided by Better Sermons.org that enables anonymous evaluation online. Access at http://www.bettersermons.org/article.php?id=3.

Listen to a Storyteller

I learned the power of story early on. When I sat in church as a small boy, if a preacher began telling a story, I looked up from my coloring book and leaned forward. My ears perked as my imagination ignited. Principles and concepts I had difficulty understanding became people, events, and pictures I could envision. As I grew older, I raided my father's bookshelves for his *Encyclopedia of 7700 Illustrations*, and Paul Harvey's *The Rest of the Story*. As I read, I constantly pulled on my mother's pants leg, "Mom! Listen to this one!"

Stories portray truth. And, they portray truth in a memorable, motivating, challenging manner.

The Bible uses narrative more than any other literary form. In fact, the whole of Scripture unfolds the single story of God's effort to redeem His fallen children. The Bible contains its nonnarrative moments, of course, but even its Beatitudes, proverbs, and precepts find their context in the story. The Old Testament invites readers to walk alongside of Noah, Abraham, and King David. Jesus takes us to that dangerous road between Jerusalem and Jericho, to the sower's field, and before the bench of an unjust judge. Paul tells and retells of the bright light on Damascus Road and of the Lord who saved and commissioned him. Neither Jesus nor biblical writers used narrative only as decoration—explaining points, then illustrating them with stories. Instead, the stories themselves teach truths, and more poignantly than would lists of precepts.

Furthermore, we live in a world of stories—the moment we slap the snooze button, the story of the day begins. One event leads to another, which leads to yet another. We speak (dialogue) and interact with others (characters), solve problems (plot), and experience life with all five senses (description). The day unfolds like a novel, not like bullet points. We live in story. For these reasons—and numerous more—effective preachers saturate their sermons with stories. Therefore, the next two exercises will help us hone our storytelling abilities. First, this week's exercise will lead us to listen to and evaluate effective storytellers. Then, next week's exercise will help us craft and tell effective stories of our own.

THE EXERCISE

1. Prepare a chart like the one below. You will use this chart to evaluate a few stories.

Plot	Characters	Dialogue	Language
Did the story introduce a complication near its beginning? What moved the story toward a resolution? How was the complication resolved? What scenes did the story progress through?	Who were the characters? What details did the storyteller reveal about them? Did the story include a protagonist and/or an antagonist? Did the storyteller speak as one of the characters, or as an all-knowing narrator?	If the storyteller used dialogue, what did the dialogue reveal about the characters? Why did the storyteller choose dialogue at particular junctures of the story?	A previous exercise taught the principle, "show, don't tell." At what points did the storyteller follow this principle? What descriptive nouns and action verbs made the story more vivid ?

2. Go to at least one of the websites listed below (or feel free to search for others). Watch or listen to stories for about forty-five minutes. As you listen, record your observations for at least one of the stories on the chart you prepared in step 1.
    *   To Listen to Stories:
        »   Enoch Pratt Library: http://www.prattlibrary.org/home/storyIndex.aspx
        »   Storyteller.net: http://www.storyteller.net/stories/audio
    *   To Watch Stories:
        »   BibleTelling Channel: http://www.youtube.com/user/BibleTelling

» Dr. Mike Lockett: http://www.mikelockett.com/video_
player.php

» Dan Lemonnier: http://www.banjotales.com

3. Reflect: What made the stories effective or ineffective?
How did these stories differ from the stories you usually tell? What did you learn through this exercise that
will enable you to tell stories more effectively in your upcoming sermons?

EXAMPLE

I watched a video of John Walsh telling, "Jack and the Robbers,"
and recorded my observations in the chart below.

Plot	Characters	Dialogue	Language
Jack's mother sent Jack to find money for his family to pay their bills (this is the story's complication). On his walk down the road, Jack encountered four animals who wouldn't normally get along with each other (a secondary complication)—a cat, dog, rooster, and donkey. They were willing to join together, however, to help Jack. They came upon a cabin and found robbers inside counting their gold. Jack had all the animals pile on one another and make noise. The frightened robbers ran and left their gold. Jack returned the gold to the bank. The bank gave Jack a big reward Jack used the reward to buy food for his friends, then to pay all his family's bills.	Jack's mother appears only briefly in the beginning to introduce the problem (bills needing paid). Jack—main character, protagonist. Cat, dog, rooster, and donkey—Jack's friends who join together to help solve the complication. Robbers in cabin—unwittingly become solution to problem. The storyteller spoke in the 3rd person, as a narrator.	The story included a great deal of dialogue—primarily between Jack and the animals. When the storyteller used dialogue, his eyes focused on an imaginary other character. And, he altered his voice to fit each character. This story used dialogue to inform listeners, and to move the plot along.	Surprisingly, the storyteller did not use much descriptive language, primarily because so much of the story was told in dialogue. The storyteller used verbal and nonverbal delivery techniques—such as changing his voice for the various characters—to add a descriptive nature to the story.

REFLECTIONS:

- I was most struck by the use of dialogue. The storyteller provided much of the story's necessary information through the characters' conversations. And, the plot unfolded through dialogue. When I tell stories, I usually just describe events and conversations, rather than actually allowing the characters to speak. If, instead, I allow the characters to speak, this will bring the stories more to life for my listeners.
- The story involved two levels of complication—Jack's family's financial need, and the animals' prejudice toward one another. The solution to the primary complication (financial need) depended on the resolution of the secondary complication (the animals' prejudice). Having two levels of complication gave the story more texture. Furthermore, the story's plot moved based on the primary complication, but the secondary complication taught a moral lesson—to solve larger problems, people need to overcome prejudice. I structure my stories too simply—thinking only of a single complication and its resolution. To improve my storytelling, I need to include more texture.
- This particular storyteller did not use as much descriptive language as many storytellers use. His speaking skills made up for the lack of descriptive language, but I wonder if his effectiveness could increase by including more descriptive nouns and action verbs. Instead of "went," for example, he could use "hurried," "ran," or "hopped."

ADDITIONAL SUGGESTIONS

1. Interview a professional storyteller. You can find a list of over a thousand professional storytellers at http://professionalstoryteller.ning.com/profiles/members. Use the search feature to search by state.
2. Listen to a preacher who tells stories well, such as Max Lucado or Fred Craddock. Observe how they tell stories, and how their stories relate to their overall sermons.
3. Eavesdrop on conversations around you, and consider

how people typically tell stories in everyday conversation. How do these differ from stories you hear in sermons or by storytellers?

"I TRIED IT"

"Traditionally, preachers use stories as add-ons to illustrate truth. We fail to realize that stories can, by themselves, *be* truth. Listening to good storytellers not only helped me be more descriptive and creative, it also helped me to bring in the audience's story as I present them with God's story. The stories I find most engaging fit this criteria. Likewise, the sermons I have presented effectively meet this criteria."

Kirk Dice, Suffolk, Virginia

"I really enjoyed watching videos of storytellers online. The stories that were most engaging to me were both casually presented, yet well-spoken. I felt like I could have been sitting in the teller's living room listening to a story he had told a hundred times. That balance of personal connection to the listener and practiced recitation seems rare. I lean toward the practiced recitation side, so I was motivated to be more personal and informal in the stories I tell in preaching."

Adam Colter, Newburgh, Indiana

RESOURCES FOR FURTHER STUDY

* *Anyone Can Tell a Story: Bob's Guide to Storytelling*, by Bob Hartman (Monarch, 2011).
* *The Art of Storytelling: Easy Steps to Presenting an Unforgettable Story*, by John Walsh (Moody, 2003).
* "Narratives: How to listen to a story ..." by Barry McWilliams. Access at http://www.eldrbarry.net/clas/gb/b19narr.pdf.
* "Dr. Fred Craddock on Storytelling in Sermons." Access at http://www.youtube.com/watch?v=DHGqfVMm_Xo.

Tell a Story

When I was in college, several guys who roomed near me in the dorm learned to play guitar. Most hours of the day, and many hours of the night, chords and discords floated throughout our wing. Some learned the instrument fairly quickly, and well. Others, though—not so well. I fit the latter category. I had never played an instrument, and I can't even sing on key. Certain that all cool ministers play guitar, though, I picked up a buddy's instrument and began strumming. "Here are the first three chords you need to learn," he said, while positioning my fingers on particular frets and strings. "But you'll have to practice. A lot." I practiced until my fingertips were so sore I could no longer type papers for class. Eventually, I learned those three chords well enough to play music vaguely similar to actual songs.

A few months into my guitar phase, I attended a concert by Christian artist Wes King. His fingers danced across the guitar strings like the wings of a thousand butterflies. Waves of magnificent melodies gushed through the concert hall. My heart raced. My fingers fluttered across my own imaginary instrument (yes, I admit it—air guitar). My head nodded and my foot tapped to the beat.

At that moment, I resolved to practice. When I returned to my dorm, I would grab that six-string and pluck away until I played like Wes King.

Another half hour into the concert, however, I stopped tapping my foot. I returned the air guitar to its air case. My head ceased nodding, and instead hung low. How could I ever play like him? Sure, I had those three chords down pat. But to play—really play—would require far more practice than I could imagine, and more ability than I could muster. So, I gave up. My guitar phase ended at that concert.

When we hear an expert doing what we want to do, the "That's amazing! I want to do that!" often regresses into "I could never be that good. I might as well give up."

Good storytellers leave their listeners spellbound. And, they leave many preachers feeling terribly inadequate. The last exercise led you to listen to storytellers online. If that exercise left you more discouraged than equipped, this week's should help.

EXERCISE, PART 1

- Before you read any further, spend about ten minutes writing a story about something that you recently experienced—perhaps a wedding or funeral, a holiday, a trip to the grocery store, or your first day at a new ministry. The story does not need to recount a momentous occasion—the common, everyday experiences of life often communicate best in sermons.

UNDERSTANDING STORY

Effective stories are well designed, described, and delivered.

Designing the Story

- *Set the Scene:* When and where does the story take place? Provide enough detail to help listeners feel like they have stepped into the story.
- *Introduce Characters:* In stories, people and/or things interact with one another—even if this only involves a person interacting with him- or herself. Introduce the characters, and provide whatever details about them that will hold significance to the story.
- *Describe the Complication:* Early in the story, introduce something that needs resolved—a conflict, tension, or difficult circumstance. Do not yet present a resolution, or the point of the story ("Let me tell you how I learned about honesty after stealing a candy bar."). Instead, only present the complication ("My

stomach growled as I walked by the store, but I had no money in my pocket.").

- *Move From Complication Toward Resolution*: Beyond just description ("Grandma prayed a lot"), stories describe particular events that unfold ("I'll never forget the time when Grandma ..."). This series of events carries the story like scenes carry a play, leading listeners from the complication toward a resolution. Therefore, sketch out the series of events that carry your story.
- *Resolve the Complication:* The complication introduced at the beginning finds resolution at the end. This resolution usually involves the solving of a problem and/or the learning of a lesson. Though it may not tie up every loose end from the story, it leaves listeners feeling like they've completed the journey.

Describing the Story

- *Use Descriptive Nouns:* Rather than, "I bought a car;" say, "I bought a 1996 Taurus with faded green paint and balding tires." The first shares information, the second paints a picture.
- *Use Descriptive Verbs:* Rather than, "I went into the principal's office;" say, "I marched into the principal's office." Or, "I crawled ... sauntered ... strutted ... moseyed."
- *Show, Don't Tell:* Recall this principle from exercise 6. Instead of telling listeners, "I was nervous," show them through word pictures what nervousness looks like— "My hand shook and beads of sweat appeared on my forehead."
- *Speak to the Senses:* What sights, sounds, smells, tastes, or elements of touch can you include in the story? "Stories must have the smell and sound and taste of life," writes Fred Craddock. "'There was this beggar sitting at the gate.' Wait a minute. Give me a chance to experience the beggar at the gate. See the rags, smell the odor, hear the coins in the tin cup, see the hollow eyes. Don't rush to the destination. Take the trip."[1]

---

1. Fred Craddock, "Preaching as Storytelling: How to Rely on Stories to Carry

- *Include dialogue:* Allow listeners to eavesdrop on conversations between characters. Dialogue makes characters more real and accessible. And, dialogue leads listeners from observing the story to participating in it.

Delivering the Story

- *Picture the Story:* When you tell the story, picture it in your mind. This will help you include vivid details and descriptions. Do not memorize the words you prepared, but the pictures you will describe.
- *Step Into the Story:* Once you picture the story, mentally step into it. This enables your movements and gestures to reflect the story. If you describe a telephone ringing in the next room, for example, you will physically turn that direction and point listeners to the telephone.
- *Trust the Story:* After we complete a story, we sometimes we feel tempted to explain it: "This story illustrates that ..." In most cases, listeners do not need such explanations, and they actually find them redundant. Stories—if designed and told well—can stand on their own.

EXERCISE, PART 2

1. Review my story from the beginning of this chapter (about learning to play guitar). Can you identify the elements discussed under "Designing the Story" and "Describing the Story?"
2. Revise the story you wrote near the beginning of this chapter. Incorporate the principles taught in the remainder of the chapter.
3. Over the next few days, tell your story in conversations with friends and family. This will reveal what aspects of the story are most and least effective so that you can make needed adjustments.
4. Find an upcoming sermon in which the story will help portray a particular truth you will preach, and include the story in that sermon.

Spiritual Freight," in *The Art and Craft of Biblical Preaching: A Comprehensive Resource for Today's Communicators* (Grand Rapids, MI: Zondervan, 2005), 492–493.

5. If you will tell other stories in this week's sermon (and you should!), prepare them according to the principles taught in this chapter.

"I TRIED IT"

"Story is where thinking and imagination collide. This exercise brought God's Word and life experiences to the center of that collision. Telling the story to my family ahead of time especially helped. From their facial expressions, I could tell if they imagined the story clearly or not. I then tweaked the story until their imaginations were moved. After I told it in the sermon, one lady said she imagined her son getting into the same mischief as I described ... then she laughed and asked how I survived childhood!"

David Caffee, Englewood, Tennessee

"I completely agree with everything this chapter teaches. I would add one additional observation from my experience. A story needs to be told well, but a story has to come from the heart. Work to make the story as vivid as possible, but never let the preparation take away from the 'realness' of the story. The magic in storytelling is when realness meets preparation—this results in a story that touches hearts."

Jeff Whitlock, Memphis, Tennessee

"This exercise inspired me. I created a modern story based on the invalid in John 5, and added elements about his emotional and spiritual struggles. By the time I revealed the text, they had already mentally stepped into his shoes. For several weeks people approached me—not to tell me that they liked the sermon, but to share with me the how it made them feel and the emotions it stirred. I have never had that type of feedback before."

Jonathan Absher, Follansbee, West Virginia

RESOURCES FOR FURTHER STUDY

- *Creating Stories That Connect: A Pastor's Guide to Storytelling,* by Bruce Seymour (Kregel, 2007).
- *Experiential Storytelling: (Re)Discovering Narrative to Communicate God's Message,* by Mark Miller (Zondervan, 2003).

- "How to Tell a Story," by Mark Twain. Access at http://www.mtwain.com/How_To_Tell_A_Story/0.html.
- "It's All in How You Tell It," by Austin Tucker. Access at http://www.preaching.com/resources/articles/11581048/page-1.

People Watch

When I think of my "sermon," I often think of a document—researched, assembled, and printed, lying on my desk waiting for me to present it. I interact with the text, study commentaries, perform word studies, organize my thoughts, outline the message, complete a five-page manuscript, then practice the sermon a few times so that I can preach it with minimal notes. If I learned from some of the other exercises in this book, I pray throughout the process. I seek God's truth from God's Word through the guidance of His Spirit. The process involves God, God's Word, and me.

Each of these elements stand critical to biblical preaching. One element, however, remains missing—my listeners. Effective preachers do not just prepare documents, they prepare for events that occur in real time and space (not just on paper) during which they lead listeners to encounter God through His Word. Our preparations, therefore, should involve more than just ourselves and Scripture. We must also consider how we can most effectively lead people—actual living and breathing people who lead dynamic lives, ask difficult questions, and face complex issues—to understand God's truth and experience Him in the process.

This week's exercise will bring us face-to-face with ordinary, complicated people who do not fit easily into categories and whose struggles seldom find solutions in three easy steps. And, it will force us to consider how we can best lead them to encounter God's truth found in a biblical text.

To accomplish this feat, we will practice the age-old sport of people watching.

CLARIFICATIONS

Before we proceed through the exercise, a few points of clarification deserve mention:

- We will not watch people to judge them. We mustn't allow pride or prejudice to enter our thoughts.
- People watching, for our purposes, involves imagination and empathy more than evaluation. As we observe people, we imagine their stories—their day-to-day existence—based on what we see and hear. Then, we envision how our sermons might connect with the people we watch.
- Artists and novelists often people watch to nudge their creativity. Perhaps they see a person in line at a supermarket with a snow shovel and three cartons of bubble gum. Around these bare facts, they build a story. We might allow people watching to stretch our imaginations in a similar manner.
- As we watch people, we must take care not to stare at any individual too long (especially a person of the opposite gender). Remain respectful and conscious of people's privacy.

THE EXERCISE

1. Complete some preparation toward your upcoming sermon. Do not yet place the final touches on the sermon, but study enough that you have a general idea of what truth you will preach, and how you will present it.
2. Choose a location where a large number of people gather or pass through—perhaps a café beside a busy street, the food court in a mall, a bustling fast food restaurant or coffee shop, a park that draws many visitors, or a city bus.
3. Bring a legal pad or electronic device to record your observations.
4. Find an unobtrusive position, then observe people for at least an hour. Consider yourself a detective. What clues do you see to peoples' stories?

5. Ask yourself questions such as these while you people watch:
   - What expressions are on their faces? Why, do you imagine, this is the case?
   - Do they rush from one place to another, or move in a more relaxed manner? What might occasion this?
   - What does their body language indicate? Do they seem nervous? Excited? Worried? Bored? Frustrated? Happy?
   - If you hear people speak, what do their words—and the way they speak these words—indicate?
   - What does their dress communicate about their personalities, backgrounds, and their perceptions of themselves?
   - Think like an artist or novelist—what stories can you build around what you have observed?
6. Ask yourself questions such as these to aid your sermon preparation (these questions require some imagination and speculation):
   - What do you imagine those you observe believe about God? About themselves?
   - What keeps them awake at night? What are their greatest fears and worries?
   - What are they most proud of?
   - What about your upcoming sermon might confuse them? What questions or comments might they have about what you plan to preach?
   - What might frighten them about the upcoming sermon?
   - What message of grace does the sermon contain for them?
   - If the people you observed heard this sermon, what truth do you most hope they would understand?
   - If they took your sermon seriously, how would it impact their lives?
   - If your congregation consisted entirely of those you watched, how would this change your preaching?
   - How could you best explain, illustrate, and apply the truth of your sermon for the people you observed?
7. When you return to your study, adjust your plans and design your upcoming sermon so that it most effectively communicates to the people of your community.

"I TRIED IT"

"I've always imagined people during my preparation, however I've primarily imagined the people in the pews—church people. This exercise made me wonder what my 'church language' and 'preaching voice' would sound like to these folks at the donut shop. Would they understand, and would the content really matter to them? Though I won't preach to the unchurched every Sunday, when they do come I want to make sure my content and delivery communicate clearly the relevance of God's Word to their lives."

Paul Viers, Abingdon, Virginia

"I've always been a big proponent of this concept of 'people watching.' Obviously, it cannot take precedent over the exegesis of a text, but learning to be 'people exegetes' or 'cultural exegetes' is indispensable in preparing a sermon that helps people find their way back to God. Much of my sermon writing is actually done in coffee shops—this allows me the opportunity to imagine that I'm writing for those very people sitting around me, which in so many ways I am."

Mark Nelson, Knoxville, Tennessee

"I tried this exercise and found it to be very helpful. 'People Watching' really helped me zero in on everyone. As I watched, I noticed most people were in a hurry and did not make eye contact with anyone. I tried to imagine how could I best communicate my sermon to people who seem to be in such a hurry."

Matthew Sullivan, Shoals, Indiana

RESOURCES FOR FURTHER STUDY

- *People Watching: The Desmond Morris Guide to Body Language,* by Desmond Morris (Vintage, 2002).
- *Preaching to a Postmodern World: A Guide to Reaching Twenty-First Century Listeners,* by Graham Johnston (Baker, 2001).
- "How to Begin People Watching." Access at http://www.wikihow.com/Begin-People-Watching.

Polish Your Thesis

In *Biblical Preaching*, Haddon Robinson offers one of the more memorable and often cited images in homiletics: "A sermon should be a bullet, not a buckshot."[1] Rather than scattered, numerous concepts, effective sermons offer a laser-like focus on a single, specific idea. We learn this principle in preaching and speech courses, but as years pass, we grow lazy and our thesis statements become hazy. This laziness leads to three common mistakes.

First, we preach too many ideas, and give each equal emphasis. A sermon becomes a collection of points—in reality, four of five brief sermons on different concepts that we happen to preach within the same thirty minutes—rather than the development of a single concept. Listeners hear a ragbag of stories, suggestions, and theories, but have no sense of the larger idea to which they contribute.

Second, we think of broad themes rather than specific ideas. When asked about the subject matter of their sermons, preachers often respond with single words—faith, perhaps. Instead, consider what precisely the text teaches about faith: "Faith blossoms as it perseveres amidst persecution." The broad theme leaves listeners in a fog. The precise thesis dissipates the fog to reveal a particular, compelling truth.

Third, we fail to word the thesis carefully. Imprecise wording leads to lengthy, clumsy statements that listeners struggle to understand and do not even attempt to remember. The best preachers, in contrast, phrase this single idea carefully. They meticulously craft

---

1. Haddon Robinson, Biblical Preaching: *The Development and Delivery of Expository Messages*, 2nd ed. (Grand Rapids, MI: Zondervan, 2001), 35.

each phrase to achieve a concise, memorable, image-inducing thesis statement. John Henry Jowett emphasized this point:

> I have a conviction that no sermon is ready for preaching, not ready for writing out, until we can express its theme in a short, pregnant sentence as clear as crystal. I find that getting that sentence is the hardest, the most exacting, and the most fruitful labour in my study. To compel oneself to fashion that sentence, to dismiss every word that is vague, ragged, ambiguous, to think oneself through to a form of words which defines the theme with scrupulous exactness—this is surely one of the most essential factors in the making of a sermon: and I do not think any sermon ought to be preached or even written, until that sentence has emerged, clear and lucid as a cloudless moon.[2]

A compelling thesis statement—that single concept around which the sermon develops, stated in the most exact, memorable sentence possible—will ring in listeners' ears long after the sermon ends.

THE EXERCISE

The exercise on the next few pages will help you develop a razor-sharp thesis statement for your upcoming sermon. After you study your text—considering its context, examining its key words, and tracing its arguments—ask these three questions to develop your sermon's thesis:

1. What question does the text answer?

If your text is the answer to a question, what is the question? Begin formulating this question with a single word that encapsulates the broad theme of the passage. If you plan to preach on Matthew 6:25–34, for example, that single term might be "worry."[3] Then, use the interrogatives (who, what, when, where,

---

2. Ibid., Robinson, 37.
3. A common mistake is to define a broad theme, but to stop at this point in the

why, or how) to build a question around the term that best reflects what the text teaches about worry. Does the text address: *Who* struggles with worry? *What* are the consequences of worry? *When* is it okay to worry? Probably, Matthew 6 best addresses, *How* can we overcome worry?

2. What answer does the text provide?

What answer does your text provide for the question described above? If we ask, "How can we overcome worry?" the text might provide this answer: "We can overcome our worries when we give attention to our pursuit of God's kingdom."

Note that this stage in the process produces a single concept, not multiple concepts crammed into one sentence. Preachers sometimes include all of a sermon's points in the thesis statement. For Matthew 6:25–34, they might state: "To overcome worry, trust God to feed and clothe you, observe from nature how He provides, and seek first His kingdom." Though the sermon may develop these three points (trust, observe, and seek), a well conceived thesis does not state all the points of a sermon—it states the overriding idea to which the points contribute. As a rule, therefore, a thesis statement will not include an "and" or commas, which indicate the inclusion of multiple ideas.

3. How can I best phrase the answer to form the thesis?

Finally, to form an effective thesis statement, refine the wording of the answer to make it as succinct and memorable as possible. To continue the previous example:

> Text: Matthew 6:25–34
> Question: How can we overcome worry?
> Answer: We can overcome our worries by giving primary attention to our pursuit of God's kingdom.
> Thesis: Worries melt into Kingdom pursuit.

Once you have developed your thesis statement, place it

---

process. The broad theme—a single word—helps send us on the path toward an effective thesis, but it is not the thesis by itself.

carefully in your sermon outline or manuscript. When you preach, emphasize the thesis when you first state it—pause before and after, and repeat it immediately. Then, try to repeat it a few more times, word-for-word, during the remainder of the sermon, so that this single idea resonates in listeners' minds.

ADDITIONAL SUGGESTIONS

The following principles will help you phrase your thesis as concisely and memorably as possible:

- *Eliminate "to be" verbs.* Forms of "be" (be, am, is, are, was, were) make weak verbs—they do not perform any action, nor do they build images. In most cases, you can adjust the wording of your thesis to include a stronger verb.
  - » Instead of: Jesus is the king of the universe.
  - » Try: Jesus reigns over the universe.

- *Use the active voice, not the passive.* In the active voice, the subject of a sentence performs the verb ("The boy threw the ball."). In the passive voice, the subject is acted upon ("The ball was thrown by the boy."). The active voice results in sharper sentences.
  - » Instead of: Servanthood is practiced by dedicated Christians.
  - » Try: Dedicated Christians serve.

- *Use few words.* A small number of carefully chosen words communicate more clearly, and listeners remember them more easily, than verbose sentences.
  - » Instead of: To persevere, we must be mindful of the calling God has placed on our lives.
  - » Try: The perseverant cling to their call.

- *State it in positive language, not negative.* In most cases, listeners will best receive our message if the thesis reflects the positive side of a teaching rather than the negative.
  - » Instead of: Those who forget God's grace fall to temptation.
  - » Try: Those who remember God's grace remain pure.

- *State it in the present tense.* State the timeless truth of the text so that listeners see its relevance for today.

  » Instead of: God provided for Abraham because of Abraham's faithfulness.
  » Try: God provides for the faithful.

- *Consider building an image.* Rather than simply stating a truth, consider hanging that truth on a memorable image.

  » Instead of: The cross solves the sin problem and gives us hope of eternity.
  » Try: The road from despair to hope passes through Calvary.

"I TRIED IT"

"Loved it ... Loved it ... Loved it! As preachers, if we're lucky we have twenty to thirty minutes a week from the pulpit to deliver an insightful and meaningful message from God's Word. This exercise helped me manage my time better by focusing the sermon on a single, carefully worded idea. The exercise was a home run!"

Randall Sidwell, Byrdstown, Tennessee

"This exercise can be applied to any Scripture, but I find it to be most helpful with difficult passages where the main idea is not so obvious (like Psalms and the Prophets). At first, I was too bent on sticking 'to the formula' (step 1, step 2, etc.), but I see this approach as a tool not a formula. Feel free to step outside the steps and to employ plenty of creative thinking. Attaining a clear, memorable thesis (and not how you got there) is the important thing."

Steve Page, Bristol, Tennessee

RESOURCES FOR FURTHER STUDY

- *Communicating for a Change: Seven Keys to Irresistible Communication*, by Andy Stanley (Multnomah, 2006).
- "Preaching the Big Idea: An Interview With Dave Ferguson," by Michael Duduit. Access at http://www.preaching.com/resources/articles/11549241/.
- "What's the Big Idea? The Sermon Thesis—Behind

the Pulpit #4," audio discussion with Wayne Roberts and Bob Turner. Access at http://theequipnetwork. com/whats-the-big-idea-the-sermon-thesis-behind-the-pulpit-4-2.

- "The Sermon Thesis ... Step by Step—Behind the Pulpit #5," audio discussion with Wayne Roberts and Bob Turner. Access at http://theequipnetwork.com/the-sermon -thesis-step-by-step-behind-the-pulpit-5.

Utilize the Five Senses

THE EXERCISE, PART 1

Throughout Scripture, God taught His truths by engaging multiple senses. For example, when He hung a rainbow in the sky, He used the sense of sight to teach Noah about His faithfulness. Stop reading at this point, and spend five to ten minutes listing other instances you recall from Scripture in which God taught using the five senses: touch, taste, sight, smell, and sound.

MULTISENSORY PREACHING

The taste of the Passover lamb. The smell of incense filling the temple. The sound of a mighty rushing wind. The touch of Jesus' hand on leprous skin. The sight of the New Jerusalem coming down out of heaven. The bread and cup—see it, hold it, taste it. Yes, God used the spoken word to proclaim His truth. He also, however, used multiple other means. God created the human body to receive information through five different senses; and, He uses all five to reveal Himself and His truth.

In contemporary churches, however, our teaching depends primarily on the spoken word. Of the five senses—the five ways God created us to receive information—we often consider only what people will hear during our sermons. If God created people to receive information through five portals, would not our preaching grow more effective if we engaged all five?

Rick Blackwood preaches for Christ Fellowship, a large church with multiple campuses in Miami. For his doctoral dissertation, he experimented to discover how the use of various senses impacts a sermon's effectiveness. One weekend, he delivered the same sermon content to three audiences, but varied the means of delivery for each. In one service, the sermon was verbal. In the next service, the sermon was verbal and visual. In the third service, the sermon was verbal, visual, and interactive (connecting with listeners' senses of sound, sight, and touch). Then, he measured how the various modes of delivery affected listeners' attention, comprehension, and retention of sermon content. To attain more accurate results, he repeated the experiment on two additional weekends.

Though Blackwood expected higher scores from sermons that engaged multiple senses, he did not anticipate the incredible degree of difference. When he added visual and interactive elements to the sermons, attention levels increased 142%; comprehension increased 76%, and retention increased 74%.[1] Simply put, the more senses we engage in our preaching, the more people will pay attention, comprehend, and retain God's truth.

Consider, therefore, your upcoming sermon. Can you help relay biblical truth by showing listeners a photograph, or by having an artist paint a picture on stage? Can you put something in people's hands—a rock, a coin, or molding clay? Can you invite listeners to write something, then bring it to a cross on stage or keep it in their pockets? Can you fill the worship center with a scent—perfume, bread baking, or myrrh? Can you fill the worship center with sounds as people enter—a waterfall, sheep bleating, or a thunderstorm? Can you engage their sense of taste with honey, bitter herbs, or roasted lamb? What can you invite people touch, see, hear, smell, and taste to emphasize God's truth?

THE EXERCISE, PART 2

1. After you complete some preparation for your sermon—enough that you have a general sense of the text's teaching and the sermon's main ideas—ask yourself these four questions (you might invite a few creative friends to brainstorm with you).

---

1. Rick Blackwood provides more information concerning the experiment and its implications for preaching in *The Power of Multisensory Preaching and Teaching: Increase Attention, Comprehension, and Retention* (Grand Rapids, MI: Zondervan, 2008).

- *Does the text contain something tangible that I can bring out in the sermon?* If the text includes a tent, light, bread, a vine, a bruised reed, clay, or a shepherd's staff, you can bring these items on stage or put them into people's hands. If the passage discusses a biblical place, you might show a photograph of the place. If the text speaks of a family tree, you can show a diagram. If the passage describes someone's clothing (maybe the high priest or a soldier), you might bring someone on stage and dress them accordingly. If the text speaks of the whole world or many nations, a globe on stage or several flags passed out among your listeners might visually reinforce the truth.
- *Can I communicate the main idea of the sermon using multiple senses?* If the sermon centers on grace, forgiveness, or purity, a particular work of art or an object lesson might reinforce the idea. If the message relates to evangelism, a testimony or drama could portray what you will preach, or a bookmark given to listeners might remind them of the main points throughout the week. If the sermon equips listeners with a godly perspective of themselves, a mirror might prove useful; if it equips them with a godly perspective of others, perhaps a window; or, if it equips them with a godly perspective of creation, maybe a telescope or photographs of nature.
- *If a particular illustration encapsulates the message of the sermon, can I reinforce the illustration using sight, hearing, taste, touch, or sound?* For example, if you tell a story about your grandmother's devotion to Bible reading, you might bring her Bible on stage. If a story tells of a basketball game, a particular food, or something that happened while you were on vacation, you could show something or put an item in listeners' hands, mouths, or ears that accentuates the story.
- *Can I lead listeners to apply the sermon immediately by doing something that involves multiple senses?* Perhaps you could give listeners a few minutes to write a letter, send a text message, journal a prayer, write a sin or temptation on a piece of paper and bring it to a cross on stage, or write a praise on a similar cross. Maybe the entire congregation can voice a prayer together, or a song, that applies the message of the sermon.

2. Based on the brainstorming you completed in step one, write your best multisensory ideas for your upcoming sermon on a chart like this:

SENSE	IDEAS TO ENGAGE EACH SENSE
TOUCH	
TASTE	
SIGHT	
SMELL	
SOUND	

3. Engage at least three of listeners' five senses in your upcoming sermon.

"I TRIED IT"

"Over a few sermons, I tried to punctuate a particular sense in each. One Sunday I had ladies bake cookies, filling the church building with the aroma—we should be sweet aroma in the nostrils of God. While I preached about Jesus calming the storm, sounds of a raging storm came through the speakers. And, during the Christmas season our congregation wrapped gifts for needy families—that Sunday these gifts were stacked fifteen feet high around the auditorium while I preached about ministering to others."

Brian Lakin, Markle, Indiana

"I really enjoyed the process of engaging several senses with my sermon. I found that when it works, it really works, and when it fails, it fails big. It's all about finding a balance. Appealing to senses while people were entering the worship space worked great, as it let them know something different and interesting was happening that Sunday. But too strong of a smell during the message served mostly as a distraction. A balance can certainly serve to enhance a sermon."

Kraig Bishop, Winchester, Virginia

"In a sermon about being 'the light of the world,' I gave everyone candles, lit other candles on stage, and played sounds of thunder and lightening over the speakers. I also turned off the lights at appropriate times. At the end of the sermon, everyone lit their own candles as I encouraged them to spread the light. I had some anxiety beforehand (this is a fairly traditional church), but was astonished at the positive response. Even days later, people spoke of what they learned from the sermon."

Steven Johnson, Clarks Hill, Indiana

RESOURCES FOR FURTHER STUDY

- *The Power of Multisensory Preaching and Teaching: Increase Attention, Comprehension, and Retention*, by Rick Blackwood (Zondervan, 2008).
- *Object Lessons: 100 Lessons from Everyday Life*, by Charles C. Ryrie (Moody, 1991).
- "The Power of Multi-sensory Preaching" by Rick Blackwood. Access at http://www.preaching.com/resources /articles/11602985.
- "Multi-sensory Learning Strategies." Access at http:// www.housing.sc.edu/ace/pdf/ASR/Multisensory LearningStrategies.pdf.

Exegete Before Sermonizing

It's important to do the right things. In many cases, it's also important to do the right things in the right order. I asked some Facebook friends to help illustrate this principle. They responded:

- First measure, then cut.
- First mix the ingredients, then bake the cake.
- First think, then speak.
- First administer anesthesia, then start the surgery.
- First put on the harness, then bungee jump.
- First tranquilize the badger, then put a sweater on it.

Though sermon preparation involves several steps, for now let's condense the steps to two: First study the text, then write the sermon. It sounds simple. Too often, though, we make decisions about the sermon—such as structure, points, illustrations, and applications—before we unpack the text. Consequently, we impose our prior thoughts onto the sermon passage instead of exposing what it actually teaches.

Biblical preachers, in contrast, begin by wrestling with the text. They exegete first, then sermonize.

THE EXERCISE

The exercise on the following pages presents a simple exegetical process—a means of interpreting a biblical text—that will enable you to preach that text's truths to your listeners. Complete the exercise early in your preparation, laying the biblical foundation for the sermon elements you will design later in the week.

The exercise builds on two assumptions. First, it assumes that your upcoming sermon will grow from a particular biblical text. If you had planned a more topical message—one that uses a variety of Scriptures to develop a topic—you might save this exercise for another week. Or, you might alter your plans by choosing a particular text that best addresses your topic, then preparing your sermon based on that text.

Second, the exercise assumes that you will use study aids such as commentaries and similar tools. Fred Craddock teaches preachers to organize their study materials by the days of the week—Monday books are the most technical and academic; Friday books are more devotional. Other books fit the spectrum in between. This exercise requires the Monday and Tuesday books. Save popular level and devotional books and websites for later in your preparation.

1. Observe the Literary Context

When we read a book other than the Bible, we do not open the book to a random page, read an isolated paragraph, and attempt to explain what the author means with that paragraph. Instead, we evaluate a paragraph according to its relationship with the paragraphs surrounding it, with the chapter in which it occurs, and with the entire book.

Biblical passages merit the same concern for context. Your sermon text does not exist in isolation. Rather, it exists in relationship with the teaching that occurs before and after it. Therefore, ask yourself: Why did the Spirit-inspired author place this paragraph where he placed it? How does it build on the paragraphs that precede it, and how does it prepare readers for the paragraphs that follow it? How does this text fit into the author's flow of thought as it progresses through the entire book? How does it relate to God's overall story of redemption through Jesus Christ?

2. Explore the Historical Context

God delivered His truth through historical people, cultures, and situations. You can understand your sermon text more deeply, therefore, by exploring the original circumstances surrounding it. From where and what situation did the author write? What circumstances did the original readers face? Why did the author write this particular book to these particular recipients? What elements of culture or history did the original author and recipients assume that contemporary readers might not catch?

3. Examine the Syntax

After observing the literary and historical contexts, turn your attention to the language, grammar, and structure or your particular text. Biblical authors—inspired and guided by the Spirit—chose words, phrases, and structures carefully. Therefore, examine them carefully

If your text is narrative, through what scenes does the narrative progress? If it is a teaching text, how did the writer arrange his logic? If it is a poem, what is the flow of emotions and/or images? Define any key words around which the text revolves. Observe nouns, verbs, and tenses. Which sentences state truths, which give commands, and which ask questions? Are the questions answered, or are they used rhetorically? Does the text repeat any particular terms, phrases, or images? Does the passage contain any promises or warnings? If so, on what are these promises or warnings based?

4. Identify the Biblical Truth

What do the contexts and syntax contribute to your understanding of the text? What truth did the original writer depict for his original recipients? What does God intend for believers of all generations and cultures to learn from this text?

AN EXAMPLE

1. Observe the Literary Context

I recently prepared a sermon about David's adultery with Bathsheba and subsequent murder of Uriah, from 2 Samuel 11. Prior chapters describe David's succession of triumphant military campaigns and the rise of his kingdom. David achieved prominence and power. Chapter 10 depicts an ongoing battle with the Ammonites that remained unfinished.

In the paragraphs after David's sin, chapter 12 offers particular insight into the reason behind David's fall. When Nathan confronted David, Nathan pointed to the ways God had blessed David. God poured His grace and favor on David and his kingdom. David, though, ignored God's grace—a lapse that left his heart vulnerable to flagrant sin (2 Sam. 12:7–9).

2. Explore the Historical Context

Second Samuel 11:1 sets the story in a historical and cultural context: "In the spring, at the time when kings go off to war, David sent Joab out with the king's men and the whole Israelite army." Research reveals three matters that help us understand the setting. First, winter rains left roads muddy and impassable, and barren winter fields provided no food for passing troops. Thus, wars often stopped in the winter. When spring arrived, roads dried and fields flourished. Battles that halted for the winter, therefore, recommenced in the spring. Second, though some kings remained behind while their armies waged war, previous chapters make clear that David typically led the charge. His decision in 11:1 to remain behind broke his normal pattern. Third, the text states that Bathsheba was "the daughter of Eliam and the wife of Uriah" (2 Sam. 11:3). Second Samuel 23 lists Bathsheba's father and husband as two of David's "mighty men," a group of gifted warriors who'd given their unbridled devotion to David. Bathsheba's grandfather—not listed here but elsewhere—was one of David's most trusted advisors. David knew Bathsheba's family—and presumably Bathsheba—well.

3. Examine the Syntax

Several linguistic and structural clues rise from the text. The term "sent" occurs eleven times in 2 Samuel 11 ("David sent Joab;" "David sent someone to find out about her;" et al.), emphasizing David's passivity that preceded his fall. Also, chapter 11 does not mention God until its final verse, while chapter 12 mentions God fourteen times. The focus shifts from David's sin in chapter 11 to God's response in chapter 12. Additionally, some scholars point to a possible chiasm in 2 Samuel 11–12, a literary device where the narrative funnels down to a central truth in the middle of the story. Central to this story stands the ominous words in 11:27, "the thing David had done displeased the Lord." Finally, after Nathan's confrontation in chapter 12, David confessed and repented, and God extended grace. Even so, David's fall brought consequences that he suffered the rest of his life. By the end of chapter 12, though, signs of hope appear. Solomon's birth reminds the reader of God's promise to keep David's descendants on the throne. And, interestingly, the last paragraph of the chapter pictures David leading his army into battle—David again leading the charge.

4. Identify the Biblical Truth

By God's grace and blessing, David rose to prominence and power. But he grew prideful and passive, forgetting God's grace. This left him vulnerable to temptation.

The universal, timeless truth that rises from the text: When we forget God's grace, we fall.

"I TRIED IT"

"This exercise requires quite a bit of time in research and reading. But, it proved to be time well spent. The beauty of the exercise is that it brings to bear a powerful spotlight that reveals careful details of context and syntax found in and around the biblical text. Soon, the light exposes the ageless, inspired, biblical truth of the text. These details, transferred onto the sermon script, quickly dance off the pulpit and into everyone's 'camcorder-mind,' where the biblical truth becomes the climax of an unforgettable sermon."

David Caffee, Englewood, Tennessee

"This exercise takes intentional time and effort, but it is well worth it. Really digging into a text, and examining its context, enables us to deliver more effective messages. I used this exercise while preparing a sermon from Romans 12, a passage where context is critical. I discovered that chapter 12 is a turning point in Romans, where Paul transitions from theology to application. I hope to continue using what I learned in this exercise in future sermons—without this kind of in-depth study, my preaching will lack depth and wisdom."

Austin Greco, Bloomingdale, Ohio

RESOURCES FOR FURTHER STUDY

- *The Modern Preacher and the Ancient Text: Interpreting and Preaching Biblical Literature*, by Sidney Greidanus (Eerdman's, 1988).
- *Text-Driven Preaching: God's Word at the Heart of Every Sermon*, edited by Daniel Akin, David L. Allen, and Ned Matthews (B&H Academic, 2010).
- "Biblical Exegesis: Discovering the Meaning of Scriptural Texts," by John Piper. Access at http://cdn.desiringgod.org/pdf/booklets/BTBX.pdf.
- "Exegesis for Preachers and Teachers of the Bible," by Dion Forster. Access at http://www.docstoc.com/docs/19591709/EXEGESIS-FOR-PREACHERS-AND-TEACHERS-OF-THE-BIBLE.

Develop Need in the Introduction

A retiree spends Friday afternoons sipping coffee and perusing the books at a local bookstore. One particular Friday, he passes a shelf that he has passed a hundred times before. He squints while skimming the same book titles he browsed through last week and the week prior. Then, like a magnet, a certain book jacket draws his gaze to its raised gold lettering: *Understanding Alzheimer's*. Why did this paperback—one he overlooked innumerable times before—suddenly catch his eye? Why does he snatch it from the shelf, race to the cashier, then devour its contents over the next four hours?

His wife's memory has grown fuzzy. Once-familiar names and faces elude her. A couple days ago, she forgot her phone number. Her doctor wants to run some tests.

Information we otherwise brush past grows suddenly critical when one element enters the scenario—need. When we *need* something—even something to which we previously gave little attention—we give ourselves entirely to it.

People listen to a sermon when they sense the sermon will address a need in their lives. Their minds, which otherwise wander from next week's ball game to the shopping list on the refrigerator to the project at work, suddenly focus on the preacher's words when they recognize the upcoming teaching will address that struggle, question, or issue that keeps them staring at the ceiling until 2 a.m.

In 1928, a famous essay by Harry Emerson Fosdick asked, "What is the Matter With Preaching?" Fosdick bemoaned the preponderance of uninteresting, insignificant sermons. He then offered a solution:

> Within a paragraph or two after a sermon has
> started, wide areas of any congregation ought to
> begin recognizing that the preacher is tackling
> something of vital concern to them. He is handling
> a subject they are puzzled about, or a way of living
> they have dangerously experimented with, or an
> experience that has bewildered them, or a sin that
> has come perilously near to wrecking them, or an
> ideal they have been trying to make real, or a need
> they have not known how to meet.[1]

I do not suggest that we choose our sermon topics based solely
on our listeners' needs. Rather, we preach the truths we discover
in our sermon texts, based on careful exegesis. I do suggest, however, that when we present these truths, we begin by showing
listeners what needs in their lives the truths will address.

For every biblical teaching—including what you will
preach this Sunday—there exists a corresponding human need.
For example:

> TRUTH: God promised that His Spirit will empower us.
> CORRESPONDING NEED: We feel feeble and
> inadequate.

> TRUTH: Christians live with an eternally significant
> purpose.
> CORRESPONDING NEED: We muddle aimlessly
> through our days and weeks.

When we raise such needs in our introductions, listeners recognize that our sermons will provide help for their struggles. So,
hungry for help, they listen.

THE EXERCISE

After you have studied the text for your upcoming sermon, proceed through this four-step exercise.

---

1. Fosdick quoted in *What's the Matter With Preaching Today?* edited by Mike
Graves (Louisville: Westminster John Knox, 2004), 9.

1. *State the main idea of the sermon.* Write in a single sentence what truth you hope listeners will absorb from your upcoming sermon.
2. *Identify what human need this truth addresses.* If every biblical teaching corresponds with a human need, with what particular need does your truth (from step one) correspond? The first two columns of the chart below provide examples.
3. *Describe the need in a manner that will relate to your particular listeners.* Write a paragraph or two that expounds on the need you identified in step two. Describe the thoughts, feelings, and/or temptations listeners often associate with this need. The third column of the chart below demonstrates this step.
4. *Include this description in your introduction.* Include the paragraph from step three in your sermon's introduction. After you preach this paragraph to your listeners—identifying the questions, fears, and temptations that burden their minds and hearts—they will lean forward, eager to hear how God's Word can help.

EXAMPLES

Biblical Teaching	Corresponding Need	Description of Need in Introduction
God designed Christians to thrive in community.	Loneliness	Though you sit this morning in the midst of three hundred people, you feel as though you sit alone. The sense is not a new one—you feel alone most of the time. You live in a neighborhood that bustles with people, you work at an office building filled with conversation and activity, you might even sit around a dinner table with family, but you feel like you face life entirely by yourself. You have no one with whom to share your questions, your hurts, your ideas—no one who understands you. You face life as the Lone Ranger. But you don't want to face it that way.

Biblical Teaching	Corresponding Need	Description of Need in Introduction
When we pursue God's Kingdom above all else, we can trust Him to care for our needs.	Worry about our lives	If I asked, "What do you worry about?" I imagine you could quickly compile a list. The stock market plunged, yet again, last week, and your 401K plunged along with it. A close friend made a decision about a relationship, and you're anxious about the outcome. Your teenager had not yet pulled into the driveway when the time for curfew arrived. You watched out the window as another ten minutes went by, then twenty, then thirty—you finally decided to call but she didn't answer her phone. You received the news, again, that the job went to somebody else. The doctor saw a spot on the X-ray. And you worry.
Through Christ, God forgives even the biggest of sins.	Ongoing guilt over past sins	All sin is rebellion against our holy God. Every one of us stumble, and all-too frequently. But some stumbles are more full-fledged plunges into vile im-morality—those sins that change the course of life, that pour buckets of tar atop our integrity, that ruin marriages and ministries and careers and oppor-tunities and witness. Those sins which, when recalled even years later, send our eyes to the floor and our gut into a twist. Yes, God forgives sin. But what about *that* one?

"I TRIED IT"

"The introduction has an importance beyond its proportionate size or length. After preaching for years we may falsely assume we are covering all the basics and that people will automatically be interested in what we say. This exercise led me to return to the 'old paths' of Homiletics I. How was I to relate the 6th commandment to a group of good people who I assume had never murdered anyone? How could I arouse the awareness that we all at times have probably treated human life as cheap? Ouch!"

Ken Overdorf, Beckley, West Virginia

"People listen when God's truth pierces their hearts and addresses their needs. A prayerfully prepared introduction, therefore, whets listeners' appetites. I applied Dr. Overdorf's exercise to a sermon series from Jonah. I developed need in each sermon's introduction as follows: The Sign of Jonah: If Jonah is only a fish story, what about Jesus' resurrection? The Prodigal Prays: What happens when life hits the bottom? A Nation Repents: Can an ungodly nation be spared? Second-guessing God: How does God deal with those chips on our shoulders?"

Tom Cash, Sault Ste. Marie, Michigan

RESOURCES FOR FURTHER STUDY

- *How Effective Sermons Begin*, by Ben Awbrey (Mentor, 2008).
- "The Fallen Condition Focus and the Purpose of the Sermon," by Bryan Chappell. Access at http://www.preaching.com/resources/articles/11550666.
- "Begin With a Puzzle: Preaching That Awakens a Hunger to Learn," by John Bell. Access at http://www.preaching.com/resources/articles/11569906.

Assemble a Feed-Forward Group

In the fall of 1999, I took a group from our church to a men's conference held in a local auditorium. The internationally known guest speaker had written several books about men's issues that had benefited my faith. The publicity for the conference highlighted the topics he would discuss—growing as godly fathers, husbands, and men of Christ. I gathered fifteen men from our church, and we sat together in a large auditorium eager to hear what he would teach.

Rather than addressing men's issues, however, the speaker used his time on stage to espouse conspiracy theories about President Clinton and the upcoming Y2K "meltdown," which the speaker felt Clinton had orchestrated and would use to seize absolute power over our country. I sank into my seat. Later, I apologized to the men who attended with me.

While this scenario exaggerates the principle, many have felt a similar frustration. We enter a presentation—or even a personal conversation—hoping to gain certain information or answers to particular questions, but the speaker talks incessantly about something entirely different. We leave irritated, with our questions unanswered and needs unmet.

Those who hear our sermons may, on occasion, experience this frustration. When we discuss topics and truths in our sermons, questions invade listeners' minds and hearts. Instead of speaking to their concerns, however, we pour rivers of information from the pulpit—matters we thought, in our study, would address listeners' concerns—and unknowingly drown them with insights they don't need and answers to questions they haven't asked. Too polite to stand, interrupt us, and ask their questions (something we might consider inviting them to do!), listeners cross their legs, allow their minds to wander, then shake our hand on the way out the door—outwardly smiling but inwardly annoyed.

If only we could talk with our listeners *before* the sermon, we could discover what questions, issues, and needs surface in their minds and hearts about our text and subject matter. Then, we could address these issues in our sermons.

This week's exercise will lead you to assemble a group for this very purpose.

THE EXERCISE

1. *Invite five to eight people from your congregation to meet with you a few days prior to an upcoming sermon.* If the sermon will address a topic that particularly touches a certain demographic, you might invite people from that demographic. For example, if the sermon will address parenting, you might invite a few parents—some new parents, some older, a single parent, and a couple expecting their first child. If the sermon does not target a particular demographic, the group might consist of a cross section of your typical listeners—including various ages, life circumstances, and levels of spiritual maturity.

2. *Give group members information to consider ahead of time.* Let group members know your basic understanding of the text and what you tentatively think the sermon will teach. Also, provide them a list of questions that will loosely guide the meeting. The best questions will pertain specifically to your text and topic. This generic list, however, may help you formulate your questions:

   • At your first reading, how does the text make you feel?
   • What questions does it raise in your mind? What seems unclear?
   • Based on your initial interaction with the text, what do you think it teaches?
   • Why do you think God included this teaching in the Bible?
   • Do the ideas raised by the text excite, frighten, or confuse you? Why?
   • If you took this teaching seriously, how would it impact your daily life?

- Where and when have you seen the truth of this text demonstrated in your own life and experience?
- What do you feel a sermon about this text should explain, illustrate, or apply?
- If you taught or preached this topic, what would you highlight?

3. *During the meeting, have someone else take extensive notes, and/or audio record the meeting.* This will free you from taking notes and allow the conversation to flow more easily.

4. *Listen and watch carefully.* Listen for group members' questions, needs, and stories from their own experiences that may be helpful to address and/or include in the sermon. (If you wish to use a particular story told by a group member, seek their permission first.) Also, watch their body language—during what portions of the meeting did people seem uncomfortable? When did they appear most engaged? Most bored? When did their eyes light up, and when did their eyes sink to the floor? When did they appear curious, and when did they appear concerned?

5. *When you design the sermon, consider what you heard and observed.* Ultimately, biblical truth should guide the sermon. The manner in which you present that truth, however, can be informed by your meeting with the feed-forward group. The group discussion should help you discern which portions of the sermon need the most explanation, what questions need answered, what needs and issues require sensitivity, and how to best illustrate and apply the teaching.

ADDITIONAL SUGGESTIONS

- The meeting with your feed-forward group will require a few days of planning and organization. You might, therefore, plan the meeting for a week or two in the future, then move ahead to the next exercise in this book for this week.
- Your group members will not have studied the text as extensively as you have—if they have misunderstandings, do not let this frustrate you. Instead, recognize that

they are encountering the text the same way the entire congregation will on Sunday. Hearing how group members first encounter the text will help you know what to explain and to spend the most time on.

- In addition to a formal feed-forward group, you might also seek people's perspectives on your sermon text and topic in an informal way. As you talk with others throughout the week, tactfully ask them questions about your text and topic: "I'm struggling with such-and-such about my sermon for this Sunday. What do you think?" Such conversations will provide you with helpful insights, and those with whom you speak will feel honored to give input into the preaching process.

- If you serve in a multi-staff situation, you might utilize other staff as a feed-forward group. One of my preaching friends completes his sermons one week in advance, and his staff reads through it with him every Monday. They respond with insights and ideas to strengthen the sermon.

"I TRIED IT"

"Utilizing a 'Feed-Forward Group' in my sermon development allowed me to hear firsthand, from my listeners, their ideas concerning my sermon passage. As I constructed my sermon, my vision of the passage expanded beyond my own. This resulted in a sermon with which my listeners more readily identified. A second, unexpected benefit was that the participants were thrilled to play a role in the writing of the sermon. They couldn't wait to see what I came up with!"

Steve Page, Bristol, Tennessee

"I met with two different groups of people—my staff and a church family that included a grade-schooler and teenagers. Each group shared their initial reaction to the text (Philippians 4:10–13), which included questions concerning the setting and context of the passage. This insight enabled me to address the context more fully with the audience than I might have otherwise and to preach, therefore, a text-driven sermon. Both groups appreciated the exercise and felt as though they made contributions to the sermon."

Harold Keck, Crawfordsville, Indiana

RESOURCES FOR FURTHER STUDY

- *The Roundtable Pulpit: Where Leadership and Preaching Meet*, by John S. McClure (Abingdon, 1995).
- "Stop Preaching in the Dark (or: Gaining Feedback Isn't Enough)," by Keith Wilhite. Access at http://www.preaching.com/resources/articles/11563837.
- "Pre-Sermon Review: A Strange Idea?" blog by Peter Mead. Access at http://biblicalpreaching.net/2010/06/28/pre-sermon-review-a-strange-idea.

Write in E-Prime

Verbs drive communication. Without verbs, nouns sit still, stagnating. Budding sentences, thirsting for life and movement, wither on the page.

"To be" verbs stand only one rung higher on the ladder of effectiveness than the complete absence of verbs. Forms of "be"—am, is, are, was, were, be, being, and been—function as verbs, but barely. They bring no movement or action. They fill an empty slot in a sentence, and make that sentence grammatically acceptable, but nothing happens in paragraphs filled with "be" verbs. Nothing leaps, speaks, or turns somersaults. Sentences remain motionless, mundane, and anemic. They just *are*.

"The dog is in the house." But what does the dog do? Does he sniff around the house, destroy the furniture, or mosey up the stairs?

"I am a teacher." Yes, but the sentence comes to life when I use stronger verbs: "I devote my life to the art of teaching;" "I earn my living in the classroom;" or "I live to see the twinkle of insight in a student's eye."

Every "be" verb wastes an opportunity to paint a picture or to propel a noun, sentence, or sermon into action.

COMMUNICATING IN E-PRIME

E-prime (short for "English Prime") refers to a method of communication that eliminates forms of "be," forcing writers and speakers to choose stronger verbs. Many communicators use "be" verbs so extensively that overcoming the habit takes much discipline. Three simple grammatical adjustments, though, can strengthen our verb choices.[1]

1. Replace Progressive Tenses with the Simple Present and Simple Past.

    > Instead of: The Spirit is empowering believers.
    > Write: The Spirit empowers believers.

    > Instead of: Paul was traveling to Ephesus.
    > Write: Paul traveled to Ephesus.

    > Hint: Progressive tenses usually follow this pattern: Subject + be verb + base wording (as in, "Paul was traveling."). The base word ("traveling") can drop the "-ing" and replace the "be" verb: "Paul traveled."

2. Replace the Passive Voice with the Active Voice.

    > Instead of: Prayer is practiced by growing Christians.
    > Write: Growing Christians pray.

    > Instead of: Evangelism is neglected by the contemporary church.
    > Write: The contemporary church neglects evangelism.

    > Hint: Move the noun that performs the action to the beginning of the sentence. Sentences written in e-prime often follow this template: the one who completes the action—the action—the object of the action (The contemporary church—neglects—evangelism.)

3. Replace Expressions of Existence, Identification, and Quality with Action Verbs in Context.

    > Instead of: The Messiah is here.
    > Write: The Messiah arrived in Bethlehem.

---

1. This section grows from classroom materials provided by Professor Ron Wheeler of Johnson University.

Instead of: Jesus is King.
Write: King Jesus reigns over the universe.

Instead of: Christians are compassionate.
Write: Christians show compassion to those in need.

Hint: Instead of listing a truth about the subject ("Christians are compassionate"), explain how the subject demonstrates that truth ("Christians show compassion...") in a particular context (" ... to those in need.").

THE EXERCISE

1. Practice the principles taught in the previous section by completing the chart below. Read the sentence in the left column that contains a "be" verb, then rewrite it in the right column in e-prime.

SENTENCES WITH "BE" VERBS	REWRITTEN IN E-PRIME
My second grade teacher was Mrs. Winchester.	Mrs. Winchester taught my second grade class.
She was always telling us to study our spelling words.	
Studying was something that didn't really interest me, though. I thought, "Studying is a waste of time."	
Still today, I am not a good speller. My reports at work are full of errors.	
It turns out that Mrs. Winchester was a smart woman!	

2. Prepare your upcoming sermon as normal, though remain conscious of the e-prime method when you put your final thoughts on paper.
3. After you complete your sermon, circle every "be" verb on your manuscript, outline, or notes. These include: am, is, are, was, were, be, being, and been (also circle any of these used in contractions, such as I'm, it's, and we're).
4. Spend at least thirty minutes rewriting sentences to eliminate as many "be" verbs as possible from your sermon.

5. Practice your sermon aloud, allowing your adjustments from step four to guide your verb choices.

When you preach the sermon, do not let your preparations from the exercise paralyze you. And, do not tie yourself to a manuscript to maintain its precise wording. Speak naturally and conversationally, confident that the exercise prepared you to communicate with more vividness and clarity.

AN EXAMPLE

The left column below contains a couple paragraphs from an Easter sermon I pulled from my files. The right column demonstrates how I could have written the paragraphs in e-prime.

ORIGINAL PARAGRAPH FROM SERMON	REWRITTEN IN E-PRIME
In Mark 16:1, three women—Mary, Mary, and Salome—are conceding defeat. Jesus had been crucified on Friday. By the time His body was removed from the cross and placed in the tomb, it was Sabbath—Sabbath went from sundown Friday until sundown Saturday. On the Sabbath day, any kind of work was prohibited, and people couldn't buy anything. Therefore, it wasn't until Sunday morning that these women could buy spices to anoint Jesus' body.	Mark 16:1 pictures three women—Mary, Mary, and Salome—conceding defeat. Soldiers crucified Jesus on Friday. That evening, as Sabbath arrived, Jesus' friends removed His body from the cross and placed it in a tomb. Sabbath stretched from sundown Friday until sundown Saturday. Jewish law prohibited buying and selling on the Sabbath, forcing the women to wait until Sunday morning to buy spices to anoint Jesus' body.
These ladies were conceding that Jesus was dead ... for good. Remember, they didn't know this was the first Easter. They weren't going to the tomb hoping it would be empty. No, they were just planning to put spices on a lifeless corpse. From all appearances, hope was gone. Death was the winner. And the situation was irreversible.	These ladies conceded that Jesus died, and that He would remain dead ... for good. Remember, they did not know that the first Easter had dawned. They did not expect to find an empty tomb. No, they just planned to anoint a lifeless corpse with spices. From all appearances, hope lost. Death won. And nothing could reverse the situation.

"I TRIED IT"

"Writing in e-prime gave me stronger, cleaner verbs. It also reduced my use of the passive voice and let me to retell the story of the text with more of a "we are there as it happens" flavor.

The congregation seemed more attentive than usual—the sermon grabbed their attention better. I noticed that in the following weeks I continued to use stronger, more descriptive words. While I will not write every sermon in e-prime, I will periodically, and the exercise has helped strengthen my writing every week."

Jim Lawler, Rushville, Indiana

"Writing and speaking with excellence requires the discipline of hard work; writing in e-prime exemplifies this principle. Though those averse to grammar parsing may find it tedious—spotting tenses and reframing them correctly takes time and focus—they will find it produces results. Surprisingly, the exercise helped in ways I had not considered. For example, it forced me to state theological truths more carefully and precisely (it did not allow cavalier theological thought!), and it helped to keep my audience's attention more effectively. In summary, this exercise proved challenging, but well worth the effort."

Kirk Dice, Suffolk, Virginia

"While I didn't enjoy this exercise as much as I enjoyed some of the others, nor did I find it easy to complete, it gave me a new appreciation for careful verb choices. Because we live in a visual society, eliminating 'be' verbs in favor of stronger verbs makes our sermons easier to grasp and follow. As preachers, we should do everything within our power to make our sermons come to life and to help our congregations understand clearly what God's Word teaches them."

Burt Brock, Morgantown, Indiana

RESOURCES FOR FURTHER STUDY

- *More E-PRIME: To Be or Not II*, ed. by Paul Dennithorne Johnston; D. David Bourland, Jr.; and Jeremy Klein (International Society for General Semantics, 1994).
- "E-Prime Tutorial," by Dan Scorpio. Access at http://www.angelfire.com/nd/danscorpio/ep2.html.
- "E-Prime." Access at http://en.wikipedia.org/wiki/E-Prime.
- "Discovering E-Prime," by Elaine C. Johnson. Access at http://www.asiteaboutnothing.net/pdf_discoveringe-prime.pdf.

Plan for Effective Delivery

My wife and I enjoy a reality show on cable television about a bakery in Baltimore that specializes in decorative, custom cakes. A team of culinary artists uses everything from blow torches to power sanders to create jaw-dropping and mouth-watering masterpieces. Past episodes have featured a seven-tiered wedding cake depicting Dr. Seuss characters, replicas of the Hogwarts castle for the premier of a Harry Potter movie, the Hubble Space Telescope for a NASA celebration, Radio City Music Hall for the Rockettes, and Wrigley Field for the Chicago Cubs.

What frightens me most about the cakes receives little attention in the show—the delivery. After the bakers spend numerous hours planning, baking, and forming their works of art, they load the cake—often in segments—onto a delivery van. I cringe as cameras show the van turning onto the busy street. I imagine a quick stop or swerve sending a carefully crafted cake smashing against the inside walls of the van. Just one mistake by the driver would leave the masterpiece in a muddled mess.

Effective delivery matters. A preacher might invest countless hours researching, crafting, and polishing a sermon outline or manuscript. By Saturday evening, the masterpiece lays glowing on his desk. Unfortunately, if the preacher does not plan for an effective delivery, the glowing masterpiece may simply flop over the rim of the pulpit on Sunday morning and land in a muddled mess before a yawning congregation.

EFFECTIVE DELIVERY

A sermon on paper contains punctuation, spacing, and marks of emphasis that help a reader discern the flow of ideas. These include paragraph indentations, commas, exclamation points, underlining, bold print, italics, highlighting, and perhaps even notes we jot down in the margins. Such markings benefit those who read a sermon, but not those who hear it. The structure, flow, and main ideas that are clear in the preacher's mind, therefore, often do not translate clearly to listeners' ears.

Competent speakers use both verbal and nonverbal indicators to lead listeners through the ideas and emphases of their messages. Though Exercise 7 ("Read the Text Well") discussed some of these factors, repeating the basic principles and adding additional details will prove helpful for this exercise, enabling us to plan ahead for an effective sermon delivery.

Verbal Elements of Delivery

- *Voice Variation:* Effective speakers vary their voices in at least three ways:
  - » Pitch: A variety in pitch pleases listeners' ears. For an exaggerated example, consider how adults speak to small children.
  - » Volume: A conversational volume will best communicate most of the sermon, but occasional variances emphasize prominent ideas.
  - » Pace: A moderate rate of speech—not noticeably fast or slow—proves effective for most of a presentation. Faster and slower speech, however, can build momentum and communicate a variance of emotions.
- *Pause*: Pauses (1) indicate the completion of one segment of a sermon and the beginning of another; (2) give listeners time to contemplate questions or ideas; and (3) bring attention to the words spoken before and after it, verbally setting apart main ideas.
- *Repetition*: Words or phrases underlined, in bold print, or highlighted on a sermon outline merit repetition in oral delivery. Repetition feels monotonous to speakers, but listeners appreciate the opportunity to hear significant ideas a second time.

Nonverbal Elements of Delivery

- *Eye contact:* By looking into listeners' eyes, speakers cultivate trust, warmth, and a relational atmosphere. The more our eyes remain on our listeners, therefore, and the less they fixate on our notes, the better.
- *Gestures:* Effective speakers use hand movements that accentuate and do not distract from their words. Planned gestures, however, appear forced and awkward. The best approach, therefore, involves simply keeping your hands in a place where they can gesture easily and naturally (not in pockets or behind the back, for example).
- *Movement:* Physical movements help communicate transitions to new ideas. For example, a preacher might stand to the right of the podium to discuss a sermon's first segment, then move to the left of the podium to present the second segment. Also, a change of position on stage can help portray movements that occur in stories. For example, if in an illustration describes a person walking from the kitchen into the living room, the preacher might take a few steps to help listeners visualize the story.

THE EXERCISE

After you complete the written preparations for your upcoming sermon, plan for an effective delivery with the four steps described on the next few pages.

1. Make notes in the margins of your sermon outline or manuscript about your delivery.
   - Note voice variations in the right margin. Consider three categories of voice intensity: reserved (less pitch, pace, and volume); conversational (moderate pitch, pace, and volume), and intense (more pitch, pace, and volume). Conversational speaking should serve as your default. Those portions of the sermon that you can best communicate in a reserved manner, however, mark with a downward arrow in the right margin. Mark those portions that merit more intensity with an upward arrow.

Voice	Pitch, Pace, & Volume	When to Use	Note in Right Margin
Reserved	Less	Use when listeners need to contemplate the idea you are presenting, and to relate emotions such as peace, quiet joy, or perplexity.	↓
Conversational	Moderate	Use during most of the sermon. This is your default voice.	(no mark)
Intense	More	Use when building momentum toward main ideas, and to relate emotions such as such as excitement, anger, or passion.	↑

- Note physical movements in the left margin. Mentally divide your speaking platform into three sections, from stage left to stage right. Based on what was taught earlier in this chapter about movement, decide where you will stand to deliver each portion of the sermon, and make the marks described below in the left margin of your sermon manuscript or outline.

Stage Position	Note in Left Margin
Stage left	←
Middle	•
Stage right	→

- Note pauses within your sermon text by placing two vertical lines everywhere a pause would benefit listeners (to transition to a new segment of the sermon, to give time to contemplate a question or idea, or to set apart main ideas).
- Note repetitions within your sermon text by writing an "R" above words and phrases that deserve repeating.
2. Practice your sermon aloud and with movement at least three times. Ideally, practice where you will preach the sermon—in your church's worship center, for example.

3. Establish "home base" for eyes and hands. As you practice the sermon, keep your eyes on your imagined listeners as much as possible—this is "home base" for your eyes. Glance at your notes as often as you need to, but return your eyes to home base as quickly as possible. Also, keep your hands at a "home base" from which they can naturally gesture—perhaps near your waist in front of your body, or at another position that feels natural to you.

4. When you preach the sermon on Sunday, don't let the delivery preparations inhibit you. And, don't fret if you miss a cue. Forget the margin notes and preach naturally, confident that your rehearsals have prepared you to deliver the sermon effectively.

ADDITIONAL SUGGESTIONS

- Video record yourself preaching the sermon a few days before you preach. Critique the video in relation to the principles discussed earlier in this chapter.
- Watch someone else preach—either live, online, or on video—and observe their verbal and nonverbal delivery. What delivery elements impact the effectiveness of their preaching?
- Take less notes into the pulpit. For most speakers, less notes allows for more movement and eye contact, and a more conversational style. Exercise 24 ("Minimize Notes") will address this issue more specifically.

"I TRIED IT"

"I carefully planned my delivery using the symbols suggested by Dr. Overdorf. I found it very helpful to think through this before delivering the sermon. I practiced beforehand and realized it was not going to be easy to do everything I had planned to do. The exercise did, however, cause me to be aware of how I deliver the sermon. As a result, I think I communicated better because I made it a point to change positions at various times in the sermon, and I was more conscious of voice inflections, pauses, etc."

Mark Overton, Louisville, Tennessee

"Old habits die hard. New habits, however, are just as hard to bring to life. While trying this exercise, I found little difficulty adding notes about delivery to my sermon. What I found challenging was retaining good eye contact afterward. The more notes I wrote on the sermon, the more fixated I became on the manuscript. I didn't want to miss a cue. My mistake was to add too much too soon. So, I've decided to progress more slowly and add only one or two new delivery suggestions at a time. When one becomes a habit, I add another."

Benjamin Abbott, Prince Edward Island, Canada

RESOURCES FOR FURTHER STUDY

- *The Moment of Truth: A Guide to Effective Sermon Delivery*, by Wayne McDill (B&H Academic, 1999).
- *Preaching With Bold Assurance: A Solid and Enduring Approach to Engaging Exposition*, by Bert Decker and Hershael York (B&H Books, 2003).
- "The Seven Axioms of Sermon Delivery," by Calvin Miller. Access at http://www.preaching.com/resources/articles/11547735.
- "Process Preaching: Oral Rehearsal," by Jerome Larson. Access at http://www.workingpreacher.org/sermondevelopment.aspx?article_id=76.

Collaborate with Other Preachers

Accomplished writers often critique one another's work before they send their manuscripts to publishers. During the 1930s and 1940s, for example, the Inklings group at Oxford gathered on Tuesday mornings at a local pub and on Thursday evenings at C. S. Lewis's college room to read their most recent drafts and to offer each other insights, suggestions, and not-so-occasional barbs. J. R. R. Tolkien first revealed portions of *The Lord of the Rings* in this circle. Such authors recognize that comrades who share an interest and passion for writing can help them brainstorm, explore possibilities, and, ultimately, sharpen their work.

Most preachers, in contrast, study alone. They prepare alone. They brainstorm alone. They formulate ideas and develop sermonic strategies by themselves. They stand in the pulpit each Sunday with a document to which no one else has offered ideas, input, or insight.

Perhaps Lewis and Tolkien have wisdom to offer such preachers.

Our sermons will strengthen as we collaborate with other preachers. Another preacher might think of a story, a quote, or a cross-reference that eluded me but accentuates a point in my sermon. When I struggle to grasp the meaning of a text, a friend may point out an element of context or research that opens my eyes. Or, this homiletic comrade might care enough to point out that an argument that makes sense to me will not make sense to anyone else. "How about trying it this way instead?" he might suggest.

We envision sermon preparation as hunkering down by ourselves in musty offices in the bowels of church buildings.

While our preparation should include such private interaction with the text and the Spirit, why not emerge from this self-imposed solitary confinement—even if just for an hour—to talk through our ideas with a couple other preachers who can bring different perspectives and experiences to the process and, therefore, sharpen our sermons?

THE EXERCISE

1. Invite two preachers to meet with you for ninety minutes so that you can offer each other ideas and insight about your upcoming sermons.
2. Complete some sermon preparation before the meeting—enough that you have a grasp of the text and at least general idea of how your sermon will proceed. If you prepare on a Monday–Friday schedule, for example, you will probably want to meet around Wednesday.
3. At the meeting, begin by praying for God's guidance. Then, devote thirty minutes to each preacher's upcoming sermon, until you have discussed all three in ninety minutes. You might divide each thirty minute segment into these four blocks:
   - One preacher provides a brief overview of his research and preparation for his upcoming sermon:
     » "In my research, I've learned this about the text …"
     » "At this point, I'm still a little confused about …"
     » "I have some ideas about how to present these truths in my sermon …"
     » "I think my thesis statement will be..."
     » "I could most use your help with …"
   - The other two preachers respond, first, with insights and ideas about the meaning of the text and the truths the sermon will present:
     » "Be sure to note how your text relates to the paragraphs around it."
     » "Paul taught something similar in one of his epistles—you might glance over at …"
     » "It's interesting how the biblical author keeps repeating the phrase …"
     » "This particular term seems critical to the text—I wonder if a word study would provide some insight?"

» "Could someone misunderstand your argument at this point? Maybe it would be clearer if you said ..."
- Next, the discussion centers on illustrations and applications that might prove useful for the sermon:
  » "I read an article in Newsweek that you could use in this sermon. I'll email it to you when I get back to the office."
  » "I once saw a preacher do an object lesson to help teach this point. He began by ..."
  » "Philip Yancey told a powerful story along these lines in his book..."
  » "Might one of your church members be willing to do a testimony about this?"
  » "If your listeners took this sermon seriously Sunday, what might they do differently on Monday?"
- Finally, brainstorm about the sermon's structure:
  » "I think the sermon could flow well by working through these four points ..."
  » "Could you divide this story into three segments, and present them at the beginning, middle, and end of the sermon?"
  » "I wonder if this application would fit better under your second point, instead of your first."
  » "This particular quote would make a great conclusion."
  » "I think the sermon would be most powerful if you held your thesis until the end."
- After discussing the first preacher's sermon in the first thirty minutes, move to the second and third preachers' sermons and follow the same process. Allow the conversation to flow naturally. Foster an open environment where each participant feels comfortable raising questions and ideas.
4. Use the insights gained in the meeting as you continue preparation for your upcoming sermon.

ADDITIONAL SUGGESTIONS

- Each preacher might send the others a synopsis of their research and sermon preparation ahead of time. This would save time during the meeting; and, since each preacher would then have a day or two to consider the others' sermons, the discussion during the meeting might be more productive.

- Though face-to-face meetings bring better communication, some preachers participate in sermon collaboration over the telephone or via webcam. Other preachers collaborate by sending one another emails throughout the week.

- If you enjoy and benefit from the collaboration described in this exercise, you might plan such meetings weekly. A next step might involve planning and preaching a sermon series together.

"I TRIED IT"

"My sermon was better when I prepared with others. Those I studied with pointed out some of the information I either overlooked or failed to grasp during my own preparation. Every preacher possesses strengths and weaknesses (one may be great with illustrations, another with application, another wordsmithing, etc.). When we study together, the resulting sermon displays the combined strength of each contributing preacher, and it minimizes each preacher's weaknesses. A few cautions: come prepared; be somewhat thick-skinned; and greatly desire to preach better."

Bob Emmert, Jefferson City, Tennessee

"Collaborating with others opened up a whole new world for me—I can't imagine, now, not working with others in sermon preparation. The discussion helped me understand the text better, gave me good ideas for illustrations, and simply gave me the opportunity to bounce my own ideas off the others. This exercise is helpful for someone trying out a preaching team for the first time, or it gives good suggestions for groups that are already functioning."

Jonathan Goss, Bluefield, West Virginia

"This exercise fit well with my normal routine of studying sermons with my staff. Through this process, we sharpen each other and encourage each other in the Word. The discussions also challenge us to think in word pictures, illustrations, and metaphors. It's part of the weekly fabric of our staff and one of the highlights for my week. As a senior minister, the collateral benefit is that we stay on the same page theologically."

Scott Sutherland, Columbia, Missouri

RESOURCES FOR FURTHER STUDY

- *Group Genius: The Creative Power of Collaboration*, by Keith Sawyer (Basic Books, 2008).
- "The Teaching Pool," by Matt Conner. Access at http://www.preaching.com/resources/articles/11602983.
- "Evaluating Collaborative Approaches to Preparing and Delivering Sermons," by Kent Walkemeyer and Tara Healy. Access at http://www.ehomiletics.com/papers/07/Walkemeyer%20and%20Healy.pdf.
- "Preachers Collaborate to Spice Up Sermons," by Lila Arzua. Access at http://articles.chicagotribune.com/2005-01-09/features/0501090505_1_sermon-worship-pastor.

Apply Specifically

Vague instructions lead to hazy obedience. Last evening, I noticed my son had spent more than his allotted time sitting behind the computer screen. "No more playing on the computer tonight," I said before leaving the room. I returned a few minutes later to find him still planted at the desk. "Didn't I tell you to get off the computer?"

"No," he responded. "You told me 'no more playing on the computer.' I'm not playing, Dad—I'm learning."

Likewise, preachers often remain too vague in our applications: "We need to witness for Christ"; "God calls us to give generously"; or perhaps, "Go now and be bold in your faith." Listeners nod their heads at such applications, but leave for the Sunday buffet with no sense of how to do what we suggested, nor any motivation to do it. By the time they finish at the buffet's dessert line, the sermon has faded into a foggy memory that will have no effect on their thoughts, decisions, or actions on Monday. They live no differently because we offered no insight, ideas, or assistance in how to witness for Christ, what generosity might look like, or how they might express their faith more boldly in their particular circumstances.

This week's exercise will help us develop specific applications for our upcoming sermons that motivate and equip listeners to live out the implications of the biblical text.

EFFECTIVE SERMON APPLICATION

Effective application exhibits these characteristics:

- *Consistency With the Biblical Text:* Life-changing application grows from a careful explanation of the biblical text. Lives change when they encounter God in His Word. Before rushing to application, therefore, impactful preachers provide the foundation of biblical theology from which application grows. Scripture is the root, application is the fruit.
- *Specific to Life:* Applications that grip listeners provide details that help listeners relate the text's teaching to their daily experiences. They describe specific situations in which people might apply the text in specific ways. For example, instead of simply preaching, "We need to witness for Christ," we can describe a particular scenario: "Perhaps the guy in the next cubicle at work does not know Jesus. You've shared numerous conversations around the coffee pot about the weather and ballgames, but you haven't yet mustered the nerve to mention your faith. Perhaps you can begin by telling of ..."
- *Stimulating to Listeners' Imaginations:* The specificity described in this chapter sparks ideas in listeners' imaginations about various ways the text might apply to them. The sermon cannot mention the particular circumstances every listener faces, of course, but by describing a few detailed scenarios, it invites listeners to dream about the implications of biblical teaching to their own lives, igniting unlimited ideas, dreams, and possibilities in each listener's mind.

THE EXERCISE

After you study the Scripture text for your upcoming sermon, answer these three questions.[1]

1. *Biblical Truth: What did God teach through this Scripture text?* Often, in a desire to preach with relevance, we give only a careless glance at the Scripture text then jump immediately to applications. Effective applications, however, help listeners

---

1. This exercise is a shortened version of a process discussed in *Applying the Sermon: How to Balance Biblical Integrity and Cultural Relevance*, by Daniel Overdorf (Grand Rapids, MI: Kregel, 2009).

imagine how a biblical truth should affect their lives. Before developing applications, therefore, we must define carefully and clearly what biblical truth we will apply.

2. *Sermon Purpose: What should my listeners think, feel, or do differently after encountering this biblical truth?* An effective sermon both explains Scripture and seeks to accomplish something in listeners' lives. What, in particular, should your upcoming sermon accomplish? To define this purpose, complete this sentence about your sermon: "As a result of this sermon, listeners should ..." Then, complete the sentence by defining what you hope listeners will think, feel, or do differently after the sermon.

3. *Sermon Application: If the sermon accomplished its purpose in specific listeners, how might it look?* After you define the sermon's purpose, imagine how it might look in at least three specific listeners' lives if the sermon accomplished its purpose in them. You might imagine actual people from your congregation, or certain categories of people—a family facing job loss, a wealthy teenage girl, or perhaps a retiree who all of a sudden has more time on his hands. How might it look—what might change in their day-to-day existence—if the sermon accomplished its purpose in them?

AN EXAMPLE

The following example builds from a sermon based on Matthew 6:25–34.

1. *Biblical Truth: What did God teach through this Scripture text?* Because they know God will provide for their needs, Christians can release earthly worries and diligently pursue God's Kingdom.

2. *Sermon Purpose: What should my listeners think, feel, or do differently after encountering this biblical truth?* As a result of this sermon, listeners should give primary attention to Kingdom pursuit rather than earthly worries.

3. *Sermon Application: If the sermon accomplished its purpose in specific listeners, how might it look?*
    *   A forty year old man lost his accounting job—a job he thought was secure, but fell victim to a faltering economy. He has a wife and two children. After encountering

Matthew 6:25–34, he gathers the family in the living room to pray. They relinquish their worries to God, and commit to trusting Him to care for their needs. During his free time—in addition to searching for a new job—he uses his accounting skills to help a local charity that had fallen behind on their bookkeeping, helps his church develop a more efficient budgeting process, and gathers a support group of others in the community who are facing job loss. He goes to bed each night less worried about his checkbook and more excited about his Kingdom pursuits.

- A seventeen-year-old girl—the only child in a wealthy family—attends church without her parents. Mom and Dad often send her to the mall with their credit cards to ease their guilt for working late. As a result of this sermon, the girl recognizes that her physical appearance—particularly her wardrobe—consumes an unhealthy amount of her time, attention, and money. She goes home and sorts through her three closets. She reduces her wardrobe such that it fills only half a closet, and takes the rest to a local mission. The mission staff allows her to hand out her clothes to a group of disadvantaged teenage girls. She smiles infinitely wider while giving away her outfits than she smiled when she bought them.

- A retiree worked for forty-five years at the same job, faithfully contributing to his retirement account along the way. He planned to provide for his and his wife's needs during their golden years and to leave a significant inheritance for their three children. The rising inflation and declining stock market, however, diminished his children's inheritance significantly. Though this causes the retired father a few sleepless nights, he vows to follow Jesus' instructions in Matthew 6 and trust in God's provision, freeing him to pursue the Kingdom. In particular, he focuses on leaving a spiritual legacy for his children. He designates an hour each morning to pray for his children and grandchildren. He pays for his grandchildren to attend retreats through their church. And, he intentionally speaks of his faith more often while in conversation with his family. He gauges his legacy more by prayers and spiritual conversations than by dollar signs and stock holdings.

ADDITIONAL SUGGESTIONS

- Early in the sermon, include some "pre-application" by raising problems and issues that the sermon will later resolve. Describe examples of circumstances and difficulties listeners face, then resolve them later in the sermon.
- To insert applications into your sermon, describe the particular scenarios you noted in the exercise: "I can imagine a seventeen year old girl who ..." Or, you might tell a story about a real person who exemplifies the truth taught: "I once knew a woman who ..." Or, you might reduce the extended scenarios into a few suggestions: "Some of us may need to go home this afternoon and examine our closets to see what we can give away. Others of us may need to consider how our gifts and abilities can contribute to God's Kingdom more than our own kingdoms."
- Consider offering a series of brief examples of how the text might apply, then an extended example.

"I TRIED IT"

"This exercise provided a needed reminder that application is the catalyst of a sermon and deserves careful attention. Without application, hearers may be inspired, but will not move to change and thus will become inoculated to sermons over time. I especially appreciate the advice about 'pre-application' to ensure a message hits home with people."

Steve Cuss, Broomfield, Colorado

"Since I read this chapter, it sticks in my mind every time I teach—application of the Word is our primary goal. I used the exercise specifically for a message on Acts 17, about the idol in Athens dedicated to the unknown God. I thought about how specific listeners could witness to those who worship other 'idols' through other religions. I prayed that the resulting message would help my listeners deal with the unsaved with grace, truth, and kindness."

Keith Ratamess, Columbia, South Carolina

RESOURCES FOR FURTHER STUDY

- *Applying the Sermon: How to Balance Biblical Integrity and Cultural Relevance*, by Daniel Overdorf (Kregel, 2009).
- *Preaching With Relevance*, by Keith Willhite (Kregel, 2001).
- "Sermon Application Help," by Justin Taylor. Access at http://thegospelcoalition.org/blogs/justintaylor/2010/05/12/sermon-application-help.
- "Toothless: The Missing Application in Sermons—Behind the Pulpit #6," audio discussion with Wayne Roberts and Bob Turner. Access at http://theequipnetwork.com/tag/sermon-application.

Preach with Women in Mind

More men than women fill pulpits. More women than men fill pews. In fact, women comprise about two-thirds of attendees in the typical American congregation. Though the "men are from Mars, women are from Venus" cliché might exaggerate the reality, male preachers and female church attenders often view life, ministry, relationships, and even God through different lenses. This discrepancy creates a communication gap that male preachers (and, perhaps, female preachers trained by male homiletics professors) must address, lest their effectiveness suffer.

Jill Briscoe begged male preachers, "Please make sure you arrest our attention, challenge our spirits, address our attitudes, and fill our souls with singing. And how are you supposed to do that? 'Well,' you may reply, 'by exegeting the Scriptures. That is what we went to seminary to learn.'

"Well now, while you were there, did anyone ever explain half the human race to you?"[1]

This week's exercise will help those who preach from a male perspective to better connect our sermons with half the human race, and two-thirds of our listeners.

PREACHING WITH WOMEN IN MIND

The paragraphs on the next few pages offer suggestions for how a preacher might relate more effectively with female listeners, based on the ways that women commonly learn, communicate,

---

1. Jill Briscoe, "Preaching to Women," http://www.preaching.com/resources/articles/11563444 (accessed April 21, 2011).

and perceive. Every person, of course—male and female—is unique. Not everything discussed will apply to every female listener. Some common threads, however, tie together the experiences and perceptions of many women—enough so that these suggestions should prove helpful.

1. Preach Relationally

Women typically give more attention to relationships than men. Men use conversation to share information, for example, while women use conversation to connect with friends. Men gather to do something—to play golf, watch a movie, or fix a car—women gather simply to enjoy the people they care about. They focus on relationships.

Ladies connect best, therefore, with preachers who speak relationally—in a conversational manner, and with a warm tone and body language. They appreciate speakers who let their guards down, laugh at themselves, and share their own stories.

Furthermore, they appreciate sermons that discuss relationships. Their ears perk when the preacher explores how Gabriel's announcement affected Mary's relationship with Joseph, or what Jesus implied when He whispered to his mother from the cross, "Dear woman, here is your son;" and to John, "Here is your mother" (John 19:26–27). Even when they hear doctrine and theology, women often wonder, "How should this affect my relationship with my friend, my mother, or my husband?"

2. Preach Authentically

A disheartening portion of women suffer the scars of abuse. Some bear the emotional scars of fathers or neighbors who treated them in an unholy manner, others hide physical scars with make up just minutes before they arrive at church. Even those who have not suffered such blatant abuse have lived enough to struggle, to hurt, and to roll their eyes at preachers who make life—even the Christian life—sound like a fairy tale. They know differently.

They appreciate preachers, therefore, who deal honestly and carefully with life's realities. They relate best with sermons that move beyond easy answers and connect Scripture with the complex, often difficult world in which they live.

3. Preach Practically

Women juggle numerous responsibilities and activities. They multi-tasked before the term became trendy. Imagine just one evening in the life of a woman in your church: She prepares a quick supper then tosses in a load of laundry just before she takes her daughter to dance lessons, then stops by the store to grab the supplies her son needs for his science project (which they will work on until 1 a.m.). While in route, she talks with others from the church committee that will oversee an upcoming prayer event, then touches base with her partner at work about the presentation they will give to prospective clients tomorrow.

On Sunday morning, this woman offers her preacher thirty minutes from her hectic life, during which she hopes to hear something from God's Word that will help her live for God from the Monday morning alarm until the Friday evening dishes are cleared. She appreciates broad concepts, but hungers for the practical applications of those concepts. "How does your theology," she wonders quietly, "make a difference where I live?"

4. Illustrate From Their World

Male preachers typically use illustrations that grow from their own interests and experiences—often the sports world, the military, or the latest leadership best seller. And, most of these illustrations quote or describe men. Many women respond with an outward sigh and an inward grumble, "Another story about baseball?!"

In contrast, the same ladies will lean forward and listen hungrily when the preacher offers a quote from a female role model, tells the story of a faithful woman, or describes a struggle that women commonly face.

In summary, to relate better with women listeners: preach with a relational tone and body language, share your own story, observe the relational dynamics within a text, discuss the relational implications of theology, speak honestly and compassionately about the difficulties women face, provide specific and helpful applications, use quotes from female role models, and tell stories of faithful women.

THE EXERCISE[2]

1. Ask five women who hear you preach regularly for feedback about how well your preaching relates to women. You might seek their input face-to-face, over the telephone, via email, or through whatever means will work best in your circumstances. Consider asking questions such as these:
   - During my sermons, when do you feel most engaged?
   - When does your mind begin to wander? When has one of my sermons made you feel, "He just doesn't understand me"?
   - When have you felt, "He just doesn't understand women"?
   - If you could stand before a room full of male preachers to advise them about connecting their sermons with women, what advice would you give?
   - If you were to give me a letter grade (A – F) to evaluate how well my sermons relate to the women in our church, what grade would you assign?

   Ask these ladies if you can contact them again after your upcoming sermon (if they will be in attendance to hear it).
2. Read over your last three sermons. Based on the discussion you had and what you learned from the women you interviewed in step one, assign yourself a letter grade (A – F) concerning how well you connected with the women who sat before you.
3. Prepare your upcoming sermon with women in mind. Do not pretend your audience consists entirely of women— recognize that men will sit before you, also (we will discuss preaching to men in Exercise 50)—but make certain that you do not neglect the ladies. In fact, intentionally design some parts of the sermon to connect with women.
4. After you preach, get back in touch with the ladies you contacted in step one. Ask them questions similar to those listed in step one, but ask them about the specific sermon you just preached. Then, invite them to assign you a letter grade (A – F) representing how well that particular sermon related to women. Compare these evaluations with the

---

2. This exercise will prove most useful for male preachers. If you are female, feel free to proceed (it will offer some help for you, also), or to complete one of the bonus exercises at the end of the book instead.

grades they assigned you in step one and the grade you assigned yourself in step two.

"I TRIED IT"

"I have always been unsure how to best relate with women listeners. This exercise resulted in objective feedback that helped me better connect my sermons with them. Their insights came through loud and clear: women want to be included, they want us to speak to their real life circumstances, and they want us to be authentic in applying the Bible to their daily lives. One woman said, 'Women like to hear sermons about women.' Just the act of consulting the ladies was affirming to them and helpful to me."

Rodger Thompson, Wichita, Kansas

"Especially as an unmarried male with a passion for seeing men develop spiritually, it is easy for me to neglect women while I'm trying to reach men. I tend to stay away from words like 'relationship' that appeal to women over men. This exercise offers a great reminder that my preaching needs balance in order to reach both men and women, and it gave helpful suggestions to keep me from neglecting a significant portion of my congregation."

Josh Lees, Winchester, Virginia

"This exercise made me realize that I wasn't connecting well with women in my teachings, and the reason was obvious: I wasn't considering them in my preparation. The ladies I spoke with said they do not want preachers to patronize them, or to guess at what they think. They'd rather us simply ask, so that we can be precise in connecting our sermons with them. Preaching with women in mind might be easier than we think."

Caleb Gilmore, Bluff City, Tennessee

RESOURCES FOR FURTHER STUDY

- *Preaching That Speaks to Women*, by Alice Matthews (Baker, 2003).
- *Shepherding a Woman's Heart: A New Model for Effective Ministry to Women* by Beverly White Hislop (Moody, 2003).

- "Preaching to Women," by Jill Briscoe. Access at http://
  www.preaching.com/resources/articles/11563444.
- "Preaching to Women," by John Sweetman. Access at
  http://www.baptist.org.au/site/DefaultSite/filesystem/
  documents/Preaching%20to%20Women.pdf.

Pray for Your Listeners

A few years ago I grew convicted to pray for those who hear my sermons. "Unless I pray for them," I thought, "how could I preach to them? Unless I present them before God, how could I present God to them?" I already prayed regularly for the church family, of course, and I prayed for my sermons. I had not, however, prayed weekly about the impact of specific sermons on specific listeners. I committed to change this.

I began arriving at the church building early on Sunday mornings—before anyone else arrived—and walking through the worship center, stopping at each pew to pray for those who would fill them a few hours later. People tend to sit in the same places each Sunday, so I could visualize individuals, recalling time I'd spent ministering to and with them—conversations we shared, hurts we revealed, and joys we celebrated. As I walked by Jeanette's pew, I envisioned the hours we spent in the hospital as her husband faded from life, and I prayed that the sermon would offer her comfort and peace. Then I stopped next to Vance and Karen's seat, recalled our premarital counseling sessions and the afternoon I led them through their vows, and prayed that the sermon would remind them of the godly basis of their new marriage. When I arrived at the back corner, where Joe sat the prior few weeks, I begged the Spirit to use that day's message to nudge Joe closer to placing his faith in Jesus Christ.

Richard Foster wrote of similar experiences,

> Some of the richest times in my pastoral ministry
> came when I would go into the sanctuary during

the week and walk through the pews praying for
the people who sat there Sunday after Sunday ....
I would pray the sermons on Friday that I would
preach on Sunday. Praying for their hurts and
fears and anxieties does something inside you. It
puts you in touch with your people in a deep, intimate way. Through prayer our people become our
friends in a whole new dimension.[1]

These times of prayer grew my heart for the people. I
preached with greater passion and compassion. My desire to
perform decreased. My desire to lead people into an experience
with God through His Word escalated. I trusted less in my own
creativity and skills, and more in the power of the Word and
Spirit to comfort, correct, encourage, and equip His church.

THE EXERCISE

1. *Study Paul's prayers.* Few pastors pray for their churches
    like Paul prayed for his. Those splendid prayers preserved
    in the New Testament evidence his hunger for their growth,
    his heart for their predicaments, and his hope that they
    would conform ever more to the likeness of Christ. Spend
    a few minutes, therefore, browsing through some of Paul's
    prayers and making notes about what and how he prayed
    for his churches.

Romans 1:8–10	
Ephesians 1:15–23	1 Thessalonians 1:2–10
Ephesians 3:14–21	1 Thessalonians 3:9–13
Philippians 1:3–11	2 Thessalonians 1:3–12
Colossians 1:3–14	Philemon 4–7

2. *Reflect on your sermon.* After you complete preparations
    for your sermon, skim through it and consider how its con-
    tent can inform your prayers for particular individuals in
    the church. If the sermon includes segments about forgiving

---

1. Richard Foster, "Centered: How Prayer Brings Authority," in *The Art and Craft of Biblical Preaching,* edited by Haddon Robinson and Craig Brian Larson (Grand Rapids, MI: Zondervan, 2005).

others, for example, or worship in the midst of heartache, these portions might address the needs of certain church members. When you pray, ask God to open these listeners' hearts during those portions of the sermon.

3. *Walk the aisles and pray.* Before you preach, walk through your worship center and pray for the particular people who will attend. Ideally, take this prayer walk a few hours before you preach. With the results of step one and step two in mind, lift these listeners before the Father and plead for His guidance, blessing, and divine work in the hearts and lives of those who will encounter His Word that day.

ADDITIONAL SUGGESTIONS

- You might complete your prayer time by kneeling where you will preach. Ask God to empower and guide you with His Spirit, to remove any barriers to communication, and to use your words to comfort, convict, and equip listeners to grow in and live for Jesus.
- Though this exercise calls for a particular time of prayer, we should never think of prayer as one step in sermon preparation. Instead, prayer should weave throughout the entire process. During the days leading into your sermon, therefore, keep your listeners in mind and continually voice prayers for them and for the sermon's impact on their hearts.
- In the moments before you preach—during those few seconds before you walk onto stage—breathe a final prayer. You might paraphrase John the Baptist's words, "May I decrease; may you increase."
- After the sermon—when the crowd has dispersed and the parking lot cleared—you might take one final walk through the worship center and ask God to keep the truth preached that day percolating in listeners' hearts throughout the day and week.

"I TRIED IT"

"From Paul's prayers, I saw how deeply he was a man of prayer, and that he knew the people he prayed for. His requests were specific, praying that their faith would grow. When I walked through our sanctuary, I was reminded of specific needs. One young husband struggles with his unfaithfulness while another attempts to win back his wife's trust. A young woman decides to change her life's direction and responds to Christ. Still another pew finds an empty space next to a faithful saint who's now going on alone."

Bill Worrell, Knightstown, Indiana

"It was enjoyable to study Paul's prayers. In eight of the nine prayers he began with thanks for his readers. We preachers need to develop a grateful attitude for God's people! It was an easy exercise—as it 'so happened,' when the assignment came I was in a series on Colossians. The sermon was 'What To Put Aside' (sexual sins, greed, bad temper, sins of the tongue, 3:5). As I 'pew-prayed,' I prayed I would be compassionate and help people prepare for Christ's coming."

Ken Overdorf, Beckley, West Virginia

RESOURCES FOR FURTHER STUDY

- *How to Pray for Your Congregation: A Leader's Guide to Praying for Your Ministry*, by Terry Gooding (Master Design, 2002; can purchase for $1 online at http://masterdesign.org/2003/08/how-to-prayer-for-your-congregation-by-terry-gooding).
- *Preacher and Prayer*, by E. M. Bounds. View entire book online for free at_http://encouragingpromises.com/P-Promises/Pr-Prom-Library/Preach-Prayer.PDF
- "Pray for Your People as You Pray for Your Preaching," audio discussion with Scott Gibson and Pat Batten. Access at http://www.gordonconwell.edu/resources/media/79.mp3.
- "How Four Specific Prayers Changed a Preacher," by Joe McKeever. Access at http://www.churchleaders.com/pastors/preaching-teaching/142171-i_prayed_for_my_preaching-and.html.

Assemble a Feedback Group

In the homiletics courses I teach, students practice preaching near the end of the semester. After a student preaches, the class discusses the sermon's merits and makes suggestions for improvement. The student who preached listens carefully to the feedback his or her listeners provide, and often takes notes on their comments. These discussions provide students immediate feedback on their preaching, and help them grow as preachers.

One semester a student came by my office a couple of hours before he was scheduled to preach. He began to speak, then hesitated. After a pause he furrowed his brow, "I don't think I can preach in class today."

"Oh?" I responded, having navigated such conversations before. "And why is that?"

"I don't mind the preaching actually—it's the discussion afterward that bothers me. This sermon is very personal. It's what God led me to say. It doesn't feel right for people to talk about what they like about the sermon, and what they think is wrong with it. I'm not preaching it to please them, anyway—I don't really care what they think about it. I just want to preach the Word of God."

This student happened to play on our college's basketball team. I asked him, "When you stand at the free throw line, holding the ball in your hands, what do you think about?"

"I just want to get the ball through the basket," he responded.

"Yes, that is your objective. What if, while watching you in practice, one of your teammates noticed a flaw in your shooting form? Perhaps your right elbow strayed too far from your body, or you didn't bend your knees enough. Would you want your teammate to help you shoot better?"

"Of course."

"The objective remains the same—make the basket. Your technique can improve, however, when people you trust offer feedback, helping you make the free throw."

He nodded, realizing what I would say next.

"Yes, you want to preach the Word of God. And, you want that Word to reach your listeners as effectively as possible. The manner in which you preach—how you organize your thoughts, how you use your voice, and even your body language—influences the sermon's effectiveness. Seeking feedback from your listeners doesn't change the objective of preaching the Word, it only helps you preach that Word better."

He flashed a crooked smile, conceded the point, and said, "See you in a couple hours."

THE EXERCISE

This week's exercise will help you to seek feedback from a few trusted listeners. This objective bears much similarity to that of our eighth exercise ("Have Listeners Evaluate You")—seeking insight from our listeners to improve our preaching—but this week's exercise uses a different method to pursue that objective. Rather than inviting listeners to complete written surveys, you will invite them to meet with you after the sermon to discuss its strengths and weaknesses.

1. Invite about five people to participate in a feedback group two or three days after your upcoming sermon. Waiting two or three days will allow the sermon to simmer in listeners' minds and hearts. Choose perceptive, kind people who you can trust to offer honest, helpful insight. Also, choose men and women from various generations and life circumstances. Let group members know in general what the meeting will involve—discussion of the sermon's strengths and weaknesses—but do not give them a specific list of questions so that they will experience the sermon in the same manner as other listeners.

2. Develop a brief list of questions to guide the meeting. You might ask:

- How would you sum up the message of the sermon in one sentence?
- By the end of the sermon, what did you understand about the Scripture text and biblical truths I attempted to explain? What did you understand about how it should make a difference in your life?
- During the sermon, when did you feel most engaged? When did your mind begin to wander? When did you want to stop me and raise your hand to ask a question, or to make a comment?
- Was there anything about my delivery—maybe something about my voice, or a particular movement or gesture that I repeat—that you found distracting?
- What two or three suggestions would you make to strengthen this sermon and/or the way I preached it?

You might also ask some questions that rise from the specific sermon you preached. For example, "What went through your mind when I told about the mother and daughter I saw at the grocery store?" Or, "I worried that my explanation of the Passover was confusing—did that part of the sermon make sense to you?"

3. After the sermon, think through each prepared question yourself. How would you evaluate the sermon? You may gain some insight by comparing your responses to those of the feedback group.

4. At the meeting with the feedback group, begin with prayer, then explain why you assembled the group. Emphasize your desire to grow as a preacher, and that their honest feedback will help. Then, work your way through the questions you prepared. Keep the meeting as informal and conversational as possible. If a question leads the conversation in a direction you had not planned, but that may provide helpful insight, allow the tangent. Your goal is to learn about your preaching, not to complete the list of questions. Take care, on the other hand, to keep the conversation moving in a fruitful direction. Listen carefully and humbly—check your ego, and resist the temptation to defend yourself. Take exhaustive notes.

5. If possible, choose two or three suggestions from the feedback group and implement them into your preaching right away. If someone commented that you tend to

speak too quickly, for example, take immediate steps to speak more slowly (perhaps with a reminder post-it note in your Bible). Then, ask the person who provided that suggestion if they noticed any improvement. Such steps will bring immediate growth in your preaching, and will show the feedback group that you valued their effort.

"I TRIED IT"

"I met with a feedback group on a Saturday morning. The discussion began slowly, but once they realized it was not a time to just criticize the sermon, we talked freely and openly about the sermon's truths and life applications. They enjoyed the opportunity to discuss these things in a deeper way. And, in this setting, they could be honest with me about what did and didn't work well, especially in regards to my stories and illustrations."

Steve Fair, Noblesville, Indiana

"I absolutely love the idea of a preacher seeking feedback on his sermons, and this exercise creates a great framework for productive feedback to occur. I think this exercise works because of the freedom it gives to listeners to be honest and constructive. It shows a vulnerability from the preacher that he really wants to get better at the craft. It obviously helps in the crafting of the sermon, but also proves beneficial for deepening the relationship between the preacher and his 'evaluators.'"

Mark Nelson, Knoxville, Tennessee

RESOURCES FOR FURTHER STUDY

- *When God Speaks Through You: How Faith Convictions Shape Preaching and Mission*, by Craig A. Satterlee (The Alban Institute, 2007).
- *The Power of Feedback: 35 Principles for Turning Feedback from Others Into Personal and Professional Change*, by Joseph R. Folkman (John Wiley and Sons, 2006).
- "Growing as Preachers Through Lay Feedback to Our Sermons," by Will Willimon. Access at http://willimon. blogspot.com/2007/10/growing-as-preachers-through-lay. html.

- "Feedback and Evaluation: Key to Relevant Biblical Preaching" (interview with Lee Strobel). Access at http://www.ministrymagazine.org/archive/2001/January/feed-back-and-evaluation.html.

Minimize Notes

Joseph Webb tells of visiting a large, metropolitan church. During the service, the preacher invited all the children to the front. She sat on the top step as the youngsters surrounded her, and for ten minutes she taught them a lesson from the Bible. She spoke naturally, with energy and laughter. She used no notes; she simply talked with the children. The adults in the pews leaned forward in their seats, riveted by her words to the children. The ten minutes passed in a flash.

Soon thereafter, the same preacher entered her pulpit, arranged several pages of a manuscript, and proceeded to read a sermon to the adults for the next twenty minutes. She attempted to read enthusiastically, but the same adults who leaned forward during the children's sermon now leaned back, their eyes lazily rotating from the floor to their watches and only occasionally toward the pulpit. The twenty minutes passed like a snail.[1]

Both sermons spoke important messages. Both required preparation. Both grew from the preacher's study, heart, and passion. Only one, however, connected with her listeners—the message spoken, not read.

A sermon is an event, not a document. Though the document aids in preparation, most effective preachers leave the document—at least most of it—on their desks, and enter the pulpit with an internalized message they can comfortably discuss with their listeners.[2]

---

1. Joseph M. Webb, *Preaching Without Notes* (Nashville: Abingdon Press, 2001), 10.
2. If you already preach without notes, feel free to bypass this exercise and complete one of the bonus exercises at the end of the book. You may, however, find that

PREACHING WITH LESS OR NO NOTES

The Spectrum

- Some preach from a *full manuscript or outline*. Every word they plan to say lays before them on the podium. This approach inspires confidence in preachers—they need not worry about forgetting a story or losing their precise wording. Too often, though, this approach inspires yawns in listeners—though the preacher attempts to deliver the sermon in an appealing manner, listeners feel read to.

- Others reduce their notes to a *one page outline*. With this approach, preachers feel less temptation to read, and don't have to shuffle papers. They can leave the one page on a podium and refer back to it as needed. On the negative side, the piece of paper still takes the preacher's eyes and attention away from listeners—the outline has a gravitational pull that draws the preacher out of the communication event.

- Some preachers use only *brief notes*, perhaps a half page tucked into their Bible, or notes made in the margins of the Bible. This method enables preachers to maintain precise wording where necessary—perhaps with quotes or statistics—and allows reminders of the major points of the sermon. Because their notes fit into a Bible, though, these preachers have complete freedom from the podium, maximizing eye contact and whole-body communication. This may be the best method for most preachers.

- Others preach with *no notes* whatsoever. This approach completely removes the temptation to read the sermon or to remain anchored to a podium. This method sacrifices, however, the ability to include a precise quote, or to have a safety valve in case a preacher's mind goes blank.

---

this exercise offers some insight and suggestions that will help you preach without notes even more effectively.

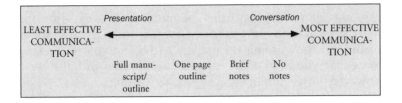

Why Minimize Notes

Preachers communicate most effectively with less notes. In fact, reflecting on the spectrum above, the further we move toward no notes, the more we connect with our listeners. This holds true for four reasons:

1. Listeners do not like to be read to. Though they want us to prepare, they also want to feel as though we speak from the heart. When we read, our pace tends to remain too steady and our pitch too consistent, unlike a lively conversation in which these vary. Most listeners respond better to conversation than to presentation.

2. When we use less notes, we can maximize eye contact. The less we look at notes, the more we look at our listeners, and the more trust, warmth, and believability we facilitate. Conversely, the more we use notes, the less we look our listeners in the eye, and we facilitate distrust, coldness, and suspicion.

3. When we rely less on notes, we can make adjustments during the speaking event. If we see puzzled looks on listeners' faces, for example, we can offer more explanation than we had planned. Or, if we see listeners leaning forward and fixing their eyes on us, this positive response can spark greater passion in our speaking.

4. When we use less notes, we are freed from the podium and we can gesture and move more consistently and expressively. Notes on a pulpit anchor us to that pulpit—though we may venture away for a short time, the anchor will always pull us back. Less notes, however—especially if the notes are brief enough to fit into a Bible—allow us to move freely.

In sum, the less we use notes, the better we connect with our listeners. Instead of being distracted by words on a page, we enter more fully into the communication event—we are more present with our listeners. Granted, we might lose some of the precise wording we prepared (though, you will retain more than you think). The enhanced connection with listeners, however, outweighs any loss of precise wording.

THE EXERCISE

1. *Commit to the sermon.* Unless you already preach with brief or no notes, commit to moving at least one notch toward that goal on the spectrum pictured on page 149.
2. *Design the sermon with logical flow.* After you study your text and compile the ideas you plan to relate, develop a preliminary map of the sermon that assures each idea logically flows into the next. Haddon Robinson tells his students, "A well written sermon remembers itself."
3. *Write the sermon fully.* Preaching with brief or no notes does not imply less preparation. Write a full sermon. Whether in paragraphs or in a detailed outline, clarify your thoughts on paper until your ideas gleam clear and precise.
4. *Internalize the sermon.* Once you complete preparations on paper, internalize the sermon—*internalize*, not *memorize*. A memorized message usually sounds canned. Instead of memorizing, therefore, learn the sermon well enough that you can stand and talk about it with the same ease you tell friends of your favorite childhood Christmas or your fumbling first date. We do not memorize such stories, we know them and tell them—an internalized sermon flows just as naturally. I use the following process, which involves practicing aloud four times and progressively weaning myself from my manuscript. Feel free to make whatever adjustments best fit your learning style and rhythms of preparation.
    - Practice the sermon aloud, reading from the full manuscript/outline. Practicing aloud helps transform written words into spoken words.
    - Practice the sermon aloud a second and third time, using the manuscript/outline progressively less—keep it close by, but use it only when you have to.
    - After the third rehearsal, you will have a sense of which parts of the sermon you struggle most to remember.

Develop a brief set of notes—preferably small enough to fit in your Bible or written in the margins of your Bible—that includes the reminders you most need.

- Practice the sermon aloud a fourth time, using only the brief notes prepared in the previous step.
- Prior to the preaching event (ideally just an hour or two before), review your full manuscript/outline. This review will give your mind a final refresher of the wording and images you prepared.

5. *Preach the sermon with less notes.* Enter the pulpit with less notes than you normally take, confident that your God-empowered preparation has equipped your God-created mind to proclaim the God-inspired Word.

"I TRIED IT"

"I have used brief notes for a couple years, and the impact has been just as this chapter describes—better eye contact and rapport with my listeners, and more comfortable and confident body language. I need the brief notes (as opposed to no notes) because we have multiple services, and I want to be careful to not skip anything, thinking 'haven't I already said that?' Also, because we use PowerPoint, the brief notes help me make certain to 'hit my marks' so the tech team can follow me."

Brian Lakin, Markle, Indiana

"Preaching with few or no notes makes for a better sermon experience for listeners and, surprisingly, for the preacher. After transitioning from manuscript-dependence preaching to few or no notes, I began enjoying preaching like I never had before. Freedom from a manuscript allowed me to develop speaking and communication skills I did not even know I had (e.g., stepping away from the pulpit; using humor) which, in turn, has helped my listeners to connect with the gospel more meaningfully."

Steve Page, Bristol, Tennessee

RESOURCES FOR FURTHER STUDY

- *You've Got to Be Believed to Be Heard, Updated Edition: The Complete Book of Speaking ... in Business and in*

Life!, by Bert Decker (Revised Edition, St. Martin's Press, 2008).

- *Preaching Without Notes*, by Joseph Webb (Abingdon Press, 2001).
- "Unscripted: Preparing to Preach Is Not Writing a Speech," by Dave McClellan. Access at http://www.christianitytoday.com/le/preachingworship/preaching/unscripted.html?start=1.
- "Preaching Effectively Without Notes," by Derek Morris. Access at http://www.ministrymagazine.org/archive/2006/October/preaching-effectively-without-notes.html.

EXERCISE TWENTY-FIVE

Talk to an Artist

Each semester I take my beginning homiletics students to the library to help them research their assigned sermon texts. This past semester, like usual, we gathered in the library's reference room, where I explained how to find and use resources such as commentaries, Bible introductions, and Bible dictionaries. While I gave this short lecture, however, my eyes were drawn to a group of four new paintings on the wall behind the students. Their vivid colors and stunning depictions of Christ captivated me. The paintings portrayed four scenes from Christ's last week, interweaving contemporary and biblical images to create a striking effect.

After I released the students into the library to research their sermon texts, I hurried to the corner of the library that displayed the paintings. I contemplated the images for a full ten minutes. Then, I noticed a printed card mounted to the right of the display, which explained that a local minister had commissioned an artist in his congregation to complete the paintings to help teach about Jesus' passion during the four Sundays leading into Easter. Each Sunday the minister revealed another painting, until the final work of art—"The God Who Is Victorious"—put an exclamation point on Easter Sunday worship.[1]

I glanced back at my students, who pored over commentaries and Bible dictionaries. While this aspect of sermon preparation stands critical to preaching God's Word in an accurate, powerful manner (and, in fact, some exercises in this

---

1. View this series of paintings at http://tonysobota.com/section/170547_Easter_
Paintings.html.

book will sharpen such research skills), I thought to myself, "What if my students could interview this artist about their sermon texts? What insight might he have into the truths they plan to preach? What images, emotions, nuances, complexities, and tones might an artist see in a text that most left-brained preachers and authors of commentaries miss?

Catherine Kapikian, director of the Center of Arts and Religion at Wesley Theological Seminary, explains, "The church, from its very conception used the visual to convey the spiritual, even something as basic as the drawings on the walls of the catacombs. To me, it has to do with the notion that you come to know God most abundantly through the use of all your senses." Preachers, therefore, "need to be educated in the nonverbal languages of the arts. They don't have a clue as to line, shape, color, value and texture ... it's as alien as Greek and Hebrew to them."[2]

THE EXERCISE

This week's exercise will send us into a realm that many preachers—not all, but many—find uncomfortable. The world of the arts feels foreign to we who relish logic and reason. A conversation with an artist, however, can open our eyes to the dynamic, majestic textures of biblical truth and mystery.

1. Ask an artist who is also a Christian—perhaps a painter, sculptor, poet, musician, novelist, or another kind of artist—to spend an hour or two talking with you about the relationship between preaching and art, and about his or her perspective of your upcoming sermon. Ideally, find an artist who participates in your own church community. If no artist attends your church, however, ask other ministers in your area about artists who attend their churches.
2. Develop a list of questions to ask the artist. Then, give the artist this list prior to the meeting, along with a basic explanation of the Scripture text(s) and truths you plan to preach.

---

2. "Preaching and the Arts" (interview with Catherine Kapikian and Laura Wyke). http://www.homileticsonline.com/subscriber/interviews/kapikian_wyke.asp (accessed May 22, 2011).

You might ask generic questions such as these about preaching and art:

- Who has most influenced you as an artist? Why has this person been so influential?
- What preachers or sermons have most connected with you? Why did they connect?
- What about preachers or sermons have most frustrated you? Why?
- How might someone approach the preaching task as an artist?
- What can preachers learn from artists?
- What would make a sermon a work of art, rather than just a lecture?
- When you want to portray a truth, question, or mystery artistically, how do you begin the process?
- What do you wish preachers better understood about communicating truth, emotion, tone, conflict, relationship, and mystery?

You might ask questions such as these about your particular upcoming sermon:

- What emotions do you sense behind the Scripture text I will use?
- What do you find most stimulating about the text and truths I plan preach? What do you find most majestic? Most perplexing? Most painful? Most joyous?
- What images, metaphors, or symbols come to mind when you consider the truths I plan to preach?
- How would you use your particular artistic medium (painting, poetry, photography, music, etc.) to portray the truths of this sermon?
- What might a preacher do in a sermon on this text that would make you think, "Yeah, he got it"?

3. When you meet with the artist, create an informal, comfortable atmosphere. Assure this artist that you hope to gain from their perspective, not to judge it. Enter the conversation humbly, seeking whatever insight you can gain from the artist you interview. Do not feel tied to the questions you prepared; instead, allow the interview to flow freely, like a conversation. Also, take careful notes.

4. Allow the insights you gained from the conversation to

inform your upcoming sermon. Perhaps the artist will suggest useful images or metaphors. Or, they might spur ideas about an object you can bring on stage or an image you can project on a screen. Maybe they will help you view your Scripture text from a different perspective—a perspective that adds new texture to your understanding and sermon.

ADDITIONAL SUGGESTIONS

1. Have an artist complete a work during the worship service—perhaps during the musical worship or even during the sermon. A painter might complete a picture on stage that adds images to the sermon, or a poet might pen a few stanzas to read after the sermon.
2. Invite artists in your community to contribute pieces to display during a specific sermon series.
3. Invite the children of your church to draw, paint, or color pictures that reinforce a particular sermon, then display the pictures on the day you preach. The invitation will inspire children to engage art; and, the raw honesty in such pictures often portrays truth in memorable ways.
4. Find a particular work of art completed by a local artist that reinforces an upcoming sermon. During the sermon, invite the artist on stage for an interview about how the piece developed.

"I TRIED IT"

"I talked with an artist friend who told me that there are a lot more people who enjoy art than what most preachers realize— we are missing a significant part of our audience when we fail to use art in our preaching. He suggested not only using art, but making sure to use something that is quality, and something that fits well with the message. Poor quality or art that doesn't really fit will hurt the sermon more than it helps. Also, he suggested that the preacher not talk too much about the art—allow the painting, poem, or whatever it is to stand on its own."

Will Pannell, Bristol, Virginia

"Artists make up a significant portion of our faith community, and we incorporate their ideas on a weekly basis. We invite them to our planning meetings for insights and thoughts on how and what is being conveyed. As I discussed my teaching with our artists, for this particular exercise, I was struck by how many different ways people can perceive one teaching. It's important for those who seek to communicate God's Word to have in mind the various ways people in our communities receive and process information—especially those who have an artistic eye."

Alan Bradford, Knoxville, Tennessee

RESOURCES FOR FURTHER STUDY

- *The Artist's Way of Preaching*, by Charles Denison (Westminster John Knox, 2006).
- "Preaching and the Arts" (an interview with Catherine Kapikian and Laura Wyke). Access at http://www.homileticsonline.com/subscriber/interviews/kapikian_wyke.asp.
- "The Sermon in Three Acts: The Rhetoric of Cinema and the Art of Narrative Exposition," by Glenn Watson. Access at http://www.ehomiletics.com/papers/06/Watson2006.pdf.

Try a Different Sermon Form

As skeletons give shape to bodies, sermon forms give shape to sermons. A skeleton determines how various body parts fit and function together, and whether that body will take the shape of a person, a dog, or a duckbilled platypus. Sermon structures, likewise, determine how the various parts of a sermon will fit and function together, and whether the sermon will take the shape of a narrative, a propositional argument, or a problem solved.

Scripture uses a variety of forms to present God's truth, such as historical narrative, parable, poetry, and prophecy. Instead of reflecting this variety in their sermons, however, many preachers construct every sermon in the same manner. They grow comfortable with one sermon form, then design every sermon, regardless of the text, with the same cookie-cutter approach.

This week's exercise will force us to consider various ways of forming an upcoming sermon.

PRELIMINARY PRINCIPLES

- *Sermon forms fall into two broad categories*—deductive development and inductive development. The difference lies in the placement of the thesis. Deductive sermons state the thesis early; inductive sermons save the thesis until the end. Deductive sermons usually divide into *points* that develop the thesis; inductive sermons usually divide into *movements* that progressively lead from problem to solution.
- *The form of the biblical text should influence the form of the sermon.* A sermon from a narrative text, for

example, might proceed in scenes. If the text presents a logical argument, then answers objections to that argument, the sermon might reflect the same structure. If the text repeatedly returns to a single idea or phrase, the sermon can follow suit. A sermon from a psalm might proceed through a series of emotions and images.

- *The sermon form should advance the truth, not overshadow it.* Some preachers grow so enamored with sermon forms that the presentation overshadows the truth. If we preach a first-person narrative sermon, for example, we do not want listeners walking away impressed by our presentation. Instead, we hope they are impacted by God's truth.

THE EXERCISE

1. Study the primary biblical text from which your upcoming sermon will grow. Give attention both to what (truth) and how (form) the text teaches.
2. Carefully read "10 Sermon Forms Anyone Can Use." An infinite number of potential sermon forms exist—in a sense, every individual sermon takes on its own form and personality. These ten possibilities, however, can help you consider various ways to structure your sermon.
3. Prepare your upcoming sermon using one of the following forms, or a variation that will best communicate the truth of your text.

TEN SERMON FORMS ANYONE CAN USE

1. The Truth Expounded

- Deductive. Begin with thesis, divide it into points. Probably use "transition with key word" at end of introduction.
- Works best with straightforward texts that present deductive arguments.
- Example from Matthew 6:1–18:
  - » INTRODUCTION: God seeks "acts of righteousness" performed only for Him (thesis). The text describes three righteous acts that we should perform for God alone (transition with key word).

» BODY: (1) Give to please God only. (2) Pray to please God only. (3) Fast to please God only.
» CONCLUSION: Restate thesis and points; closing illustration and challenge.

2. The Truth Constructed

- Inductive. Each point adds a word or phrase to the thesis, constructing the thesis throughout the sermon. The final point completes the thesis.
- Works best with texts that inductively build arguments over series of verses or paragraphs, or brief texts (such as Proverbs) in which the sermon unpacks just a sentence or two.
- Example from Acts 1:1–11:
  » INTRODUCTION: How can we fulfill our mission in Christ?
  » BODY: (1) God empowers us ... (2) To witness for Him ... (3) Near and far (thesis completed).
  » CONCLUSION: Closing illustration and challenge.

3. The Truth Spiral

- Deductive. Begin with the thesis, then circle back to the thesis after each point.
- Works best with texts that repeatedly cycle back to their main ideas.
- Example from Psalm 136:
  » INTRODUCTION: God's love endures forever (thesis).
  » BODY: (1) God works wonders in the universe (His love endures forever). (2) God protects and leads His people (His love endures forever). (3) God provides grace and life (His love endures forever). (4) God deserves our thanks (His love endures forever).
  » CONCLUSION: Closing illustration and challenge.

4. The Process of Elimination

- Inductive. Begin with a question, then work through wrong answers until you reach the right answer at the end.

- Works best with texts that present a series of possibilities before stating their main ideas.
- Example from the book of Ecclesiastes:
  » INTRODUCTION: Where can we find meaning in life?
  » BODY: (1) Wisdom? No. (2) Pleasure? No. (3) Wealth? No. (4) Career? No. (5) Anything in this life? No.
  » CONCLUSION: Only a relationship with God brings meaning to life (thesis).

5. The Unfolding Plot

- Inductive. Follow the pattern of a narrative text—the sermon's movements reflect the key scenes of the narrative, culminating with the thesis.
- Works best with texts that proceed through a series of scenes (narratives), emotions (such as Psalms), or ideas that are resolved at the end.
- Example from Genesis 22:1–19:
  » INTRODUCTION: How can we obey God when obedience seems beyond reach?
  » BODY: (1) God's commands may seem preposterous (God asked Abraham to sacrifice Isaac). (2) Obedience may seem unattainable (Abraham saddled up, put Isaac on altar). (3) Obedience hinges on our trust in God's provision (Abraham trusted God would provide).
  » CONCLUSION: We obey God as far as we trust Him (thesis).

6. The Problem Solved

- Inductive. Begin with a problem, end with its solution. In between, movements discuss causes and/or implications of the problem, and lay the basis for the coming solution.
- Works best with texts that deal with obvious problems, then teach principles that lead to solutions.
- Example from 1 Corinthians 5:
  » INTRODUCTION: Unrepentant sin infects a church community like cancer.

» BODY: (1) The community suffers the consequence of an individual's unrepentant sin. (2) The evil must be purged from the community. (3) The purging purifies the church. (4) The purging hopes to lead the sinner to repentance.
» CONCLUSION: Godly churches love enough to discipline (thesis).

7. The Paradox

- Probably inductive. Show how two ideas commonly considered antithetical are both true, and even complimentary. The sermon changes an "either/or" into a "both/and."
- Works best with texts that clear up common misunderstandings about seemingly opposing ideas.
- Example from James 2:14–26:
  » INTRODUCTION: Which matters most in the Christian life, our inner faith or our outward works?
  » BODY: (1) Does faith matter most? Yes. (2) Do works matter most? Yes.
  » CONCLUSION: A living faith includes both inward commitment and outward expression (thesis).

8. The Contrast

- Probably deductive. Present a contrast, usually from bad to good: "It's not this [movement 1], it's this [movement 2]."
- Works best with texts that present a contrast, such as the vice/virtue lists in the epistles.
- Example from Galatians 5:13–26:
  » INTRODUCTION: The Spirit enables change (thesis).
  » BODY: (1) By the Spirit we put off sinful desires. (2) By the Spirit we bear the fruit of Christlike character.
  » CONCLUSION: Closing illustration and challenge.

9. The Interrogation

- Deductive or inductive. Develop the sermon around

questions about the thesis (if deductive) or the text (might then be inductive).
- Works best with texts that are difficult to understand, such as prophecy and apocalyptic literature.
- Example from 1 John 2:18–26:
  » INTRODUCTION: Much speculation circulates about the antichrist.
  » BODY: (1) Who is the Antichrist? (2) What does the Antichrist do? (3) When will the antichrist appear? (4) Where will the antichrist appear? (5) Why does the Antichrist matter? (6) How should we respond to the Antichrist?
  » CONCLUSION: When lies circulate, cling to the Truth (thesis).

10. The Story

- Inductive. Form the sermon around a story or intertwined stories. In *Creative Anticipation*, David Enyart describes six kinds of narrative sermons:[1]
  » Simulating the Narrative: The shape of a narrative text shapes the sermon.
  » Sustaining the Narrative: The story is the sermon; the preacher never leaves the story (can be either first or third person).
  » Supplementing the Narrative: Though the sermon consists primarily of a story, it is supplemented with occasional explanation and application.
  » Segmenting the Narrative: The story is broken into segments; between segments comes another story or biblical exposition. The two tracks converge at the end.
  » Sequencing the Narratives: Multiple narratives are told sequentially, each teaching the same truth from a different perspective.
  » Suspending the Narrative: One or more stories are left unresolved.
- Works best with narrative texts, though can be used with

---

1. David A. Enyart, *Creative Anticipation: Narrative Sermon Designs for Telling the Story* (Philadelphia: Xlibris, 2002).

other texts/theses that can be wrapped into a narrative.

- Example from Genesis 18:1–15; 21:1–7 (Sustaining the Narrative, first person):
  - » INTRODUCTION (out of character): Are some things too powerful even for God?
  - » BODY (in character): (1) When God promised Sarah and me a son, we laughed. (2) We could not fathom God giving us a son in our old age. (3) The day Isaac was born, Sarah was amazing. (4) As we held our son, we looked at each other, and laughed.
  - » CONCLUSION (out of character): "Anything God has ever done, He can do now. Anything God has done anywhere, He can do here. Anything God has done for anyone, He can do for you" (A.W. Tozer, thesis).

"I TRIED IT"

"The benefit of the exercise for me was that it caused me to look at a familiar text (John 13:1–17) in a different light. I am one who is comfortable with my normal method of study and preaching. This exercise helped me to look deeper into how the text relates to us. It helped me to ask questions that I understood my listeners would be asking, and allowed us to struggle together with those questions and find the answers together in the text."

Drew Mentzer, Danville, Illinois

"Trying a different sermon form made for a fun and interesting week. I had done first-person messages before, but this time I did more of a story form. Preparing for it made me think in different ways. The people seemed to really enjoy it, and they listened intently for what was coming next. I kept the identity of the main character (Samuel) hidden for a while. I could see them trying to figure out who the story was about. Using this sermon form really kept them involved in the message."

Randy Overdorf, Elizabethton, Tennessee

"This exercise reminded me that I need to use different outlines to keep from getting lazy. Exploring different sermon structures helps keep me sharp, and results in clearer, better sermons. In addition to the possibilities listed in this chapter, I would also mention the SUCCES outline offered by Chip and Dan Heath in *Made to Stick*, and the approach taught by Robert Smith, Jr., in *Doctrine That Dances*. Smith's insights forced me to see Scripture and sermon structure in a fresh way."

Kirk Dice, Suffolk, Virginia

RESOURCES FOR FURTHER STUDY

- *The Shape of Preaching: Theory and Practice of Sermon Design*, by Dennis Cahill (Baker, 2007).
- *Determining the Form: Structures for Preaching*, by O. Wesley Allen, Jr. (Fortress, 2008).
- "The Four D's: Design," by Mary Hinkle Shore. Access at: http://www.workingpreacher.org/sermondevelopment. aspx?article_id=21.
- "Preaching by Design," by Dennis Cahill. Access at http://www.preaching.org/preaching-by-design.

Explore the Original Context

I sometimes tell this fictional story to preaching students:

Not long ago I ventured into a musty closet tucked in a corner of our college's Old Main Building, which our founder constructed in 1905. I needed an old college catalog for a research project, and someone suggested that I look in this closet. While I shuffled through its stacks of books, notebooks, and folders—most of them decades old—a yellowed, dusty paper fluttered to the floor. Curious, I unfolded it, and found this brief note:

> Dear Marge,
>   I hope all is well with you and the others at the college. Let everyone know that I miss them.
>   I am doing fine. Please tell Mom that I love her. I miss you, and hope to see you all again soon.
>   Love Always,
>   Harold

The note offered a simple message. Harold sent greetings to Marge, his friends, and his mother. He hoped to see them soon. I stuffed the letter in my back pocket then continued my research.

That evening while I prepared for bed, I found the note again. "I wonder who Marge and Harold were?" I thought. I noticed a date scrawled at the top: "July, 1943."

The next day I visited the college's historical room. I scanned a photograph of the entire student body from 1940—just a handful of students in those days. The picture included a young man named Harold and a young lady named Margaret.

They stood a row apart—smiling, tall, and attractive. In the 1941 picture, taken a year later, Harold and Marge stood next to each other, and shared a last name. In the 1942 and 1943 pictures, however, Marge stood alone. Her shoulders slumped and the smile had disappeared.

I then pulled a binder from a shelf that contains the college's old newsletters. I found Harold and Marge's engagement announcement in a 1940 publication, and their wedding picture in 1941. An announcement in 1942 revealed that Harold had been drafted to serve in World War II. The newsletter dated October, 1943, was dedicated to Harold's memory—he died on the battlefield.

I read the letter again, penned by Harold to his new wife just weeks before his death. The note had not changed—its message remained simple and uncomplicated. An awareness of the context, however, gave the words texture and depth. I now understood Harold's letter as it connected with a larger story, filled with romance, fear, and heartache.

Paul wrote Timothy. Moses preached to the Israelites. Jeremiah prophesied to Judah. Luke recorded the story of Christ for Theophilus. A Roman prison. The shadows of Artemis's temple in Ephesus. East of the Jordan River after forty years wandering the wilderness. Jerusalem with the Babylonians bearing down. The Mediterranean world blossoming with new churches. AD 66. 1400 BC. 600 BC. AD 70.

Too often, we read biblical texts as though they occurred in a vacuum, void of context, emotion, and personality. The careful interpreter recognizes, however, that God revealed His truths through particular people, places, and cultures. To fully understand a text, therefore, requires an exploration into its original context. The exploration may not change the meaning of the words on the page, but it will add texture and depth to them. This awareness of the story behind the text will transform black and white letters into high definition cinema.

THE EXERCISE

Near the beginning of your preparation for your upcoming sermon, complete the following four steps:

1. Read through the primary Scripture text(s) on which you
   will base your upcoming sermon. As you read, compile a
   list of matters to research and questions to answer. Give
   special attention to the people, places, and particulars of
   culture and history related to your texts.
   - *People.* Who wrote the text? What can we learn about
     the author from other biblical texts, history, or church
     tradition? To whom did the author write this text?
     What can we learn about this original audience? What
     kind of relationship did the author and recipients
     share? Does the passage mention anyone in addition
     to the writer and original readers? What can we learn
     about these individuals from other biblical texts, his-
     tory, or church tradition?
   - *Places.* From where and under what circumstances
     did the author write? Where and under what circum-
     stances did the original recipients live? Do these places
     appear elsewhere in Scripture? What historical events
     occurred at each place? How did their cultures func-
     tion in regard to economics, education, politics, re-
     lationships, and religion? What was the topography
     and climate of each place? How did these impact the
     cultures, histories, and daily lives of their inhabitants?
     Does the text mention any additional locations? If so,
     what can you learn about them? Where, geographi-
     cally, were these places? What relationship did they
     have with the locations of the writer and recipients?
   - *Particulars.* What historical or cultural details arise in
     the passage that might influence how we understand it?
     These might involve farming techniques, financial mat-
     ters, relationships between people of different strata of
     society, or family dynamics. Often such particulars shed
     light on a Scripture passage. For example, why did Paul
     tell Timothy to "get here before winter?" (2 Tim. 4:21).
     Why did John say that Jesus "*had* to go through Samaria"
     when he traveled from Judea to Galilee? (John 4:4, em-
     phasis mine). How would a cripple like Mephibosheth
     have existed from day to day? (2 Sam. 9). How would
     a tax collector like Levi have obtained his job, related
     with the government, and related with his fellow citi-
     zens? (Mark 2:13–17). What educational, cultural, and

religious influences might Moses have had while Pharaoh's daughter raised him in Egypt? (Exod. 2:10).

2. Gather whatever study materials you have available. These might include Bible dictionaries, Bible encyclopedias, commentaries, books related to historical or cultural backgrounds, Bible study software, and/or websites.[1]

3. Comb through your resources to find whatever information you can about the people, places, and particulars of culture and history that surround your primary text(s). Allow the list you compiled in step one to guide this research.

4. Use at least two insights you gained from your research in your upcoming sermon.

"I TRIED IT"

"It was exciting to carry out a thorough exploration of the original context because as I dug, the research revealed a treasure of background information that clarified the text and its setting for me. The golden nuggets of information added true dimension to my sermon and definitely boosted my confidence as I preached. Congregants came to me and explained they enjoyed hearing the background details because it provided them a 'fuller understanding' of the verses."

David Caffee, Englewood, Tennessee

"This chapter served as a timely and helpful reminder in regard to my sermon preparation. Exploring the text's original context helps safeguard us from anachronistic preaching and teaching, while at the same time unlocking more accurate parallels and insight for appropriate contemporary application. For the preacher who does the digging, important social, historical, psychological, and literary observations emerge from the background and bolster both our understanding as well as the homiletic potential of the text at hand. This exercise should play a permanent role in the sermonic process."

Jared Wortman, Durham, North Carolina

---

1. The *Zondervan Illustrated Bible Backgrounds Commentary* offers particular help with historical and cultural context. Websites such as studylight.org and followtherabbi.com also provide helpful resources.

RESOURCES FOR FURTHER STUDY

- *The World Jesus Knew: Beliefs and Customs From the Time of Jesus*, by Anne Punton (Monarch, 2010).
- *Dictionary of New Testament Background*, edited by Craig Evans and Stanley Porter (InterVarsity, 2000).
- *Studying the Ancient Israelites: A Guide to Sources and Methods*, by Victor Matthews (Baker, 2007).
- *Manners and Customs in the Bible: An Illustrated Guide to Daily Life in Bible Times*, 3rd ed., by Victor Matthews (Baker Academic, 2006).
- Access research, articles, and lessons provided by That The World May Know Ministries at www.followtherabbi.com.
- "Preaching in High Definition," by Jere Phillips. Access at http://www.preaching.com/resources/articles/11600640.

Hang the Sermon on an Image

Logic paired with images communicates better than logic alone. When benevolent organizations want to explain the needs in third-world countries, for instance, they use few facts and statistics. Instead, they feature images and stories, which captivate people and convince them to help. Furthermore, people remember in images. If you ask a grown man about his first car, his mind fills not with printed words but with the picture of that faded-yellow jalopy he saved his yard-mowing money to buy. When people reflect on events of the past—a first job, a first kiss, or the dreadful ten days spent in the hospital during college, their minds stroll through a gallery of pictures.

To convince listeners of biblical truth, therefore, and to create experiences they remember, sermons need to pair facts and logic with images. In fact, a sermon will often best reach listeners if the entire message hangs on a single image—a dominant metaphor, story, or picture that frames the rest of the sermon.

For example, David could have began the twenty-third Psalm by stating, "The Lord provides for my needs, leads me, and treats me tenderly." Instead, he offered the image, "The Lord is my shepherd," and allowed that picture to frame the remainder of the psalm. Other psalms revolve around metaphors such as, "God is my rock," or "God is my fortress," which present more expansive views than, "God is dependable," or "God protects me." In the prophets, God sent Jeremiah to a potter's house, and Ezekiel to a valley of dry bones—His messages to His people in these instances revolved around each image.

A sermon, likewise, often relates truth most effectively if framed by a single, dominant image. Usually, this dominant image comes near the beginning of the message, then the remainder of the message grows from it. For example, on the Sunday following September 11, 2001, I began my sermon with the following image:

> Over the last five days we've watched as workers sift through the rubble, searching for survivors and beginning to clean up the horrible wreckage left behind by the gruesome act of terrorism. I can't help but think of a spiritual analogy—in a sense, all of America is sifting through the rubble. We're full of questions, doubts, and fears. Why did this happen? How could God allow it to happen? Is God trying to teach us something through this? Was this God's will? Is it okay to be angry? Would it be okay for the United States to retaliate? This morning we will sift through this rubble that plagues our minds and hearts, attempting to answer at least some of the questions that remain behind.

Each point in the sermon, then, grew from the image of sifting through rubble.

In some cases, the dominant image might come near the end of a message. In one sermon, the preacher connected the Tree of Life in Garden of Eden with the Tree of Life in the New Jerusalem. He had two trees on stage with him. Near the end, the preacher stood between the two trees with his arms outstretched, symbolizing the cross of Jesus which bridges the gap. The entire sermon hung on that image, though he did not finalize the image until the end.

THE EXERCISE

After you research the primary text(s) for your upcoming sermon, proceed through these four steps to hang your sermon on an image.

1. *Define the central idea of the sermon.* As specifically and concretely as possible, state your sermon's thesis. More than just

a word ("forgiveness"), state a complete, declarative sentence ("God calls us to forgive others as He forgives us.").[1]

2. *Move from idea to image.* The three methods below can stimulate your brainstorming and help you find an image—such as a metaphor or story—that best pictures your central idea. These are not three sequential steps, but simply three different ways to spur ideas.

   - Examine the words in your thesis and consider what images they evoke. From the example above—"God calls us to forgive others as He forgives us"—allow the term "call" to roll over in your mind. The word carries different nuances than would "suggest" or even "command." Does it bring to mind the image of a referee? An auctioneer? A parent? A motivational speaker? Allow your mind to wander. Or, you might focus on the term "forgive." What pictures or stories does this evoke? Perhaps you consider a canceled debt, recall a spat with a childhood friend, or remember a story about someone who granted forgiveness in a painful circumstance.

   - Generalize the central idea. The thesis that you stated specifically, now state more generally. For example, "God calls us to forgive others as He's forgiven us" might become, "Give what you have received." This more general idea, then, can inspire particular images—perhaps believers functioning like a pipeline rather than a reservoir, or a child who receives an allowance then immediately gives it to a needy person.

   - Brainstorm about where a dynamic similar to your central idea appears elsewhere in life—perhaps in nature, families, friendships, athletics, business, science, history, politics, food, movies, television shows, or literature. The chart on the next page contains examples.

3. *Choose the most effective image.* Considering your particular personality, audience, and sermon, which image will most effectively encapsulate the message? Remember, this image will frame the entire sermon, not just illustrate a particular point or segment in the sermon.

---

1. Review Exercise 12, "Polish Your Thesis," for help with this.

Sermon/Central Idea	Dominant Image
Jesus died in our place.	In Dickens's *A Tale of Two Cities*, a good man trades places with a scoundrel and goes to the gallows in his place.
We endure difficulties when we view them from the standpoint of eternity.	Your perspective of a football game differs depending on where you sit. Choose the chair that will give you the best overall perspective, perhaps in the press box.
Godly parents train their children then release them in the Lord.	A mother eagle nurtures her young, then sends them from the nest that they might fly.
From Romans 14–15 (meat offered to idols): Love provides the balance on decisions about disputable matters.	A tightrope walker often uses a balance bar to keep from falling to one side or the other.
From Ecclesiastes: Worldly pursuits leave us empty, escalating our hunger for the eternal.	Hemingway's *The Old Man and the Sea* describes an epic battle between man and fish, but the man's victory proves empty in the end. However, literary scholars believe Hemingway included images of Jesus' crucifixion in the story.[2]

2. See Exercise 51 for more about Ecclesiastes and *The Old Man and the Sea*.

4. *Hang the sermon on that image.* Design your sermon such that the entire message hangs on the image you chose. You will probably want to introduce the image early in the sermon, then return to it throughout. Depending on the sermon's structure, this image might introduce each segment ("The second reason to choose a chair in the press box ...").

"I TRIED IT"

"I used this exercise with two sermons. The first explored the image of falling at Jesus' feet. I concluded that we need to fall at His feet now, or face the judgment of being under His feet one day. The second was about God knowing the number of hair on our heads. I brought my wife's hairbrush on stage, and talked about how much the hair in the brush means to me simply because it's hers. God knowing how many hairs we have shows how special we are to Him."

Burt Brock, Morgantown, Indiana

"I think most preachers, myself included, sometimes secretly wish that all our people wanted in a sermon was a precise parsing of Greek verbs and exposition. But the reality is that our culture latches on to images in marketing and media, so why not in sermons? When I used this exercise, I found that people remembered the sermon better, because the main idea connected with an image. I also found that I remembered the sermon better, too!"

Caleb Gilmore, Bluff City, Tennessee

"During a series on the armor of God from Ephesians 6, I came to the sermon about our 'feet fitted with the readiness that comes from the gospel of peace.' I used the image of shoes—the basis for our standing firm and being ready for whatever comes along. The congregation really resonated with the image—it gave them a visual, and something to think about and remember."

Mark Behr, Grand Rapids, Michigan

RESOURCES FOR FURTHER STUDY

- *Preaching and Teaching With Imagination: The Quest for Biblical Ministry*, by Warren Wiersbe (Baker, 1997).
- *Imagining a Sermon*, by Thomas Troeger (Abingdon Press, 1990).
- "Learning to Preach With Image," by Jason Moore and Len Wilson. Access at http://www.religiousproductnews.com/articles/2007-July/Supplement/Learning-to-Preach-with-Image.htm.
- "Metaphor: The Most Common and Complex of the Homiletician's Tools," by Calvin Pearson. Access at http://www.ehomiletics.com/papers/05/Pearson2005.pdf.

Expand Your Multicultural Awareness

Ronald Allen tells of a boat ride he took on the Caribbean during a trip to Jamaica. Looking over the side of the boat, he could see fish moving beneath the surface. They all looked similar—like shadows of various sizes, but without definite shape or color. A few minutes later, however, he donned goggles and leaped into the water. Now beneath the surface, he could see the fantastic variety of fish—each distinctive in size, with brilliant colors and unique shapes. "Preachers sometimes view the congregation from the surface," Allen explains. "The listeners appear to be much the same. But when preachers penetrate below the surface of the congregation, a more complex picture comes into view …. The typical congregation contains many different kinds of people who are defined by many different traits."[1]

I read Allen's story and considered his proposition, but thought, "This may be true in Miami or New York, but not in most churches I've been to." Then, I considered the church I attend. We are a relatively small, white, middle class, suburban congregation. Or, so I thought. I glanced around the next Sunday and realized that within a few feet sat people of Korean, Jewish, Hawaiian, African American, Chinese, Mexican, Haitian, and Filipino ethnicities. Even those I thought of generically as "Caucasian" hail from various backgrounds—Irish, French, German, Polish, Italian, and others.

Furthermore, I considered all the cultural differences related to gender, economics, and education. And, our

---

1. Joseph Jeter and Ronald Allen, *One Gospel, Many Ears: Preaching for Different Listeners in the Congregation* (St. Louis: Chalice Press, 2002), 5.

congregation includes some with mental and physical disabilities, others of various religious backgrounds, and people from multiple generations. Some in our church grew up in New York; others hail from the Appalachian Mountains, Southern California, and the Midwest.

Every listener interprets life, relationships, and even the Bible through a particular grid—a grid constructed from the various cultural elements in their background and experience. No two grids are exactly alike.

Unfortunately, most of my sermons and lessons reflect only my grid—my culture. My illustrations and applications, for example, often relate to white middle-class fathers of young children who have been in church their entire lives, enjoy sports, and work in white-collar environments. I fail to connect as well as I could, therefore, with those who interpret life through different grids. I have a feeling I am not alone in this oversight.

CONNECTING WITH A MULTICULTURAL AUDIENCE

Minor adjustments in what we preach, and how we preach it, can make a noticeable difference in how well we connect with people of various cultural backgrounds.

- *Connect With Hospitality.* From the pulpit and through personal greetings, extend a courteous welcome to everyone present, just as you would for guests in your home. Furthermore, preach and teach about hospitality, and practice what you preach by inviting people of various backgrounds into your home.

- *Connect With Story.* Most cultures are more story-oriented than western cultures. Western preachers who rely heavily on logic and propositional argument, therefore, can increase their multicultural effectiveness by using more stories. Furthermore, stories invite listeners into shared experiences, thus drawing people of various backgrounds together. If these stories grow from cultures different from the preacher's, the multicultural effectiveness escalates— telling a story from Mexican history, for example, rather than American history.

- *Connect With Celebration.* Preachers often tie their sermons to holidays and annual rituals common to their culture—American preachers often mention American holidays. Could a similar connection be made to a Chinese holiday, or an Italian custom? Imagine a preacher saying, "Ruth—one of our church members—grew up in a village in southern India. She explains that every Easter the Christians in her village would get together and ..."

- *Connect With Needs Raised.* Effective sermons demonstrate how biblical truth addresses human needs. Preachers often describe only those needs that arise from their own cultural circumstances. Instead, consider the needs of those of various backgrounds—someone for whom English is a second language, a person who faces life in a wheelchair, or a teenager who has grown up in the foster care system.
- *Connect With Applications.* Just as needs vary among different listeners, so varies the ways people should apply biblical truth to their circumstances. Applications should uniquely equip diverse segments of your listeners to live for Christ. While preparing a sermon about courage, for example, consider how Christlike courage might look for the second generation of an immigrant family, a pregnant sixteen-year-old from a wealthy family, or a woman working in a male-dominated environment.
- *Connect With Illustrations.* In a sermon, Alice Matthews told a story about sewing. She then made the offhanded comment, "This was my sweet revenge for all the football stories I have heard over the years." She received a standing ovation.[2] Preachers with multicultural awareness mine stories from a variety of cultural circumstances and backgrounds.

THE EXERCISE

Proceed through the following four steps to prepare your upcoming sermon with greater multicultural awareness.

1. Consider your own culture. Down the left side of a piece of paper, list the various elements that contribute to your own

---

2. In "Preaching in a Multicultural World," by Daniel L. Wong. http://www.preaching.com/resources/articles/11569912 (accessed June 22, 2011).

understanding of life and God. Include, but do not limit yourself to, your gender, ethnicity, education, economics, family of origin, present family, place of upbringing, present home, and religious background.

2. Develop a chart that compares your culture to your listeners' cultures. For every element you listed in step one, list what variables exist among those in your congregation. The chart below provides a couple examples.

Me	My Listeners
Caucasian American	Korean, Jewish, Hawaiian, African American, Chinese, Mexican, Haitian, Filipino
Youngest of four children, parents still together	Only child, adopted, divorced parents, deceased parent(s), raised by single mom, raised by single dad, raised by grandparents, raised in group home, raised by succession of foster families
Etc.	

3. Choose the five individuals from your church whose cultural backgrounds are most unlike yours, and send each a brief questionnaire through email, Facebook, or however is easiest in your circumstances. Consider including questions such as these:
   - How, when, and where have you felt closest to God?
   - How do people from your cultural background worship differently than we do at our church?
   - What prominent stories, rituals, or holidays in your background have influenced your perspectives of life and God?
   - What do you wish others in the church understood about your cultural background?
   - How does my preaching differ from the preaching you experienced growing up?
   - What have I said or done in a sermon that offended you or made you feel left out?
   - How could I better connect my sermons to your circumstances?

4. Reflect on the bullet points in the previous section ("Connecting With a Multicultural Audience") and what you learned from previous steps in this exercise, and include

in your upcoming sermon at least two deliberate efforts to connect with a multicultural audience.

ADDITIONAL SUGGESTIONS

- Invite people from different cultural backgrounds into a study group for an upcoming sermon.
- Learn to say a few words—such as "Hello," "Good morning," or "God loves you"—in the various language groups represented in your church. Then, say these phrases during a church service.
- Invite people of various backgrounds to bring something on stage with them that represents their culture, like a photograph, an article of clothing, or an artifact. Have them describe its significance.
- Invite people of different backgrounds into your home for dinner so that you can discuss their cultural insights.
- Plan a potluck dinner, and invite people to bring food that represents their heritage.

"I TRIED IT"

"This exercise humbled me, and convicted me of how narrow my preaching has been. I imagine one might argue that their congregation is not diverse enough to warrant effort in this area. Yet, another could argue that our churches are not diverse precisely because we have not made efforts to be more multicultural in our preaching. This is certainly true of me. Our congregation has a surprising amount of diversity, but my preaching did not reflect it. Reading the results of the questionnaire was painful, but wonderfully enlightening. I will continue to do this on a regular basis."

Brian Walton, Winchester, Kentucky

"This exercise was extremely helpful. I used to minister in a setting that included several international students; and, I presently minister with several from Jewish, American, and Asian heritages. We have done a lot of pot luck dinners and other activities to bring them together. The exercise helped me to recognize how the diversity should affect my preaching and teaching. I've really been emphasizing that we are one in Christ, no matter where we're from."

Keith Ratamess, Sevierville, Tennessee

RESOURCES FOR FURTHER STUDY

- *One Gospel, Many Ears: Preaching for Different Listeners in the Congregation,* by Joseph Jeter and Ronald Allen (Chalice, 2002).
- *Preaching to Every Pew: Cross-Cultural Strategies,* by Thomas Rogers (Fortress, 2001).
- "Choices for Congregations: Creating Multicultural and Multigenerational Congregations," by George Bullard. Access at http://bullardjournal.blogs.com/.m/bullardjournal/mtoc062002_post.doc.
- "Preaching in a Multicultural World," by Daniel Wong. Access at http://www2.tyndale.ca/~dwong/viewpage.php?pid=22.

Design Careful Transitions

I just finished reading a historical novel set in World War I. The author's description of the various battles, strategies, and movements reminded me of the importance of bridges to military strategy. To an extent, whoever controlled the bridges controlled the movement of the war.

Sermons need bridges. Sermons include series of segments, such as introductions, points or movements, and conclusions. Effective preachers build bridges between these segments with transition statements—a few words or sentences that logically and smoothly connect a previous section to an upcoming section. Transition statements serve as bridges.

Furthermore, transition statements serve as signposts. A signpost points back to where a traveler has been, and points ahead to where the traveler will go. In a transition statement, a preacher can remind listeners where they have been—"Thus far, we have learned x and y ..."—and point to where the sermon will take them next—" ... we will now learn z." Like a tour guide, the preacher stops at the signpost and gathers the congregation, debriefs about the trip taken to that point, then previews the remainder of the journey. Transitions serve as signposts.

Additionally, transition statements serve as corridors. Tom Long pictures sermons as houses. Each major segment of a sermon compares to a room in the house. One room offers explanation of the text. Another room contains a story. A third room challenges listeners to consider the implications of the text on their lives. Additional rooms represent additional sections of the sermon. A series of corridors connects the rooms.

These corridors are transition statements by which the preacher leads listeners from one room to the next. If the preacher does not build corridors into the sermon, listeners will not make the journey from room to room.[1]

Carefully designed transition statements—which function like bridges, sign posts, and corridors—result in clear, understandable sermons. If a lack of clarity is a weakness in your preaching, therefore, give more attention to crafting transitions between the major sections of your sermons. Well thought-out transition statements ensure that each segment flows naturally and logically into the next, and they give listeners the opportunity to catch their breath, reflect on where the sermon has come, and look ahead to where the sermon will go. A sermon that flows smoothly does so on the crest of its transition statements.

KINDS OF TRANSITIONS

In *Christ-Centered Preaching*, Bryan Chapell outlines five types of transition statements:[2]
- *Knitting Statements.* Knitting transition statements reach back to the previous section and point toward the coming section, knitting the two together. They often use the formula of "Not only … but also …": "Not only does love necessitate compassion, but also, love necessitates sacrifice." Or, they might use the formula of "If … then …" to lead from one point to the next: "If the Spirit empowers us, then we must rely on His strength."
- *Dialogical Questions.* These transitions voice questions raised by the previous section that the coming section will answer. For example, "God answers prayer. How do we explain those times, however, when our prayers seem to go unanswered?" This type of transition may be the most effective option because it enables the preacher to voice the congregation's unspoken questions, which makes the sermon conversational and meaningful for listeners.
- *Numbering and Listing.* Some sermons divide easily

---

1. Tom Long, *The Witness of Preaching*, 2nd Ed. (Louisville: Westminster John Knox, 2005), 187–188.
2. Bryan Chapell, *Christ-Centered Preaching: Redeeming the Expository Sermon*, 2nd Ed. (Grand Rapids, MI: Baker, 2005), 262–265.

into numbered points, such as "three characteristics of Christ's love," or "four reasons God calls us to forgive others." In such cases, these numbers should appear in the transitions. Numbered transitions work best, however, when paired with other types of transitions. For example, a preacher might pair numbering with dialogical questions: "Yes, God answers prayer. This is the first lesson in our text. How do we explain those times, however, when our prayers seem to go unanswered? Thankfully the text provides a second lesson that addresses this very question."

- *Picture Painting.* If the entire sermon hangs on an image or metaphor, the transitions can grow from that image. For example, in a sermon designed around the image of God building the church: "God built the church by designing its blueprint. Furthermore, He continued building the church by laying its foundation."
- *Billboards.* A billboard transition statement typically occurs during an introduction. It previews all the points or movements that the sermon will include. For example, "In our text today we will discover three elements of faith—belief, trust, and obedience." This transition should not be used in inductive sermons, or others that build suspense or contain surprise twists. Aside from these exceptions, however, billboards provide listeners a clear preview of the sermon's main points.

THE EXERCISE

1. Informally, ask a few people who hear you preach regularly, "Would you say that clarity is a strength or weakness of my preaching?" Their answers will give a strong indication of how well you transition between the segments of your sermons.
2. Review your last three to five sermon outlines or manuscripts. Highlight or underline the places where you intentionally transitioned from one major idea to the next. For each transition, consider other ways you might have transitioned more effectively. Also, note places where you should have included a careful transition, but did not.
3. After you map out your upcoming sermon, decide how you

will transition between each major segment. Review Bryan Chapell's five possibilities; however, do not feel confined to these if other options come to mind. In most cases, a sermon will flow most clearly if it uses only one kind of transition statement between major sections—between every point, for example, you transition with dialogical questions (the Billboard is the exception to this principle— if you use this transition at the beginning, you will need an additional type throughout the sermon).

4. Write transitions for your sermon that bridge each major segment to the next.

"I TRIED IT"

"I really appreciated this exercise. I find that I often get in a rut when it comes to transitions. I use the same types of transitions almost every time, and they aren't always the best ones. This chapter has opened my eyes to other types of transitions. It has also made my sermons more logical and easy to follow."

Joseph Schmidt, Kewanee, Illinois

"When I reviewed my recent sermons, I discovered that I had given great care to opening 'hooks' and to conclusions that drove home my points. In the bodies of the sermons, however, I noticed my tendency to move quite rapidly from point to point without signaling to the audience that a change had occurred. My transitions were abrupt, unclear, and clumsy. I found that my sermons felt more like Sunday School lessons, and didn't flow well. This exercise helped me think more carefully about how I transition between points, resulting in better flowing sermons."

Bob Emmert, Jefferson City, Tennessee

RESOURCES FOR FURTHER STUDY

- Though no book is devoted entirely to transition statements, two books cited in this chapter contain chapters with helpful discussions about transitions: *The Witness of Preaching*, by Thomas Long (chapter 7); and *Christ-Centered Preaching*, by Bryan Chapell (chapter 9).

- "It'sAllAboutFlow,"byBillMiller.Accessathttp://highpow-erresources.com/2011/09/the-importance-of-transitions/.
- "Transition Words." Access at http://larae.net/write/tran-sition.html.
- "Moving Together," by John Osborn. Access at http://www.ministrymagazine.org/archive/1981/March/moving-together.

Encourage Texting During Your Sermon

"Everyone please take out your phones and be sure they're turned ... *on*." The announcement earns scattered chuckles and raised eyebrows from an increasing number of congregations, as church leaders wrestle with how they might present Christ in the midst of, and to, contemporary culture—a culture permeated by social media channels such as Facebook, Twitter, and texting. These channels of communication, in and of themselves, are neither right nor wrong. They sit as tools on people's computers and smart phones ready for use. Whether they advance the Kingdom of God or the kingdom of darkness depends on who engages them and for what purpose. We must consider, therefore, how we can use such tools to advance the Kingdom of God. And, more specifically, how can we use them to advance our preaching?

This week's exercise will lead us to use a particular tool that most of our listeners already carry with them into our worship centers every Sunday—their phones. We will invite them to interact with our sermons via text messaging. Inviting such interaction deserves consideration for at least four reasons:

- The invitation, because of its novelty, will grab people's attention—particularly those who rely heavily on electronic communication throughout the week
- It will encourage participation from those too shy to interact in church otherwise. Someone who never approaches you after the service with a question may feel more comfortable sending that question as a text message.
- The exercise will promote a sense of community among the congregation, as it allows listeners to participate in, and give input to, the preaching event.

- The opportunity to interact with the sermon will facilitate more active listening—people will pay better attention when they know they can make comments or ask questions.

ONE CHURCH'S EXPERIENCE

Greg Lee ministers with the Suncrest Christian Church in St. John, Indiana. Greg recently posted on Facebook, "Sunday we'll talk about relationships. During the services we'll answer questions that you text to us. If you want to get a head start, you can begin text messaging your questions now to xxx-xxxx."

After I saw his post, I asked him how he uses text messaging in his preaching.

How often do you invite your listeners to text their questions to you?
We have used texting probably six to ten times in the last couple years. We tend to group them—to invite texting multiple times within a particular message series. So, this is the third or fourth series in which we've used texting.

Do you see the questions ahead of time?
No. We have the text messages sent to our sound/projection booth. Someone there receives them, then puts them on the screen at the end of the service. I see them for the first time when the congregation sees them. This adds some positive drama—people know that this puts me on the spot! Also, it adds some grace to the conversation—people know they aren't going to get a well-researched answer to a difficult question. This doesn't stop them from asking difficult questions, though. People have asked some very raw and challenging things.

Do you answer every question that is asked?
We try to answer as many as we can. We do have someone screen them. Usually, though, the screener just weeds out questions that are too similar to one another.

Your church meets on multiple campuses—how has this dynamic affecting the texting?
We get better response at the large campus than our smaller

campuses. We are confident it has to do with anonymity at a larger campus.

Logistically, how do you pull this off during a service?
We've learned some tricks to setting it up well. Sometimes we publicize it in the days ahead, and even let people send texts early. On Sunday, we announce it at the beginning of the service, and keep the phone number where they send their texts on the screen the whole time. People find it ironic and humorous that we actually tell them, "Get your cell phones out and make sure they're turned on for the service today."

Who receives the text messages?
When we started, we just used a staff member's cell phone in the booth. People would send text messages to his phone, and he would type the questions into the computer to project onto the screen. Now we use Google Voice, so the messages come straight into the computer, and we don't have to publicize the staff member's cell phone number.

How have your people responded?
The whole church loves it when we do it. We would do it more often, but it always takes more time than we imagine in the services. I usually preach for thirty minutes, but if we're having people text in questions I cut that to around twenty, so that we can spend ten minutes answering questions.

THE EXERCISE

1. Consider

How could you use text messaging to facilitate interaction with your congregation? Consider these possibilities:
- You might invite listeners to text their questions or comments about the sermon topic, then answer them at the end of the service. If your worship center has a screen and projection system, you could post the questions on the screen.
- Listeners could send texts in response to a particular question that relates to your sermon. For example, "Which element of the fruit of the Spirit do you find most elusive?" "What term or phrase most leaps out at

you from the Scripture text?" or "What are the most significant words of encouragement you have ever received?" Listeners will enjoy seeing their own and others' responses to such questions.

- Listeners might text in prayer requests or comments that will add to elements of the service outside of the actual sermon. During the musical portion of worship, for example, worshippers might text in an attribute of God that has been most evident to them during the prior week, or a blessing from God for which they are particularly grateful. As these appear on the screen in front of the congregation, the sense of communal worship will swell.
- You could challenge listeners to send a text to another person (not to be seen by the entire church) as a way of applying the sermon. For example, at the end of a sermon about encouragement, you might challenge listeners to send text messages to friends who need their spirits lifted. Or, after a sermon on evangelism, you might challenge them to text their unbelieving friends, inviting them to church the following Sunday. These challenges will prove most effective if you give the congregation two or three minutes during the service to actually send the text messages.

2. Publicize

If possible, let the congregation know a few days prior that they will have the opportunity to send text messages, what you will invite them to text, and to what number they can send the texts.

3. Receive

During the worship service, have someone so designated receive text messages and screen them. If you have projection equipment available, this person might then project the text messages on the screen. If you do not have such technology, this person can compile the messages on a document, then give the document to you when appropriate. If you are uncomfortable with the logistics and technical aspects involved, ask someone in your church who has such knowledge for help (hint—start with your teenagers and college students!). You might consider using Google Voice or Wiffiti (http://wiffiti.com)–an application that turns your screen into a bulletin board on which people can post comments or questions via text messages.

4. Respond

Depending on how you choose to use text messaging, respond in some manner during the service. If listeners texted questions, for example, allow around ten minutes near the end of the service for the questions to appear on the screen, and for you to respond.

"I TRIED IT"

"I asked church members who are in small groups to text in testimonies about the value of small groups. Their responses were posted on the main screens during my sermon. This was the first time it had been done in our adult worship gathering. We received a good response. The format we used was not very convenient, but the overall result was effective. I love the audience participation aspect of it."

Adam Colter, Newburgh, Indiana

"Our congregation got a big kick out of the idea of texting me during the sermon. Most of their texted questions were asking for more information about how the sermon related to them directly. We do not have the resources to put the texts up on the screen, but it was still good to hear what people were thinking and to have the chance to respond to them directly. I think the exercise will help me be a better communicator in the future."

Mark Overton, Louisville, Tennessee

RESOURCES FOR FURTHER STUDY

- *The Hidden Power of Electronic Culture: How Media Shapes Faith, the Gospel, and Church*, by Shane Hipps (Zondervan, 2006).
- "Do We Need Twitter in Worship?" by Taylor Burton-Edwards. Access at http://www.umc.org/site/apps/

nlnet/content3.aspx?c=lwL4KnN1LtH&b=242986
7&ct=6968881.

- "The Tech Effect: Technology is changing the way we preach. Is this a good thing?" Interview with Shane Hipps, John Palmieri, and Jarrett Stevens. Access at http://www. christianitytoday.com/le/2007/summer/1.28.html.
- "Thumb Wars: Can text messaging and Twitter enhance worship or just interrupt it?" by Tyler Charles. Access at http://www.christianitytoday.com/le/preachingworship/ worship/thumbwars.html.

Assign Biographies to Children

One of the more worn clichés in Christian circles claims, "I'd rather see a sermon than hear one any day." Preachers might find this thought threatening—if nobody wants to hear a sermon, then we'll end up in the unemployment line. Yet, as with many clichés, the statement holds some truth. In response, therefore, we should do more than just update our resumes. We should include more in our sermons for people to see.

Listeners need to understand biblical truth, and to see that truth in the flesh—to observe how it shows up in the real lives of real people. This is one reason that Paul, as he drew his letters to a close, often included names and a few words about people, partners, and comrades. A careful consideration of these names reveals that Paul typically, in a sly manner, gave his readers final pictures of people who embodied what he taught in the letter.

Biblical truths come to life when we wrap them around stories of people. Listeners lean forward in their seats when we describe men and women of faith. Abstract truth grows tangible when we put flesh on it.

But what people, you might ask, should we talk about? Where do we find stories of men and women who put flesh on biblical principles? Though numerous answers apply, this week's exercise will lead us to tap one resource we often neglect—and to tap it in a way that facilitates interaction, interest, and even education. We will invite children to read biographies of great Christians from history, then incorporate these bios into upcoming sermons. In addition to strengthening our sermons, this approach will allow a few children to give input into our preaching, expose the congregation to some key figures from church history, encourage children to read, and give these children and their families a sense of ownership of the particular sermons with which they help.

LESSONS FROM BIOGRAPHIES

Christian history brims with stories of believers who personify biblical truth. And, thankfully, biographers have told many of these stories. The chart below offers some examples of biographies we might invite children in our churches to read, and truths these stories can illustrate in our sermons.

A Biography Of ...	Can Illustrate ...
Dietrich Bonhoeffer	Discipleship, Community, Sacrifice
Corrie ten Boom	Compassion, Forgiveness, Daring
David Brainerd	Courage, Evangelism, Legacy
William Carey	Missionary Work, Passion, Great Commission
Amy Carmichael	Compassion, Evangelism, Perseverance
George Washington Carver	Science, Creation, Education
Elisabeth Elliot	Surrender, Courage, Forgiveness
Jim Elliot	Mission, Sacrifice, Self-Denial
Francis of Assisi	Compassion, Justice, Poverty
Billy Graham	Biblical Authority, Evangelism, Integrity
Martin Luther King, Jr.	Reconciliation, Commitment, Sacrifice
Eric Liddell	Priorities, Convictions, Mission
David Livingstone	Courage, Perseverance, Evangelism
Martin Luther	Faith, Passion, Bible Accessibility
George Muller	Faith, Orphan Care, Education
John Newton	Grace, Life Change, Redemption
Florence Nightingale	Compassion, Servanthood, Calling
Joni Eareckson Tada	Overcoming, Disabilities, Determination
Hudson Taylor	Mission, Vision, Faith
Mother Teresa	Compassion, Humility, Charity
William Tyndale	The Bible, Bravery, Commitment
George Washington	Leadership, Courage, Perseverance
George Whitefield	Revival, Evangelism, Preaching

THE EXERCISE

1. Look ahead to what you plan to preach in the next four to eight weeks. Consider what broad topics you will discuss, such as faith, grace, courage, holiness, or sacrifice.

2. Find biographies written for children about two or three figures from Christian history who exemplify the principles you will discuss. The chart on the previous page provides a few examples, but do not feel limited to these. You might find such biographies in a local library, or you can purchase them—most are between five and ten dollars (see "Resources for Further Study" on page 200 for websites where you can purchase children's biographies). If you have homeschool families in your church, check with them—Christian homeschoolers often read such biographies as a part of their curriculum, and may have books available to borrow.

3. Invite children—one for each biography—to read the biographies. Children between the third and seventh grades will probably be most willing and interested. Let each child know your plans—that you hope to discuss the person from their book in a particular upcoming sermon, and that you need their help to learn about that person. Make certain to tell each child when they will need to complete the book.

4. Meet with each child at least a week prior to the sermon in which you will discuss their historical figure. Encourage the child to tell you what he or she learned from the biography. Be ready to ask questions to keep the conversation flowing. Listen especially for specific stories from the biographies that might be useful in a sermon.

5. Find a way to incorporate what each child learned into the appropriate sermon. Consider these ways to use their stories:
   - You might just tell in the sermon what the child told you: "Johnny Madison recently read a biography of Francis of Assisi, and Johnny told me that Francis..."
   - If the child is willing, he or she could prepare a two or three minute presentation, and come on stage to present it during your sermon.
   - You might interview the child on stage, which may prove more comfortable to the child than giving a presentation. It will help to give the child the questions ahead of time.
   - You might video the child discussing his or her historical figure. This approach may make the process less nerve-wracking for the child, and will allow for a few "takes" and editing, if necessary.

"I TRIED IT"

"For a sermon about integrity, I invited two children to read a biography about Billy Graham. One of the two completed the reading (I bribed them with ice cream!). He wrote a short piece about the book, and I quoted it in the sermon. When I mentioned that this young man had helped me with this part of the message, the people perked up and really began to listen. People love to see kids involved!"

Nathan Crowe, Galax, Virginia

"I attempted this exercise twice. The first time didn't go very well—the exercise takes a fair amount of organizing and planning, and I hadn't done this sufficiently. The second time, I asked our children's minister to read a children's book during their programming—a book that related to a sermon I would be preaching soon. She also talked to the children about the book afterward to get their comments and questions about it. This worked well—it provided me with some helpful comments and illustrations for the sermon."

Jason Warden, Knoxville, Tennessee

RESOURCES FOR FURTHER STUDY

- "Illustrating Sermons With Biography," by Bill Whittaker. Access at http://www.preaching.com/resources/articles/11578565.
- "Church History for Children," by Simonetta Carr. Access at http://simonetta-carr.blogspot.com/2010/11/church-history-for-children.html.
- You can purchase Christian biographies written for children at these websites:
  - » http://www.graceandtruthbooks.com/category/biographies-for-youth
  - » http://www.christianfocus.com/series/show/7/-/d_series
  - » http://www.ywampublishing.com/c-39-hero-biographies.aspx
  - » http://www.childrensbibleclub.com/menandwomen-faith/menwomenfaith.htm

Craft Evocative Words

"The difference between the right word and almost the right word," said Mark Twain, "is the difference between lightning and the lightning bug." Some words electrify listeners and thunderously split the sky. Others flutter through the night quietly, unnoticed, offering only an occasional flicker. Some phrases evoke passion, anger, shock, conviction, contemplation, or memories. Others simply take up space.

While attending seminary, I read a book of sermons by the renowned Scottish preacher James S. Stewart. His word crafting left me in awe. For example, in his famous sermon "Vanguard and Rearguard," Stewart described God's constant presence with His children:

> The Lord our vanguard! Has not that been your experience on the road? Can't you look back today and put your finger on place after place and say, "Here, and here, and here I was 'to grace how great a debtor'—here and here God has prepared the way for me"?
>
> Take the longest view. Look back on the whole course of your life. Has not God always been beforehand with you? And if you love Him today, is it not because—as St. John puts it with great simplicity—He has always loved you first?
>
> Think of the surprises that His grace has so often brought to you. At birthdays and Christmas seasons you prepare surprises for the children and those you love. You smuggle things into the house. You keep them locked away. You guard your secret well. And then when the happy morning comes, you bring out the thing you have prepared, a glad, loving surprise. Is not that what the great Father of heaven does times without

number for His children? And is not half the magic of life just this, that it is so full of the thrill of discovery—and all because a God of love is going on before?[1]

Few preachers give such attention to their word choices. We rattle off in a cluttered mess of twenty words what we could have said sharply in seven. Rather than engaging our listeners with stimulating, unique ideas, we send their minds wandering with our vague platitudes.

Every word we speak either blurs or clarifies, bores or evokes. This week's exercise will lead us to choose more evocative words for our upcoming sermons.

CRAFTING EVOCATIVE LANGUAGE

Omit Unneeded Words

Our sermons lose their evocative potential when we clutter them with unnecessary words. Even the most poignant, stimulating nouns and verbs become diluted with unneeded adjectives, adverbs, redundancies, and qualifiers. For example, a speaker might begin, "I am really very excited to speak to this rather large crowd. Though, like you probably are, I'm also a little tired after last night's really long sermon!" The sentence sharpens if we delete terms like very, really, and probably: "I am excited to speak to this crowd. Though, like you, I'm also tired after last night's long sermon!" Consider these additional hints:

- Phrases such as "who is" and "which were" are often unneeded. "His sister, *who is* a member of the same class …" could be shortened to, "His sister, a member of the same class…"
- Some preachers clutter their speech with unnecessary phrases like "the fact that" or "the idea of." "We will talk today about the idea of grace" would have more punch if simply, "We will talk today about grace."
- Many two-word phrases used in common vernacular are redundant, and need only one word. Examples include empty void, advance forward, alternative option, blend together, tiny speck, and joint collaboration.

---

1. James S. Stewart, *The Gates of a New Life* (Edinburg: T & T Clark, 1987), 85.

Replace Clichés With Unique, Expressive Phrases

Lazy communicators from all walks of life wrack their brains to say something original, then in the nick of time they grasp at straws with clichés, failing to move out of their comfort zones. Effective communicators—who are few and far between—go for broke to avoid clichés like the plague. They get up bright and early to prepare well, lest their messages fall on deaf ears, and so that their presentations never contain a dull moment and their listeners swallow them hook, line, and sinker. (Yes, this paragraph contains twelve clichés!)

We should avoid clichés because over familiar language fails to evoke passions, memories, or intrigue. Clichés evoke only blank faces and glazed eyes. In contrast, fresh language and expressions—which do require significant thought, effort, and practice—engage listeners. Effective communicators, therefore, use words that express how they uniquely feel, experience, and perceive.

The two websites below can help communicators avoid clichés. The first contains an extensive list of common clichés; the second contains a tool in which you can paste your text (perhaps a few paragraphs from a recent sermon?), then the tool highlights any clichés in your text.

- http://www.clichesite.com/alpha_list.asp?which=lett+1
- http://cliche.theinfo.org/

Speak With Specificity

- Use specific theological language. Preachers have a few fallback phrases—religious clichés—that ooze with significance, but with overuse grow stale in listeners' ears: "Accept Jesus as your Lord and Savior," "We're atoned by the blood of the Lamb," or perhaps "It's not a religion, it's a relationship." Such phrases roll from our lips without concrete explanation (what do these heavily-loaded religious terms imply?). And unfortunately, because of their overuse, they can send minds wandering rather than soaring. Before using such expressions in sermons, therefore, careful preachers force themselves to craft crisp, meaningful phrases that communicate the same vital principles but in fresh ways.

- Use specific nouns. The more specific our nouns, the sharper the images we build. Often our nouns give listeners only broad categories—dogs, for example—instead of a particular image—a thirteen-year-old cocker spaniel who trots with a limp. The first shares information, the second evokes a picture. Consider these additional examples:

Broad	Specific
Recently	Last Tuesday
Award	Trophy
Tree	Weeping willow
A drink	Cranberry juice

Choosing specific nouns often eliminates the need for adjectives. Instead of a purple flower, for example, the single noun "violet" portrays a more concise and evocative image. We can better describe an expensive sports car as a Porsche.

- Use specific verbs. As with nouns, specificity strengthens verbs. Rather than "went," did you drive, hurry, fly, mosey, or rush? Rather than "see," do you investigate, skim, observe, glimpse, or scrutinize? Choosing specific verbs often eliminates the need for adverbs. Instead of "walked hurriedly," for example, you can say "rushed." Or, instead of "think carefully," say "consider."

Replace Explanation With Experience

Fred Craddock bids preachers:

Go through your sermons sometime on a rainy day—when nobody is expecting you to do any calling or anything—and look at the words. How many words in there just don't have any pulse? No nerve twitches. You say them, and it's nothing. "Stewardship." The seventeenth time you say that in a sermon it's kind of dull. Sort of like it was the first time you said it. Do you have another word?

You can say "all people are mortal," and put it to a vote, and it will pass. But nothing happens. But if you say, "Jimmy Hubbard was killed this morning on his bicycle while he was delivering papers ..." Concrete, specific—this creates experiences."[2]

---

2. Fred Craddock at the 2003 North American Christian Convention, Indianapolis, IN, in workshop "Taking P301 Again for the First Time, Part 2."

Sermons that speak in vague principles leave listeners yawning. Sermons that speak to listeners' experiences, however—the heartaches, joys, and nitty-gritty of life—evoke passions, memories, and commitment.

THE EXERCISE

1. Visit http://www.enhancemyvocabulary.com/triple-words. html and spend around five to ten minutes skimming lists of evocative words that can give your preaching more flavor.
2. Read a sermon by a preacher known for word crafting, such as James S. Stewart, Frederick Buechner, or Charles Spurgeon. An online search will reveal numerous such sermons available. As you read, note the use of evocative language. What words evoke emotions, memories, and images?
3. As you prepare an outline or manuscript for your upcoming sermon, keep the principles learned in this chapter in mind as you choose your words.
4. After you complete preparations for your upcoming sermon, read back over your outline or manuscript, and find at least ten instances where you can:
   • Omit unneeded words;
   • Replace a cliché with a unique, expressive phrase;
   • Speak with more specific theological language, nouns, and verbs; and
   • Replace explanation with experience.

"I TRIED IT"

"Ouch! This lesson exposed my bad habits developed through years writing sermons too quickly, which resulted in less than evocative language. The suggestions in the lesson are very helpful. Although the time and effort needed to produce explicit terminology is challenging, I also find it stimulating. I once simply asked myself, 'What do I want to say to the people?' Now I find myself asking, 'How can I communicate my thoughts more powerfully and vividly portray the message of God's Word to His people?' Thanks, I needed that!"

Jeff Brunsman, Mount Gilead, Ohio

"My dad was not just a preacher. He was a master story teller. His greatest strength lay in telling a story filled with language that evoked the imagination and invoked emotion. Both laughter and tears were commonplace when he spoke. Even before my own call to ministry, I understood the power of the right word. This exercise benefits all who wish their own preaching to penetrate the souls of their listeners as my dad did."

Josh Lees, Winchester, Virginia

"Words are the tools of our craft. Just as a sharp knife enables a wood carver to transform a block of walnut into a masterpiece, precise and evocative words enable preachers to capture attention and transform hearts. Dr. Overdorf's exercise exposed my habit of entering the pulpit with dull and lifeless terms and expressions. I plan now to spend an additional fifteen minutes each week sharpening my words upon completion of my sermon manuscript, in hopes that fresh, razor-specific words will pierce the souls of my church members and inspire deeper commitment to Jesus, the master soul carver."

Greg Robbins, Heath, Ohio

RESOURCES FOR FURTHER STUDY

- *The Elements of Style: Fiftieth Anniversary Edition*, by William Strunk and E. B. White (Longman, 2008).
- *The Gates of New Life*, by James S. Stewart (T & T Clark, 1999).
- "The Preacher as Poet," by Peter K. Stevenson. Access at http://www.ministrytoday.org.uk/magazine/issues/41/286.
- "Preaching from Comp 101," by Eric Van Meter. Access at http://www.ministrymatters.com/all/article/entry/58/preaching-from-comp-101.

Consider the Text's Literary Form

If this chapter began with the phrase, "Once upon a time, in a land far, far away ...," what would you expect to read? Or, what would you expect if it began, "Dearly beloved, we have gathered together today in the sight of God and in the presence of these witnesses ...;" or, "Knock, knock ...?" In each case, the opening words give clues to what you will hear—a fairy tale, a wedding ceremony, or a joke. And, they suggest what to listen for—we listen to a fairy tale expecting a fictional story with a moral loosely weaved in, to a wedding ceremony expecting an exchange of vows and a final pronouncement of husband and wife, and to a joke waiting for a punchline. The way we listen and what we listen for varies depending on the literary form of a presentation.

The Bible uses a variety of literary forms—poem, parable, prophecy, proverb, and many others.[1] Each form speaks with a different voice. And, for every passage, the Spirit-inspired author chose a particular literary form because of the voice with which it speaks. When Jesus told a parable, for example, He chose that approach because it carried His message in the manner He wanted to present it—in a way that a poem or proverb could not. To understand a biblical text, therefore, an interpreter must give careful attention to the literary form of that passage. With what voice does it speak? With what framework should we listen? What should we expect to hear?

---

1. Scholars generally use the term "genre" to refer to larger categories and "literary forms" to refer to classifications within these categories. For example, "narrative" is a genre; "miracle story" is a literary form within that genre. For the sake of simplicity, this chapter will use the phrase "literary form" to refer to both.

Likewise, to preach a text biblically, a preacher must give careful attention to a passage's literary form—both to interpret the text correctly, and to design the sermon in a manner that respects the text's form. Biblical preaching recreates the intended impact of a text. That impact depends both on content and the way biblical writer presented that content. Biblical preachers allow texts to speak in their own voices—they allow parables to speak as parables and prophecy to speak as prophecy.

This principle does not imply that a sermon's form must mimic the form of the preaching passage. When preaching from one of Paul's prayers, for example, the preacher does not have to "pray" the whole sermon. Instead, the preacher should discern the *rhetorical function* of a text's literary form, and replicate that function in the sermon. For example, a parable uses familiar images to stimulate thinking and to challenge assumptions. A psalm uses carefully crafted words, phrases, metaphors, and other images to stir emotions and imaginations. A narrative presents a series of scenes that unfold to picture a biblical truth. Biblical preachers design sermons from such passages that seek to function in the same ways. Ultimately, we ask ourselves: How can we design a sermon that creates the same impact that the text creates with its literary form?

PREACHING FROM TEXTS OF VARIOUS FORMS

The charts found on the next few pages list some of the more prominent biblical literary forms, and insights and suggestions for sermons that grow from such texts.

Literary Form	Insights and Suggestions for Preaching
Epistle	Pay special attention to the occasion and purposes of the letter, and of your particular text. How do these parallel your contemporary circumstances? Seek analogies between the original situation and the circumstances churches face today. Epistles are pastoral in nature. Leaders respond to churches' needs through the written word. Whether teaching, confronting, or encouraging, the author does so in the context of a pastoral relationship. Sermons on the epistles need to reflect the same feeling and intent.

Literary Form	Insights and Suggestions for Preaching
Epistle	Often writers of epistles responded to circumstances, or even direct questions, from the recipient churches. Reading an epistle compares to overhearing one side of a phone conversation. Because of this dynamic, a sermon might be structured as responses to particular circumstances or questions. The thanksgiving/prayer sections found in many epistles serve at least three functions. They: demonstrate the writer's heart for the recipients, encourage and inspire the recipients, and preview the major themes that the letter will address. Resulting sermons can carry the same tones and themes. Teaching portions of epistles often present logical arguments—either deductively (stating the main point first) or inductively (leading from a question/problem to the answer). Sermons on these passages can proceed in the same manner.
Gospels, narratives	Narrative portions from the Gospels can be preached similarly to other narrative texts (see section on the next page about preaching narratives). Generally, the sermon's form can unfold just as the narrative text unfolds, scene by scene. Most portions of the Gospels, including the narrative portions, point to Jesus' identity and glory. Ask yourself, therefore, what does this narrative reveal about Jesus? Then, design the sermon to reveal this particular aspect of Jesus' identity. Interpreters consider two different audiences of Gospel texts. First, they consider the immediate audience described in the text—the Pharisees, perhaps, or Jesus' disciples. Second, they consider those for whom Matthew, Mark, Luke, and John wrote. Preachers often neglect this second audience. Why did the church in these decades after Jesus' life need to hear what the Gospel writers penned? Why does the church today need to hear it?
Gospels, teaching sections	Teaching sections, such as the Sermon on the Mount or Jesus' extended discourses in John, usually follow a sequence of logic. They sometimes unfold deductively—the teacher presents the major theme in the beginning, then unpacks it. Sometimes they unfold inductively—the teacher presents a series of arguments that climax in the overall truth. The resulting sermon can reflect the same logical flow.

Literary Form	Insights and Suggestions for Preaching
Gospels, teaching sections	Extended teaching sections need to be understood as whole entities. Though you might preach one portion of the Sermon on the Mount, for example, relate that portion to the overall themes of Jesus' whole sermon. Though exceptions exist, sermons from teaching sections are usually best structured around propositions, following the text's approach of leading listeners through a sequence of truths. Teaching sections often lend themselves to verse-by-verse exposition in which the sermon simply walks through the text giving comments, illustrations, and applications along the way.
Gospels, miracles	In most cases, the stories of Jesus' miracles focus only secondarily on the miracles themselves. Primarily, they spotlight Jesus, revealing His power, compassion, and character. Likewise, the sermon should focus on the same truth about Jesus. Consider beginning the thesis statement with "Jesus is ...," "Jesus has ...," or "Jesus does ..." Gospel writers tell of Jesus' miracles to accomplish some purpose in their readers—often to inspire awe or worship. Preachers should identify that purpose and seek to accomplish the same in their listeners. Jesus' miracles usually overcome some conflict or a person's helplessness. The sermon can make connections with parallel circumstances in listeners' lives, then explain how Jesus provides the solution. Thus, the sermon will move from a feeling of conflict or helplessness to a sense of victory.
Narrative	Rather than providing a snapshot—a frozen, single frame in time—a narrative provides a running video. It moves, picturing a series of events that lead to a conclusion. To understand a narrative, observe its literary features: setting, conflict, scenes, plot progression, turning points, climax, and conclusion. Furthermore, take note of dialogue, repetitions, and those scenes in which the author slows the narrative and provides details. The sermon's structure can reflect all of these features. The narrative comes to life—both for the preacher and the listener—when it grows from a careful understanding of its historical and cultural contexts.

Literary Form	Insights and Suggestions for Preaching
Narrative	Narrative texts naturally lend themselves to the use of stories in the sermon, or sermons that consist entirely of a single narrative. Biblical narratives describe characters that mirror contemporary listeners' struggles and hopes. Preachers should connect their listeners with the biblical characters' dilemmas and emotions. A narrative text contains a beginning, middle, and end. The resulting sermon can parallel these.
Psalms, hymns, and other poetic sections	Psalms and other poems express and evoke deep emotions and memorable images. A resulting sermon, therefore, should connect with listeners' emotions and evoke images in their minds. Poems in the Bible often progress from disequilibrium to resolution (though the resolution does not always feel complete). A sermon from the poem can progress similarly. Sermons on poetic texts should equip listeners to express their prayers and worship. The use of contemporary poetry serves as a natural way to illustrate poetic texts. Poetry uses careful, imaginative, picturesque language. Though it may be difficult to emulate this for an entire sermon, the preacher can deliberately use such language at appropriate places in the sermon. Poetic texts often have dominant images or metaphors (such as a shepherd or a fortress). Sermons can revolve around these images.
Prophecy	Prophecies contain an abundance of literary techniques such as parallelism, metaphor, and hyperbole. When the text contains these, the sermon might, too. Take note of the prophet's purpose—what is he trying to accomplish in his listeners with this particular prophecy? How can you accomplish the same in your sermon? Prophecies tend to offer direct words from the Lord and they leave no doubt concerning God's character and His desires for humankind. A sermon from a prophecy should, likewise, leave little doubt concerning God's character and expectations.

Literary Form	Insights and Suggestions for Preaching
Prophecy	Prophecies must be understood within their contexts, particularly when dealing with Old Testament prophecies, which tell of God's enforcement of the old covenant. When designing sermons on such passages, the preacher must account for the transition to the new covenant, in which many specific condemnations or promises from the old covenant no longer apply directly. They do, however, reveal the character of God.
Proverbs	Proverbs are brief sayings to help people with the nuts-and-bolts of wise living. Sermons from proverbs should offer a great deal of practical teaching for listeners' daily lives. Proverbs do not promise ("this is what will happen") or command ("this is what you must do") but they describe ("this is how things typically work out"). Sermons from proverbs, therefore, should not offer illegitimate promises or commands. Proverbs send listeners' minds searching for examples. The sermon should provide an abundance of them. A preacher might approach a sermon from a proverb by playing "devil's advocate"—raising objections to the proverb and discussing them from a biblical standpoint. A sermon from a proverb might contrast biblical wise sayings with contemporary proverbs, such as: God helps those who help themselves; he who dies with the most toys wins; good things happen to good people; or, what you see is what you get.
Revelation and other apocalyptic literature	Though apocalyptic passages sometimes speak of the future, they seldom give precise roadmaps of future events. Their primary purpose is to give hope to readers who face serious difficulties, reminding them of God's ultimate power and victory over evil. Sermons from such passages, therefore, should pursue the same purposes. Apocalyptic literature uses highly symbolic language and images. Preachers should carefully research what such images symbolized in the ancient world before jumping to conclusions too quickly about their meanings. Apocalyptic passages contrast how things are (affected by the powers of evil) with how things ultimately will be (with God conquering and reigning). The preacher could design a sermon around the same contrast.

Literary Form	Insights and Suggestions for Preaching
Revelation and other apocalyptic literature	Apocalyptic literature addresses matters on a cosmic scale. It does not deal with minor inconveniences of life, but the major influence that Satan has on the world, and the infinite power of God that will overcome it. The sermon should speak to the same grand themes.

THE EXERCISE

1. Identify the literary form of your upcoming sermon's primary text.
2. Determine the rhetorical function of that literary form. What does this particular literary form—whether narrative, poem, prophecy, or another form—intend to do in listeners? List your conclusions on paper.
3. Consider why the biblical author chose this particular literary form for this passage.
4. Design your upcoming sermon so that it reflects the rhetorical function of the text's literary form. If the literary form functions to intrigue or inspire awe, for example, how can you design your sermon such that it intrigues or inspires awe? The conclusions you listed for question two, the preceding chart, and the "Resources for Further Study" listed on page 214 should provide some help.

"I TRIED IT"

"It's tempting to write each sermon in the form most natural to my own communication style, forgetting that God has already chosen a *particular* way to communicate each part of His Word. I've found that carrying over the rhetorical function of the text not only helps me be more true to Scripture, but also improves retention with my listeners. The next time someone reads the prophetic passage I preached from last week, they'll already have some of the tools needed to understand the text in its original context, regardless of whether they remember my exact application point or illustrations."

Scott Kenworthy, Indianapolis, Indiana

"Paying special attention to the literary form of the text and the suggestions in this chapter proved helpful in my own sermonic development. Not only did heightened emphasis on the text's form help shape the sermon, but it also ensured that the sermon mirrored the original text's concern and emphasis. The preacher who takes the time to implement these suggestions will find that listening carefully to the literary form will deeply influence the way a sermon is preached and heard."

Jared Wortman, Durham, North Carolina

"The biblical writers were concerned not just with what they said, but how they said it. Knowing how each genre works, therefore, remains an indispensable tool for any interpreter. Such knowledge aids in sermon design. I applied this information to a Mother's Day sermon taken from Proverbs 22:6, an often misinterpreted text. I explained that proverbs are general truths, not universal commands or promises from God. I also made my points proverbial in form—short pithy statements. The congregation was very receptive to the message and learned something about wisdom literature."

Harold Keck, Crawfordsville, Indiana

RESOURCES FOR FURTHER STUDY

- *Preaching With Variety: How to Recreate the Dynamics of Biblical Genres,* by Jeffery Arthurs (Kregel, 2007).
- *The Sermon as Symphony: Preaching the Literary Forms of the New Testament,* by Mike Graves (Judson, 1997).
- *Preaching and the Literary Forms of the Bible,* by Thomas Long (Fortress, 1988).
- "Striking all the Chords of the Text: Preparing Homiletics Students to Preach Genre-Sensitive Sermons," by Ken Langley. Access at http://www.ehomiletics.com/papers/03/Langley2003.pdf.
- "Form Fit Preaching: How the Genre of the Biblical Text Should Shape Sermon Structure," by Jeffery Arthurs. Access at http://www.christianitytoday.com/le/2008/winter/8.41.html?start=1.

Include Immediate Application

When I was twelve, my next-door neighbor and I learned to play golf. We drug an old set of clubs out of the basement, borrowed an instructional book from the library, and bought a bag of plastic practice balls. Each evening after supper we read a few pages from the instruction book then took the rusty clubs and plastic balls to the front yard. Sometimes we took the book with us. We read its pages, studied its diagrams, then grabbed clubs and slapped at balls, trying our best to apply what we learned from the book. Though neither of us ever received an endorsement deal from Titleist or an invitation to the Masters Tournament, we managed each evening to send the ball a little further and a little straighter.

If we had read the instruction book but never picked up a club, we'd never have learned the game. If we had read from the book one evening, but waited a few days before implementing what we learned, our skills would have gradually improved, but only with sluggish progress. Accelerated progress came when we read about the golf swing then immediately, with these principles and diagrams fresh in our minds, applied what we learned.

A similar principle holds true when people study music, math, painting, and numerous other fields. We learn best when we immediately implement what we learn, turning abstract concepts into concrete experiences.

How might this concept influence our preaching? How can we challenge our listeners not only to apply a sermon, but to apply it immediately? Are there ways listeners can apply what they learn before they even leave the worship center? This week's exercise will lead us to consider such possibilities.

EXAMPLES

How listeners can immediately apply what they learn varies a great deal from sermon to sermon. The examples below, however, may help spur ideas for your upcoming sermon.[1]

- *Writing:* Often, we can challenge listeners to apply the sermon immediately in writing. In a sermon about hospitality, for example, have listeners write the names of three people they will invite into their homes over the coming three months. In a sermon on encouragement, provide cards, envelopes, and stamps, then give them time to write brief notes of encouragement to others who need their spirits lifted.

- *Prayer:* The most appropriate immediate application might involve prayer. In a sermon about worship, you might have listeners list the three attributes of God that have been most obvious to them lately, then give them two minutes to pray and worship God for these particular attributes. Or, in a sermon about guilt and forgiveness, allow people a couple of minutes to confess their sins to God, then to thank Him for His grace.

- *Texting:* As Exercise 31 described, sending text messages can provide opportunities for immediate application. When the application involves interaction with other people—expressing gratitude to them, perhaps, or inviting them to something—consider offering your listeners a couple of minutes during the sermon to send text messages.

- *Two minute drills:* When the application centers primarily on knowledge and content—helping listeners understand a concept or equipping them to explain a truth—allow them two minutes at the end of the sermon to write everything they can remember about the topic, or to verbally explain the concepts to someone sitting near them. This will help cement the concepts in their minds and prepare them to explain the truths in their own words.

- *Case Studies:* Describe a scenario in which listeners could

---

1. The book and online articles listed under "Resources for Further Study" on page 218 provide numerous additional examples. Though they pertain more directly to the classroom, many of their ideas can find use in the pulpit, as well.

apply what the sermon teaches, then have them write or discuss their response to that scenario. For example, if the sermon equips listeners to overcome worry, describe a situation that might make them anxious, then allow them time to consider and discuss how they might overcome worry in that particular situation. To vary this approach, you might describe the scenario at the beginning of the sermon, then have listeners discuss their responses at the end.

THE EXERCISE

As you prepare for your upcoming sermon, consider these four questions to include immediate application. The first three of these questions also appeared in Exercise 20, "Apply Specifically." To these we now add a fourth that considers immediate application.

1. *Biblical Truth: What did God teach through this Scripture text?* Often, in a desire to preach with relevance, we give only a careless glance at the Scripture text and jump immediately to applications. Effective applications, however, help listeners imagine how a biblical truth should affect their lives. Before developing applications, therefore, define carefully and clearly what biblical truth we will apply.

2. *Sermon Purpose: What should my listeners think, feel, or do differently after encountering this biblical truth?* An effective sermon both explains Scripture and seeks to accomplish something in listeners' lives. What, in particular, should your upcoming sermon accomplish? To define this purpose, complete this sentence about your sermon: "As a result of this sermon, listeners should ..." Then, complete the sentence by defining what you hope listeners will think, feel, or do differently after the sermon.

3. *Sermon Application: If the sermon accomplished its purpose in specific listeners, how might it look?* Once you define the sermon's purpose, imagine how it might look in listeners' lives if the sermon accomplished its purpose in them. You might imagine actual people from your congregation, or certain categories of people—a family facing job loss, a wealthy teenage girl, or perhaps a retiree who all of a sudden has more time on his hands. How might it

look—what might change in their day-to-day existence—if the sermon accomplished its purpose in them?

4. *Immediate Application: What can my listeners do during the preaching event to begin applying what they have learned?* What can I have them write, pray, text, or discuss that will enable them to immediately apply what the sermon has discussed? How can my listeners demonstrate—before they even leave the worship center—that the sermon is accomplishing its purpose in them?

"I TRIED IT"

"In my sermon, I emphasized that we live for God. So, I challenged my congregation to think of areas in their lives in which they could involve God more. At the end of the service, I allowed a few moments of silent prayer for them to speak with God about those areas. While they prayed, I could see expressions on several people's faces that showed they were really thinking about the challenge and the prayer. The immediate application helped the point to hit home."

Nathan Crowe, Galax, Virginia

"I completed this exercise while preparing a sermon for the anniversary of the September 11 tragedy. I preached about the ever-present, long-lasting joy that is our resource and strength through all circumstances. I decided the best immediate application would involve prayer. So, during the sermon I directed the congregation through a time of personal prayer in which we focused on our nation's needs. Also, our elders were available after the service to pray with people in our prayer room."

Bill Worrell, Knightstown, Indiana

RESOURCES FOR FURTHER STUDY

Though the field of homiletics offers resources about application (see suggested resources in Exercise 20), it offers little about providing immediate ways to apply truth during the preaching event. Much has been written along similar lines, however, in the field of education, often under the label of "active learning." The suggested resources, therefore, come from the education field.

- *Active Learning: 101 Strategies to Teach Any Subject*, by Mel Silberman (Allyn and Bacon, 1996).
- "Active Learning for the College Classroom," by Donald Paulson and Jennifer Faust. Access at http://www.calstatela.edu/dept/chem/chem2/Active/.
- "Great Active Learning Strategies," by Jeri Asaro. Access at http://www.inspiringteachers.com/classroom_resources/tips/curriculum_and_instruction/great_active_learning_strategies.html.

Teach Preaching to High Schoolers

When speaking recently at Johnson University, Bob Russell observed, "Not everyone is called to preach. But, more are called than who respond." He then added, "I fear that there is not the gentle persuasion toward the preaching ministry that there was years ago." If Russell's observation rings true—and I fear it does—existing preachers need to take more deliberate action to pass the baton of ministry to the next generation. This week's exercise will provide one means to encourage the potential preachers in your church. These potential preachers might include high schoolers or adults in whom you sense God kindling a passion for ministry. By giving them basic instruction in homiletics, you will offer these promising ministers the opportunity to experience the exhilarating, burdensome joy of preaching.

Charles Spurgeon proclaimed, "A man who has really within him the inspiration of the Holy Spirit to preach, cannot help it, he must preach. As a fire within his bones, so will that influence be until it blazes forth." The Holy Spirit kindles this fire daily within the hearts of some—not all, but some—who sit in church pews each Sunday across the world. We who lead these churches and sense God stirring the hearts of aspiring preachers have an opportunity of eternal significance—the opportunity to fan that kindling fire into a flame that burns for the preaching of the Gospel of Jesus Christ.

THE EXERCISE

1. Develop a curriculum to teach preaching fundamentals to

those who have no prior training. About three to four hours of teaching should prove sufficient. These teaching times should not consist entirely of lecture—instead, alternate between instruction and times when you allow participants to implement what you have taught. For example, you might discuss writing a thesis statement for fifteen minutes, then allow them fifteen minutes to write thesis statements for their own sermons. See a suggested curriculum below.

2. Plan when and where you will offer the training. You might consider a single Saturday morning workshop or a series of lessons that occur once a week for a month.

3. Invite those from your church in whom you see ministry potential. Though the title of this chapter refers to high schoolers, feel free to include any others who might benefit from such teaching—perhaps adults who show ministry potential or others who would appreciate training on preparing biblical messages. Additionally, feel free to invite people from other churches in your community. Do not fret if the response isn't as large as you hope—even just one or two participants will make the effort worthwhile.

4. Prior to the training, encourage each participant to identify the passage of Scripture from which they will write their sermons during the training, and to read through the passages several times. You might even loan them commentaries to read.

5. Conduct the training at the scheduled time. Consider the instructional times more "lab" than "lecture," as you walk with participants through the process of preparing a sermon.

6. In the weeks following the training, you might provide an opportunity for each participant to preach the sermon they prepared—perhaps during a youth worship service, or at a specially planned event at which all the participants preach to one another and their family and friends.

POSSIBLE CURRICULUM FOR TEACHING PREACHING

The curriculum assumes that the teaching will occur during a Saturday morning workshop, from 9 a.m. until noon. Feel free to adjust it to best fit your circumstances.

EXAMPLE WORKSHOP SCHEDULE	
9:00 – 9:10	Welcome and Introduction
9:10 – 9:25 (9:25 – 9:40)	Study the Text and Define the Thesis (Participants Work on This Aspect of Their Sermons)
9:40 – 10:00 (10:00 – 10:20)	Choose a Sermon Form (Participants Work on This Aspect of Their Sermons)
10:20 – 10:35 (10:35 – 10:50)	Develop Applications and Illustrations (Participants Work on These Aspects of Their Sermons)
10:50 – 11:00	Break
11:00 – 11:15 (11:15 – 11:30)	Prepare the Introduction and Conclusion (Participants Work on These Aspects of Their Sermons)
11:30 – 11:45	Sermon Delivery
11:45 – Noon	Q and A

Example Teaching Outline

The content for each teaching session in the example grows from other chapters in this book. To prepare your lessons, you might begin by reviewing Exercise 4 ("Remember the Fundamentals"), then review the other exercises as they're listed in the outline.

I.   Study the Text and Define the Thesis.
   A. Study the text (see Exercise 14 of this book).
      1. Observe the literary context.
      2. Explore the historical context.
      3. Examine the language, grammar, and structure of the text.
   B. Define the thesis (see Exercise 12).
      1. What question does the text answer?
      2. What answer does the text provide?
      3. How can you best phrase the answer to form the thesis?
II. Choose a Sermon Form (see this section of Exercise 4)
   A. The sermon form is a vehicle to present the thesis.
   B. Sermons typically develop deductively (thesis early) or inductively (thesis late).
      1. Deductive sermons.
         a. Introduction: state the thesis.
         b. Body: draw points from the thesis.
         c. Conclusion: restate the thesis and review points.

    2. Inductive sermons.
        a. Introduction: describe a problem/issue to solve.
        b. Body: draw clues ("movements") from the text to help solve the problem.
        c. Conclusion: state the thesis (the solution to the problem).
  C. Example outlines (see examples provided in Exercise 4).
III. Develop Applications and Illustrations.
  A. Develop applications (see Exercise 20).
    1. What did God teach through this Scripture text?
    2. What should your listeners think, feel, or do differently after encountering this biblical truth?
    3. If the sermon accomplished this purpose in specific listeners, how might it look?
  B. Develop illustrations.
    1. Illustrations help listeners understand biblical truth and/or help them see how the truth should make a difference in their lives.
    2. Illustrations might include stories, analogies, quotes, statistics, or poems.
    3. The best illustrations grow from life experience; those from books, movies, or similar sources are also helpful.
    4. Illustrations—especially stories—are most effective when told well (see Exercises 10 and 46).
IV. Prepare the Introduction and Conclusion.
  A. Prepare the introduction (see this section in Exercise 4).
    1. Capture attention.
    2. Develop a sense of need (see Exercise 15).
    3. Indicate how the sermon will proceed.
  B. Prepare the conclusion (see this section in Exercises 4 and 47)
    1. State or restate the thesis.
    2. Tell an illustration that brings the sermon to a focus.
    3. Offer a closing challenge.
V. Sermon Delivery (see Exercise 18).
  A. Verbal aspects of delivery.
    1. Vary pitch, volume, and pace.
    2. Make effective use of pauses.
    3. Repeat important phrases and sentences.

B. Nonverbal aspects of delivery.
  1. Maintain as much eye contact as possible.
  2. Allow natural hand gestures to reinforce what you say.
  3. Allow physical movements to reinforce what you say.

Sermon Preparation Worksheet

You might give participants a worksheet like the example below. Then, as you teach the various aspects of sermon preparation, they can use the worksheet to prepare their own sermons. Leave enough room on the worksheet for students to write.

Biblical Text:
Thesis:
Sermon Form:

INTRODUCTION
  Capture Attention:
  Develop Need:
  How Sermon Will Proceed
  (if deductive, state thesis; if inductive, state problem):

BODY
  Point/Movement 1:
    Explain From Text:
    Illustrate:
    Apply:
  Point/Movement 2:
    Explain From Text:
    Illustrate:
    Apply:
  Point/Movement 3:
    Explain From Text:
    Illustrate:
  Apply:

CONCLUSION
  Thesis:
  Illustration:
  Challenge:

"I TRIED IT"

"I found the process of teaching preaching a high school student helpful in a personal way. In teaching preaching, all the basics of good preaching resurfaced in my own practices—good exegesis and hermeneutics, knowing the audience, and bathing it all in prayer. I tried hard to set the student up for success and engaged in thorough evaluation afterwards. The best indicator of the quality of the experience was him asking if we could do it again. I was thrilled to comply."

Adam Colter, Newburgh, Indiana

"I spent my teaching time with a 'twenty-something' firefighter from our congregation who is preparing to sell out and move his family to the mission field in Africa. We had a wonderful time together as we discussed preaching fundamentals. We actually worked on a sermon series together and each week I would add another piece of sermon development to the process. The young man was surprised of the amount of time and work that goes into a sermon. The exercise was fun and we both learned a lot. I plan to do this again in the near future with more students."

Harold Keck, Crawfordsville, Indiana

RESOURCES FOR FURTHER STUDY

- *Biblical Preaching: The Development and Delivery of Expository Messages*, 2nd Ed., by Haddon Robinson (Baker 2001).
- *Preparing Expository Sermons: A Seven-Step Method*, by Richard Ramesh (Baker, 2001).
- Visithttp://www.workingpreacher.org/sermondevelopment .aspx to view a series of brief articles by Mary Hinkle Shore on "The Four D's: Discovery, Development, Design, and Delivery" (see menu of articles on left side of the page).
- "Teaching First-Year Preaching," by Sidney Greidanus. Access at http://www.ehomiletics.com/papers/03/Greidanus2003.pdf.

Analyze a Movie

Karl Barth instructed his students to hold the Bible in one hand and a newspaper in the other. Newspapers, he taught, hold great sway over society's perspectives and values. Those who teach God's Word—though they submit to and are formed by the Bible—should understand and evaluate the world's perspectives so that they can best communicate with people and reshape their values according to biblical truth.

What held true of newspapers in Barth's day holds true of the entertainment industry today. Television, film, and popular music form our culture's perspectives, values, and worldviews. Believers must not blindly accept what this industry churns out; yet, we must not remain blind to the ethics it professes, the questions it raises, and the influence it holds.

Acts 17 describes Paul interacting with the people of Athens and demonstrating an awareness of their culture, commenting on their idol dedicated to an unknown God and quoting their own poets and philosophers. He observed their culture so that he could engage that culture with Gospel truth. He paid attention to the conversations taking place in the marketplace and in the circles of philosophy so that he could enter these conversations with the good news of Jesus.

Preachers today, likewise, should pay attention to our culture's conversations so that we can infuse them with the Gospel of Christ. Many of these discussions take place on screens—smart phones, laptops, and televisions. The most in-depth conversation, however, occurs on the big screen. Hollywood writers and producers enthrall audiences with two hour, one-way conversations in which they tackle significant issues and dilemmas common to the human condition, such as life and death, love, greed, ultimate meaning, and forgiveness. Unfortunately, they often approach these issues from a less-than-biblical standpoint. As preachers, therefore, we can observe what issues the film industry raises, then equip our listeners to interpret them through Christian lenses. Often, we can respond to films: "Right question. Wrong answer." Even so, we can thank the film industry for raising the questions and providing us the opportunity to shed the light and grace of Christ onto significant issues.

To be fair, sometimes Hollywood provides the right answers, giving compelling pictures of biblical truth. Some films demonstrate the power of forgiveness and reconciliation, for example, the dangers of greed, or the destruction caused by adultery. Furthermore, a growing number of Christians in the movie industry deliberately produce films that reveal godly virtues such as sacrifice, integrity, and perseverance. Just as we critique ungodly values portrayed on film, we should celebrate the godly values. Either way—whether we critique or celebrate, we must enter the conversation.

THE EXERCISE

Movies represent our culture's conversation—this exercise will enable you to enter that conversation. You will view a movie, interpret it through biblical lenses, then consider how it can inform an upcoming sermon.

One suggestion: You will find this exercise most beneficial if you complete it with a friend or two. Watch a movie together, then get a cup of coffee and discuss it.

1. *Choose what movie you will watch.* You might consider a movie near the top of the current box office charts (see http://movies.yahoo.com/mv/boxoffice), or another film that you have heard people discuss. If a movie has created a buzz in religious circles—especially if some from your congregation have specifically asked you about it—it may prove beneficial to choose that film.[1]

---

1. If you fear that watching such movies will compromise your integrity, you might just read about a movie instead. Several available resources will give you

2. *Research the movie before watching it.* Search particularly for interviews with the cast, director, or screenwriter. An online search of "interview *xyz* movie" usually returns multiple, helpful resources. Such interviews often include questions such as, "What were you trying to teach through this movie?" and "What do you hope the audience takes away from this film?" The movie makers' responses to such questions reveal insights about a movie's intended message. You might also perform an Internet search for Christian discussions of the film.

3. *View the movie and take notes.* Resist the temptation to escape into the movie, or to simply be entertained. Instead, watch to learn—consider yourself a researcher and evaluate what the particular film contributes to, or how it reflects, society's perspectives, values, and longings. You might consider these questions:

    *   What in the movie grabbed you? What intrigued you? What made you uncomfortable?
    *   What in the movie rings true with your own experiences in life and faith? What does not ring true?
    *   Who is the movie's hero? What is the hero's flaw? What is the hero's goal or desire?
    *   What choices did the hero make, and what values drove these decisions? How does the hero change during the course of the movie?
    *   Who or what is the hero's adversary? How does the hero confront the adversary?
    *   What issue or struggle common to humanity does the movie portray?
    *   What does the film reveal about the worldviews of those who made it?
    *   What spiritual elements does the movie portray, and in what light does it portray them?
    *   What does the movie celebrate? What does it condemn?

4. *Identify the film's most prominent message.* Those who make movies bring certain perspectives and assumptions to the process. And, they portray certain truths and ideas

---

a good sense of the movie's perspectives, such as http://www.pluggedin.com and http://www.crosswalk.com/culture/movies. Or, if you prefer, feel free to bypass this exercise and complete a bonus exercise from the end of the book.

through their work. After you watch the movie, therefore, reflect on it: What is the film's overall theme or message? If the movie illustrates a truth or idea, what might that truth or idea be? Sometimes, one of the film's main characters (usually the hero) will voice the movie's overall message near the end—either in a conversation or as a voiceover. Or, you might discern this message by reflecting on the main character's journey—what did he or she learn or teach others through the course of the film? Often, a film's overall message can be phrased such that one thing leads to another: Greed leads to destruction. True love liberates those in bondage. One who works hard overcomes obstacles. In *Hollywood Worldviews*, Brian Godawa offers these examples from some popular movies of the last twenty-five years:[2]

- *Shrek*: Fear of differences leads to alienation.
- *Dead Poets Society*: Conformity kills the spirit, but individuality frees it.
- *Jurassic Park*: Unfettered technology turns against humanity.
- *The Truman Show*: True freedom is found in controlling one's own destiny.
- *Amadeus*: True freedom is found in accepting one's fate or destiny from God; trying to control one's destiny leads to slavery.
- *Babe*: Biology can be transcended by personal choice.

From a biblical perspective, the message may or may not be true. At this point, however, simply identify what message the movie teaches.

5. *Compare this message to biblical truth.* Unless we carefully critique a film's message—and, unfortunately, most Christians fail in this—its lessons can worm their way into our thinking, values, and worldviews without our realizing it. (How many churches have embarked on building projects based on the wisdom of Kevin Costner? "If you build it, they will come!") Therefore, consider:

- What does the movie teach or symbolize that reflects biblical truth? What does it teach or symbolize that opposes biblical truth?

---

2. Brian Godawa, *Hollywood Worldviews: Watching Films With Wisdom and Discernment* (Downers Grove, IL: InterVarsity Press, 2002), 44–45.

- How might Scripture correct any misunderstandings demonstrated in the film? Or, how might the film illustrate something that Scripture teaches?
- If the film served as the starting point in a conversation about Christianity, how might such a conversation proceed?

6. *Consider how these insights can inform an upcoming sermon.* At least four ways exist to utilize insights about a movie in a sermon:
   - Dialogue with the movie throughout the sermon. Acknowledge early in the message that you will provide a biblical response to the issues raised in the film. Then, design the sermon as a conversation between the movie and your Scripture text. Each major segment of the sermon might raise a different issue from the film, then provide a biblical response.
   - Use the film as the sermon's introduction. Describe the overall message you believe the movie teaches or the issue it raises (including examples from the film), then spend the remainder of the sermon responding from your sermon text.
   - The film—or a particular scene from it—might illustrate a point in your sermon. With this approach the film has a less pervasive role in the sermon, serving like any other illustration to shed light on a particular point. If the film has been released to video, and if you have projection equipment available, you might show a clip from the movie.[3]
   - Particularly if the movie contains questionable content and you do not want to inadvertently endorse the film, you might discuss its worldviews and issues without mentioning it by name. You could begin, "A popular theme in contemporary movies and novels is ..." Or, "I once saw a film in which the main character said ..."

---

3. Be aware of copyright laws before showing a movie clip. You might consider services such as Church Video License International (http://www.cvli.com) or Christian Copyright Solutions (http://www.copyrightsolver.com).

"I TRIED IT"

"I watched a film with some friends about a secret agency that controlled people's fates. Afterward, we discussed how the things of the world—even our curiosity about things like fate—should point us to God (Rom. 1). Unfortunately, films like this one try to point our curiosity away from God. Our best response isn't to ignore such films, but to explain how their teachings fail to measure up the truth (1 Pet. 3:15). Christ-followers can gently show that the world's philosophies are only a shadow of the truth God freely reveals through the light of Scripture."

Benjamin Abbott, Prince Edward Island, Canada

"I do most of my preaching to high schoolers, so I took a group to a popular movie, then afterward we went out for pizza and discussed the film. We talked about the movie's messages and themes, and why they felt the movie was popular. It was an eye-opening conversation! Now, after they watch movies, they want to come and talk with me about the message they believe the movie is teaching. It has opened up great doors for spiritual conversations."

Billy Knieriem, DeLand, Florida

"I decided to watch a few movies and draw conclusions from them collectively. Based on those I watched, I noted that today's society views God as a personal entity, to be molded into what each individual wants God to be. Also, I observed the world-view that God accepts any behavior as long as an individual believes they're a good person. Finally, I noted the recurring theme that any emptiness in a person's life is filled with self-gratification. Unfortunately, such movies create false realities that leave people wanting when they reenter the real world."

Steven Johnson, Clarks Hill, Indiana

RESOURCES FOR FURTHER STUDY

- *Hollywood Worldviews: Watching Films With Wisdom and Discernment*, by Brian Godawa (InterVarsity Press, 2009).
- *Reel Spirituality: Theology and Film in Dialogue*, by Robert Johnston (Baker, 2006).

- "How to Dissect a Movie." Access at http://www.the-filmforum.net/?page_id=2.
- "And Now, A Word From Your Culture," by Terry Mattingly. Access at http://www.tmatt.net/tmatt/freelance/future.htm.
- "Discerning Worldviews in Movies: Theology, Philosophy, and Psychology in *Star Wars*," by Chuck Edwards. Access at http://www.worldviewweekend.com/worldview-times/article.php?articleid=2524.

Swap Pulpits

I recently ate lunch with a friend who spends hours in the gym lifting weights. As he lifted his fork to his mouth—a fork carrying only green, leafy vegetables—his biceps bulged from beneath the sleeves of his t-shirt. He can barely find pants that fit his massive legs without dwarfing his tiny waist. His rippling abs ... Well, you get the picture. Though I may exaggerate the reality just a bit, my friend knows his way around free weights and exercise routines.

As he explained over lunch, however—his salad, and my greasy pizza dripping with mozzarella and pepperoni—"routine" is an enemy of bodybuilding. Because the human body adapts so quickly, weight lifters alter their exercises and schedules frequently. Otherwise, their bodies would become accustomed to the routine and their muscles would cease growing. Experienced bodybuilders, therefore, might complete a particular set of exercises, in a particular order, for two or three weeks. Then, they alter the exercises and the order. My friend explained that he will even work out at different gyms on occasion just to mix up his routine.

Some preachers fall into routines that limit their growth. Their minds slip into autopilot each Monday as they begin piecing together their upcoming sermons. They know their listeners so well that it takes little thought to fashion just the right explanation, humor, and emotional tugs that will leave their listeners nodding, chuckling, or weeping on cue.

Like bodybuilders, preachers who want to grow can benefit from varying their routines. This week's exercise will lead us to vary a significant part of our weekly preaching—the audience to whom we preach. Preparing a sermon for a different congregation will force us to take our minds off of autopilot and carefully consider how to best communicate to a particular audience, thus exercising those communication and audience analysis muscles that may have shrunk from a lack of use.

THE EXERCISE

1. Choose a preacher with whom you can swap pulpits for a Sunday. You will probably want to approach a preacher with whom you already have a relationship, and who shares your basic theological convictions.
2. Find a date that works for both of your calendars and commit to exchange pulpits for that day.
3. Investigate the congregation where you will preach. If they have a website, browse through any information you can find about their history, vision, leadership, and ministries. If the church ministers in a community different from yours, browse through the latest census numbers to get a feel for their demographics and how these compare with your own community (www.census.gov).
4. Plan a lunch meeting with the other preacher at least a couple weeks before you will swap pulpits. Discuss each of your congregation's histories, values, dynamics, and needs. You might also discuss what each of you has preached in recent months, and any relevant logistics: When during the service will you preach? Will you need to do anything in addition to preaching during the service? Do you need to discuss your sermon with the church's staff or worship planning team ahead of time? What technology is available, and would you like to use it? End this meeting by praying for one another.
5. Prepare a sermon that unpacks an appropriate biblical text and speaks relevantly to the congregation to which you will preach. Resist the temptation to boast about your own church, to exalt yourself, or to "wow" the church with your homiletical prowess. Instead, lean toward simplicity as you exalt Christ, encourage the congregation, and equip them with biblical truth and application that will help them live for Jesus.
6. On the day of the pulpit swap, arrive early at the church where you will preach so you can mingle with people before the service begins. Then, preach your sermon with

the confidence that God's Spirit will work through you to speak the message the congregation most needs on that particular day.

7. During the week following the pulpit exchange, debrief with the other preacher. You might meet again for lunch, speak on the phone, or just swap emails.

ADDITIONAL SUGGESTIONS

- The pulpit exchange will prove most valuable if you swap with a preacher who ministers in a setting different from yours—perhaps in a community with a different ethnic makeup or economic situation. Or, you might swap pulpits with a preacher who is significantly older or younger than you.

- Some ministers who swap pulpits also bring their choirs and worship leaders with them.

- You might consider a group pulpit exchange. Perhaps five or six ministers will all put their names in a hat and randomly choose who will preach at which church on a particular Sunday.

- Preachers whose churches support a common ministry—such as a church camp or a homeless ministry—might do a group pulpit swap as a fundraiser for that ministry. Each church could take up an offering for the ministry on the Sunday of the exchange. A variation of this idea would involve a "Mystery Pulpit Exchange" where church members do not know who will preach for them until that minister arrives.

- A group of preachers might each prepare one sermon to contribute to a series, then rotate through the churches until each church has heard every preacher and every sermon. If four preachers enter such a partnership, for example, the rotation of preachers continues for four weeks, with each minister preaching the same sermon four times, but to four different congregations (that preacher's own church plus three others).

"I TRIED IT"

"Swapping pulpits is a win for everybody! It blesses the

congregations and each preacher. As an outsider, I had the opportunity to praise the good work being done by the church
I visited and to remind them that our congregations are connected as the body of Christ. The personal benefit was that it
allowed me to use one of my stronger messages that had already been tested and preached. This saved a great deal of time
and actually allowed me to rest and get a jump start on some
long-term planning."

Paul Wingfield, St. Louis, Missouri

"When doing this exercise, the other preacher and I studied
together and preached on the same text. We ended up with
different outlines, but similar subject matter. The congregations both appreciated the experience. It was helpful for me
to research the other congregation and its surrounding community—it helped me to step into the pulpit more confidently."

Steve Fair, Noblesville, Indiana

"I've participated in several pulpit swaps, and have enjoyed
them. A few suggestions I'd offer: First, make certain to lift
up Christ, not yourself. It's tempting when visiting a church to
attempt to impress the people there. Second, preach an encouraging message, not a controversial one. This is not the time to
tackle confusing issues or difficult doctrines. Third, if you're
using PowerPoint, take your own wingman—someone who
knows your pacing and habits. Exchanging pulpits with another preacher can be a blessing for all involved!"

Ken Runyon, Roanoke, Virginia

RESOURCES FOR FURTHER STUDY

- "Local Pastors Reflect on Pulpit Exchange," by Carl
  Nielsen. Access at http://santamariatimes.com/lifestyles/
  faith-and-values/religion/article_22b42d30-47ac-11e0-
  8417-001cc4c03286.html.
- "Choir, Pulpit Swaps Make a Comeback in Bir-
  mingham," by Greg Garrison. Access at http://blog.
  al.com/living-news/2009/10/post_6.html.
- "Maryville's Pulpit Swap Unites Congregations," by
  Leita Crossfield. Access at http://www.heraldnet.com/
  article/20080419/NEWS01/813903686.

Illustrate with Video

THE EXERCISE, PART 1

1. Browse the SermonSpice website (http://www.sermonspice. com) and watch two or three videos. Perhaps:
   - "Get Service" at http://www.sermonspice.com/product /14972/get-service
   - "Together (Team Hoyt)" at http://www.sermonspice. com/product/108/together-team-hoyt
   - "That's My King!" at http://www.sermonspice.com/ product/114/thats-my-king
   - "Who Was Jesus?" http://www.sermonspice.com/product /5314/who-was-jesus

2. Browse the WingClips website (http://www.wingclips. com) and watch two or three clips from movies. Maybe:
   - From *The Karate Kid* at http://www.wingclips.com/ movie-clips/the-karate-kid-1984/wax-on-wax-off
   - From *Apollo 13* at http://www.wingclips.com/movie-clips /apollo-13/getting-home
   - From *Cloudy With a Chance of Meatballs* at http://www .wingclips.com/movie-clips/cloudy-with-a-chance -of-meatballs/your-choice
   - From *Courageous* at http://www.wingclips.com/movie -clips/courageous/carjacking

3. After viewing a few videos and movie clips, reflect on these questions:
   - What truths do these videos teach?
   - What are the advantages and disadvantages of using video to help teach a truth?

- How might you use such videos as a part of your preaching?

ILLUSTRATING WITH VIDEO

Jesus ministered in a culture saturated with oral storytelling. Thus, He told stories. He painted verbal pictures of kings and judges, widows and farmers, mustard seeds, wedding parties, rebellious children, and loving fathers. His stories—relevant to His culture both in content and presentation—pointed listeners toward eternal truth.

Likewise, preachers throughout the generations have told stories, breathing life into propositional truth and giving it voice, emotion, and expression.

Story carries the same power today that it has for centuries. Today's storytellers, however, have additional options for portraying stories. Most notably, they can portray truth on film. Because preachers have long told stories in sermons, and because today's stories often appear on film, an increasing number of preachers use video illustrations in their sermons. They simply show stories, rather than telling them. This week's exercise will lead us to consider this possibility for our upcoming sermons.[1]

THE EXERCISE, PART 2

1. Identify the central theme of your upcoming sermon. Because listeners remember video illustrations more so than other illustrations, videos work best if they relate to the heart of your message rather than to a secondary subpoint.
2. Find or create a video to illustrate your central theme. Consider these possibilities:[2]
   - Locate a brief, professionally produced video intended for Christian teaching and preaching (such as what you watched on the SermonSpice website). You can purchase

---

1. If you do not have access to video projection equipment, you might turn to the end of this book and complete one of the bonus exercises instead of this exercise.
2. The websites listed under "Resources for Further Study" on page 243 will prove useful for this part of the exercise. You might also ask friends who often watch movies for help: "I want to illustrate such-and-such-point with a video. Do you recall any movie scenes that relate?"

such videos for a nominal fee, and this fee includes the rights to show the video.

- Choose a short clip taken from a motion picture or television show (like you watched on the WingClips website). Clips purchased from WingClips or similar organizations come with the rights to show the video. Before using a clip intended only for personal use, however—such as from a DVD or a downloaded movie or television show—make certain to obtain the legal rights to show the clip. You might consider services such as Church Video License International (http://www.cvli.com) or Christian Copyright Solutions (http://www.copyrightsolver.com).

- Engage a few gifted people in your church to film a video of their own that helps illustrate the sermon. This video might include someone giving a testimony, a "man on the street" series of brief interviews, or perhaps a metaphor that sheds light on your central theme—a father teaching his son to hit a baseball, a dog chewing on a bone, or a toddler trying to stand or walk.

If you do not feel confident with the technology involved, find a friend to help. Likely, someone in your church has the ability to locate, download, or otherwise arrange a video for you to use in a sermon.

3. Choose where in your sermon to place the video. As with any illustration, placement is key. If the video pictures a problem that the sermon will address, but does not resolve the problem, the clip may function best in the introduction. If it illustrates the answer to the problem, it may function best in the conclusion. If it fits best in a particular point or movement of the sermon, place it there.

4. Communicate with the person who will operate the projection equipment during the sermon. Give the person clear instructions regarding when to show the video, what cue you will give, and (if playing a clip from a longer video) precisely where to begin and end the segment. You might practice together prior to the sermon.

ADDITIONAL SUGGESTIONS

In an article published on PreachingToday.com, Kenton Anderson offered these suggestions:

1. *Keep it legal.* We must respect copyrights. Using clips taken from copyrighted motion pictures without consent of the rights holder is theft. Gaining consent usually requires paying a fee. Blanket licenses can be easily and inexpensively obtained from the Motion Picture Licensing Corporation [http://www.mplc.com]. Whatever the fee, it will not equal the cost of losing integrity.

2. *Keep it short.* Using a movie clip often requires contextual set-up for the scene, how it fits into the overall plot. If the clip requires too much explanation, it probably isn't worth using. A clip of more than two or three minutes (10 percent of the sermon duration) will probably damage the sermon itself. Shorter is always better.

3. *Keep it flowing.* Smooth transitions in and out of the video are critical. In most cases it is best to use the video clip as a lead-in to the sermon or as a post-sermon piece. Either way, videos need to fit the flow of the overall worship experience, or they could be more trouble than they are worth.

4. *Keep it clean.* Remember that showing a movie clip in church is equivalent to offering a blanket recommendation for the whole movie. The clip we show might be clean, but what about that graphic sex scene forty-five minutes later in the movie? If we can't recommend the whole movie, then we should not use it at all.[3]

"I TRIED IT"

"This exercise reminds us of the power of stories. Stories connect and stimulate in ways that nothing else can. People remember, discuss, and contemplate stories long after our three points have faded. In our media-drenched culture, this exercise reminds us that we have the opportunity to tell stories in ways that few other generations have had opportunity. I was prompted, by this exercise, to utilize a film clip which showed the flip-side to God's biblical vision. It was a great set-up for the rest of the message."

Andy Hudelson, Spring Hill, Tennessee

---

3. "In the Eye of the Hearer: Visuals That Support Rather Than Distract From the Word," by Kenton Anderson. http://www.preachingtoday.com/skills/2006/october/170--anderson.html (accessed September 29, 2011).

"I needed a quick way to introduce a new sermon series on James titled: *Living Large in Shanty Town.* Shanty Town, a place of hopelessness and broken dreams was to be a dramatic metaphor for this fallen world in which we all live. James tells us how we can 'live large' in Shanty Town as children of the King. I chose a video illustration from Bluefish TV titled, 'The Mission of the Church Matters.' In three minutes and 45 seconds I dramatically introduced the people to the whole thesis for the series. Bluefishtv.com is an excellent source."

Rodger Thompson, Wichita, Kansas

RESOURCES FOR FURTHER STUDY

Resources About Using Video Illustrations

- *Digital Storytellers: The Art of Communicating the Gospel,* by Len Wilson and Jason Moore (Abingdon Press, 2002).
- *Silver Screen, Sacred Story: Using Multimedia in Worship,* by Michael Bausch (The Alban Institute, 2002).
- "The Art of Video Sermon Illustrations," by Don Pucik. Access at http://www.preaching.com/resources/articles/11547716.
- "Why Use Video in Preaching?" by George Temple. Access at http://www.preaching.com/resources/articles/11547709/.

Resources With Suggested and/or Downloadable Video Illustrations

- A series of books published by Zondervan between 1999 and 2005: *Videos That Teach.*
- A series of books published by Group Publishing between 2001 and 2006: *Blockbuster Movie Illustrations.*
- **SermonSpice:** http://www.sermonspice.com
- **WingClips:** http://www.wingclips.com
- **Bluefish TV:** http://www.bluefishtv.com/Store/Browse/Video_Illustrations
- **Highway Media:** http://www.highwaymedia.org/Sermon-Illustrations-C16.aspx
- **ImageVine:** http://www.imagevine.com/movies/christian-movies.aspx
- **MovieMinistry:** http://www.movieministry.com

Conduct E-Interviews

When I began writing Exercise 14 of this book ("Exegete Before Sermonizing"), I wanted to illustrate the importance of doing the right things in the right order. I got stuck. The river of ideas that sometimes flows—or, that I hear flows for some people!—had run dry. I turned to Facebook. "Help me with an illustration," I pecked out on my keyboard. "In what circumstances would it be important to do the right things, *and* to do them in the right order?" My friends didn't fail me. My favorite response was, "First tranquilize the badger, then put a sweater on it."

I have sought similar input through phone calls and conversations over lunch. The more I communicate with others about what I plan to preach, teach, or write, the sharper my content and the better it connects with my audience. Seeking such input, however, can consume more time than we have to spare. The use of technology such as Facebook, Twitter, email, or online blogs—though admittedly less personal than face-to-face conversations—can give preachers quick, easy means to seek input while we prepare our sermons. We might ask our friends to help with an illustration, what aspects of a text or a principle they find most challenging, or how a biblical truth might apply in their particular circumstances.

Consider these benefits of using technology to invite listeners to participate in our sermon preparation:

- The process can bring big results for little effort. An email or Facebook posting might take ninety seconds to type and post, but it reaps involvement with and information from a substantial number of friends.

- By inviting our listeners' input, we help transform the preaching event into a community-building experience. People appreciate the invitation to participate. And, if you use their stories or quotes during your sermon, they will sit up straighter and smile when they hear their words spoken from the pulpit.
- Our friends' thoughts and questions can help us discern what aspects of a sermon need more or less attention.
- We can build momentum toward a sermon by initiating conversation about it before we even preach it.
- When we have gotten stuck while searching for an elusive illustration or application, our friends' collective wisdom can bump our minds and imaginations back into motion.

THE EXERCISE

After you study your sermon text and complete some preparation for your sermon, proceed through these three steps.[1]

1. Consider what input from others will prove most helpful for your sermon preparation. You might invite your friends to:
    - Respond to questions about the text. If you plan to preach about the parable of the good Samaritan, for example, you might ask, "What do you think was going through the priest's and Levite's minds as they passed by? What do you think was going through the Samaritan's mind? How might you have felt if you had been in the crowd listening to Jesus tell this story?"
    - Ask their own questions about the text. Tell your friends what biblical text(s) you plan to use, and explain the basic direction you think the sermon will go, then allow your listeners to raise any questions they have about them.
    - Share stories. A few years ago, I sent a note to our church email list that said, "I'm preaching this Sunday about

---

1. If you do not have access to the technology described in this chapter, you might invite a friend who does have such access and expertise to help you. Your friend can post your question for you on his or her Facebook page. For example: "Preacher Bob wanted me to ask you this question ..." Or, feel free to skip this exercise and complete one of the bonus exercises at the end of this book instead.

God answering prayer. Has there been a time in your own life and experience when you knew God answered a specific prayer? If so, send me the story." Within hours, my inbox brimmed with stories from church members.

- Share struggles, challenges, or potential applications. You might ask, "If you attempted to live out this particular Christian truth, what changes might that require? What would be most difficult about these changes? In your particular circumstances at school, work, your neighborhood, or in your family, how might it look if you took this truth seriously?"

2. Choose what technology will best serve your circumstances. If you have a church email list, you might send your questions through it. If you have a Facebook or Twitter account, and you are connected with a substantial number from your church, you might post your question there.

3. When you receive responses, allow your listeners' questions, comments, and stories to influence your study and preparation for the sermon. A responder might raise an issue that you had not considered, or share a story that will help illustrate a truth you plan to preach. A friend's question might indicate that you need to offer more explanation of a particular principle than you had planned. (Ask permission before quoting someone or telling their story.)

ADDITIONAL SUGGESTIONS

- The previous exercise invites your listeners' participation. On some occasions, you might find it helpful to seek assistance from fellow preachers instead. They might provide needed insights about a text or illustrations to support your sermon.
- When you ask questions, ask with humility, from the standpoint that you do not yet know the answers. Your listeners might feel intimidated to discuss biblical or theological issues with you. Make clear that you are genuinely interested in their opinions and insights.
- In addition to seeking input as you prepare a sermon, you can also use technology to gather feedback after a sermon. If the sermon issued a particular challenge, for example—perhaps to fast for a day or to read a certain

number of chapters from the Bible—you could invite people to describe their progress on Facebook posts.

- From a pastoral standpoint, Facebook, Twitter, and similar social media outlets can help you keep in touch with church members. Their posts can give you pastoral knowledge of their joys, hurts, and questions. And, you can make comments on their posts to express care and to celebrate with them when appropriate. This electronic communication should never replace face-to-face pastoral care, of course, but it can supplement it.

"I TRIED IT"

"I found conducting e-interviews a rather humbling experience. As a preacher it's hard to admit that other people might have better ideas, sermon thoughts, or points than you do. It's humbling to allow them into the sermon preparation, tipping them off ahead of time about the topic of the sermon. It's humbling but then again, God gives grace to the humble so I guess being humbled isn't such a bad experience after all."

Burt Brock, Morgantown, Indiana

"Inviting friends into the sermon preparation was enjoyable. In anticipation of a sermon on missions, I sent electronic notes to our missions team, asking them for personal insights. I wanted to know why they were personally motivated toward missions. I asked what 'thought nuggets' had crystallized in their minds about missions. And, I asked what misconceptions they think others have. I could not use all their comments, but it gave them an investment in a sermon about something very important to them. My sermon was strengthened by their convictions."

Brian Lakin, Markle, Indiana

RESOURCES FOR FURTHER STUDY

- *The Church of Facebook: How the Wireless Generation Is Redefining Community*, by Jesse Rice (David C. Cook, 2009).
- *Thy Kingdom Connected: What the Church Can Learn From Facebook, the Internet, and Other Networks*, by Dwight Friesen (Baker, 2009).

- "Facebook Sermon Prep," by Bill White. Access at http://www.christianitytoday.com/le/2010/fall/facebook sermonprep.html.
- "Facebook in Sermon Preparation," blog entry and discussion. Access at http://biblicalpreaching.net/2010/02/05/facebook-in-sermon-preparation.

Go to Work with a Church Member

A friend and recently retired colleague of mine, David Enyart, tackled an interesting project as a part of his doctoral studies. He spent twenty days visiting the workplaces of various members of the church where he preached. He shadowed someone who worked in a school cafeteria, rode shotgun with a truck driver, and spent days in various factories. He witnessed first-hand what his congregants faced on a daily basis—tyrannical bosses, stress, boredom, even physical danger. One church member, in particular, encountered harassment on the job site because of his faith—his coworkers left explicit pictures in his locker and toolbox, and made a game of embarrassing him with their filthy jokes. "With my newly gained insights," David wrote after the experience, "I more fully understood the complexities of living and working as a faithful believer in the secular workplace. I was able to crawl into their *frame of reference*—to see the world a little more through their eyes. When we stand for a while in another person's shoes, we realize more fully how they pinch!"[1]

Sometimes we think of our listeners only as we see them on Sundays—attending church services, convening committee meetings, and bustling through religious activities. Our sermons, therefore, connect with their church lives: "Today our challenge is to serve more faithfully. Perhaps you can volunteer for the nursery, lead a cooking team for our Wednesday night meals, or serve as a greeter on Sunday mornings." Such needs

---

1. David Enyart, *The Homiletical Review Notebook* (Knoxville, TN: Tennessee Valley Publishing, 2003), 83.

may exist, but our listeners spend most of their lives outside the walls of the church building. How might the challenge to "serve more faithfully" play out when they leave the safe haven of church and encounter the knotty business of life in their homes, neighborhoods, and job sites?

For this week's exercise, we will visit at least one church member in his or her work environment, where believers face the tensions, dilemmas, questions, struggles, and celebrations that mark the daily walk of a disciple.

THE EXERCISE

1. Choose whom you will visit. Consider someone who works in an industry common to your community, and who would enjoy your visit. Ask if you can visit their workplace, and when would be most convenient. Make certain not to intrude. And, do not stay too long—perhaps just an hour or two during which your friend can show you around and describe his or her typical day. You might visit in the late morning, then take your friend to lunch afterward. Rather than just visiting one person, you might set aside an afternoon or an entire day to visit a few church members, perhaps including a stay-at-home mother, a retired person, or others who may not go to nine-to-five "jobs" every day but who work, struggle, and face life's dilemmas nonetheless.

2. Prepare ahead of time. Learn all you can about the church member's occupation and their particular workplace. A simple Internet search will often reveal helpful information. Also, compile a list of questions to ask. You might consider questions such as these:
    - What does a typical day look like for you?
    - What are the most and least enjoyable aspects of your job?
    - What are the most and least fulfilling aspects of your job?
    - How well do people get along with one another at your workplace?
    - How is the relationship between the workers and the supervisors or bosses?
    - What workplace politics have you experienced?

- When you wake up in the morning, are you excited to go to work or do you dread it? Why?
- When have you most felt like quitting?
- Would you like to continue in this career, and/or at this particular company, for a long time? Why or why not?
- What hopes do you have for your future career? What fears do you have?
- What about your job is most challenging to your faith?
- When have you felt most tempted to compromise your Christian convictions at work?
- Has there been a particular sermon or study in the past that helped you live as a Christian on the job?
- What particular questions or dilemmas do you face at work for which you would appreciate biblical guidance?
- How could I, as a preacher, better equip you to live faithfully on the job?

3. As soon as you return from your visit, write and mail a thank-you note—handwritten on a card—to the person you visited.
4. Based on what you learned, consider how your upcoming sermon can best equip your church members to live for Christ on the job. Include at least two illustrations or applications that deliberately focus on Monday – Friday rather than on Sunday. Ask yourself, "What can I say to my listeners this Sunday that will survive the Monday morning alarm?" Additionally, consider planning an entire sermon series that equips your church members to live out their faith on the job. The series might present a theology of work, tackle issues such as honesty and relational struggles that are common in workplaces, and help your listeners pursue their jobs as a way to extend the Kingdom of God.

"I TRIED IT"

"I job shadowed a man in our congregation who is a vice president of a Fortune 500 company. I found the experience highly useful and insightful. He excels at challenging those who work under him—constantly helping them to improve and grow in excellence. I witnessed multiple conference calls in which he helped managers keep their efforts in line with their corporate mission. His example encouraged me to be a better leader and a more challenging preacher—should we not be even more driven toward our values and mission?"

Scott Sutherland, Columbia, Missouri

"I spent time on the job with one of my best friends in the church. Needless to say, I was already somewhat familiar with his job and work environment. However, getting to watch him at work added on layers of detail and plain old reality that I would not have been aware of otherwise. It also convinced me to go to work with our church members more and more."

Jonathan Absher, Follansbee, West Virginia

"One of our church members is on staff at a large local university. He was very gracious in letting me come and spend the morning with him. Not only did I get to know him better in his own environment, but seeing how he interacted with the students and other staff members was very encouraging! I came to learn more about his job, and ended up learning more about his passions, his heart, and his life."

Billy Knieriem, DeLand, Florida

RESOURCES FOR FURTHER STUDY

- *Work and Leisure in Christian Perspective*, by Leland Ryken (Wipf & Stock, 2002).
- *The Other Six Days: Vocation, Work, and Ministry in Biblical Perspective*, by R. Paul Stevens (Eerdmans, 2000).
- "Preaching and the World of Work," by William Hinson. Access at http://www.preaching.com/resources/articles/11563548.
- "Preaching About Work," by John Roxborogh. Access at http://www.roxborogh.com/elders/preachingabout-work.htm.

Employ Purposeful Humor

I have long admired Bob Russell's preaching. During his ministry at Southeast Christian Church in Louisville, Kentucky, the congregation grew from 120 to 18,000 attenders each weekend. Russell humbly explains that God grew the church, yet most any observer recognizes that God performed a great deal of this work through Russell's biblical, relevant preaching.

As a college student, I listened to several of Russell's sermons, and noticed a certain rhythm in his use of humor. Soon thereafter, I visited the church in Louisville, and decided to track his humor on the back of my bulletin. Like clockwork, laughter rippled through the worship center every five minutes. As a seasoned preacher, he sensed the rhythms of effective communication.

Russell seldom tells jokes. Instead, he tells stories from life and experience that illustrate the truths he preaches. He simply includes comments, details, and verbal pictures that tickle listeners' funny bones and amplify biblical truth.

God did not call many of us to serve as standup comics. He called us to preach His Word. Those who preach His Word most effectively, however, use humor as one tool to facilitate meaningful communication.

HUMOR IN THE PULPIT

What Is Humor?

Pulpit humor includes those elements of a sermon that listeners find comical, to which they respond with an amused roll of the eyes, a polite chuckle, or all-out laughter. But what, precisely, elicits such responses? Preacher and comedian Ken Davis explains, "Basically it comes down to three things. Exaggerating, taking something that's real and blowing it out of proportion. Truth, taking a look at something you might not otherwise have even paused to look at, something you didn't even see, and when you see it you realize it's funny. And then surprise. Surprise is the joke, the punch-line kind of funny."[1]

Furthermore, Davis explains the difference in "high risk" and "low risk" humor. High risk humor involves telling a joke that depends on a punch line. If the punch line fails—if the joke falls flat—the resulting awkward silence saps the sermon of its momentum and, frankly, the preacher has wasted precious pulpit time on a joke that didn't work. Preachers should use high risk humor with care.

Low risk humor, on the other hand, involves stories or observations that demonstrate those truths and incongruities of life that catch people off-guard. Unlike a joke with a punch line, the power of such stories does not depend solely on the congregation's laughter—even if people don't laugh, the story still makes a point.

Why Use Humor in Preaching?

If humor involves risk—whether high or low—why take the risk? Of numerous reasons, four rise to prominence.

- *Humor can advance truth.* Faithful preachers do not use humor simply to make people laugh, to feel good about themselves, to fill time, or to feed their egos. Rather, they use humor when it helps advance biblical truth. If an amusing story will help people better understand God's truth, the story deserves a place in the sermon.
- *Humor can build rapport.* Effective communicators use humor to build relational bridges to their listeners. Laughter opens a window of intimacy, even if only briefly. Once the window opens, we can step through it with God's great truth in all of its gravity and significance.
- *Humor can lower defenses.* Particularly when we deal with difficult or heavy subjects, humor can help disarm

---

1. "Humor That Connects," interview with Ken Davis. http://www.preaching-today.com/skills/humor2004/200403.2.html (accessed November 1, 2011).

potentially defensive listeners. When people laugh, they settle more comfortably into the conversation, and grow more open to new insights and information.

- *Humor can demonstrate joy.* Unfortunately, some view Christianity as an entirely somber existence. The use of humor in preaching demonstrates that our faith includes great joy. Perhaps more so than any other gathering, a gathering of Christians should exhibit the joy—even the laughter—of lives redeemed by Christ, filled with the Spirit, and blessed with the hope of our eternal inheritance.

THE EXERCISE

1. *Consider what makes you laugh.* Watch a few clips from Christian comedian Ken Davis' channel on YouTube.com (http://www.youtube.com/user/KenDavisComedy). As you watch, consider: What makes him funny? How does he describe characters, develop stories, and make observations? How does he use surprise, truth, and exaggeration? How does he use his voice and body? Also, over the next couple days, notice what makes you laugh, perhaps in conversation, while watching television, or when reading. Why did you laugh? Was it irony? Incongruity? A truth viewed from a new perspective? How does this humor differ from what you observed in Ken Davis?

2. *Consider what you say that makes others laugh.* Using humor well requires that we recognize our own personalities and styles. When do people laugh at what you say? Is your sense of humor a "deadpan" approach, sarcasm, exaggeration, storytelling, joke telling, or observational? What you do well in conversation, you can do well in preaching. What you do not do well in conversation, however, you will not do well in preaching.

3. *Determine what truth your sermon will advance.* Humor should advance the truth we preach. Therefore, before inserting amusing stories or comical comments into our outlines, we must identify clearly what biblical teaching our sermon will proclaim. The truth comes first.

4. *Determine what humor might help advance that truth.* What have you witnessed or experienced in life that both

furthers the sermon's truth and will amuse your listeners? What comments have you heard from others, what have you read or observed on television or at a movie, what bit of irony or incongruity has grown obvious to you, what reality might you exaggerate (with a wink to your listeners, of course), or what comical detail might you add to a story or a paragraph that will elicit a smile from your listeners and help ingrain biblical truth into their hearts? If all else fails, websites, books, or magazine articles with sermon illustrations often include some intended to make people laugh.

5. *Determine where the humor will best fit in your sermon.* Location matters. Even a funny story, if told at the wrong moment, may cause discomfort or offense. Therefore, take care to place that amusing antidote or funny story where it fits the natural flow of the sermon. Humor often works well near the beginning of a message, to help establish rapport between the preacher and the congregation. It also can illustrate points, or lead well into emotional or challenging parts of the sermon. Following a humorous story about parenting, for example, the preacher might say, "Though we laugh, we also recognize that the struggles that many parents face are no laughing matter. Perhaps you are dealing with ..." In contrast, humor attempted immediately *after* emotional or challenging segments may appear to trivialize them.

6. *Be careful.* We should avoid humor about a person's ethnicity, politics, or weight. And, sexual innuendos should remain off limits. If an attempt at humor feels borderline—you wonder if it might offend—delete it from your outline before you enter the pulpit. Furthermore, take great care when using humor about another person. Good-natured teasing between friends might be safe, if you feel confident the other person will enjoy the joke as much as everyone else. If any chance exists, however, that the joke will make its object feel uncomfortable, don't use it.

7. *Practice.* Using humor well requires timing and a careful choice of words. Therefore, practice the story, observation, or joke. After you practice it a few times—revising it each time as you learn what works best—bring it into the preaching event with confidence.

"I TRIED IT"

"My bread and butter tends toward research and application. Often, I would tell a humorous story to open, then once I had that out of the way, I became serious. Thanks to this chapter, I deliberately added more humor throughout. Humor does break down barriers to the heart. Because of this, people responded better to this sermon than to any I have preached previously."

Josh Lees, Winchester, Virginia

"I found this exercise to be challenging, because my humor is usually in the form of a joke. With this exercise I had to be more creative in using a story or statement that added humor to the message. I have found that some of the best laughter has been in reply to some almost off handed comment that I made instead of a joke. I also was reminded how different people respond to humor. With multiple services, what one group (younger) finds humorous, another group (older) may not. Even humor needs to be relevant to the audience."

Drew Mentzer, Danville, Illinois

RESOURCES FOR FURTHER STUDY

- *Laugh Your Way to Grace: Reclaiming the Spiritual Power of Humor,* by Susan Sparks (Skylight Paths Pub., 2010).
- *The Art of Using Humor in Preaching: Toward a Methodology Which Equips Pastors to Use Humor Intentionally in Preaching,* by Bradley Rushing (Lambert Academic Pub., 2010).
- "Dr. Fred Craddock on Using Humor and Emotion in Sermons." View video at http://www.youtube.com/watch?v=bT1DA-e2nos.
- "Using Humor in the Pulpit," by V. Neil Wyrick. Access online at http://www.preaching.com/resources/articles/11547245.
- "Using Humor in Preaching: An Interview with Bob Russell," by James R. Barnette. Access online at http://www.preaching.com/resources/articles/11563744.

Preach in Dialogue

Often the most compelling elements of a story come in its dialogue. One person speaks, another responds, and a conversation—a journey toward discovery—ensues. Through the dialogue, the audience gains insight into characters' thoughts, struggles, and idiosyncrasies. Non-dialogue portions of a story consist of narration—a person talking about what happens, simply sharing information. When dialogue begins, the story transforms from narration into a personal experience for the audience, who now encounters the characters firsthand, rather than through the narrator's perspective. As novelist Anne Lamott explained, "Good dialogue is such a pleasure to come across while reading, a complete change of pace from description and exposition and all that *writing*. Suddenly people are talking, and we find ourselves clipping along."[1]

Scripture uses dialogue extensively. Old Testament narratives contain conversation between characters, and the prophets often presented their teaching as dialogue between God and His people. The Gospels include conversations that Jesus shared with various groups—His disciples, the crowds, Pharisees and teachers, and others. In Acts, Luke often used the Greek term *dialegomai* (discuss, reason, argue) to describe Paul's ministry. In the Thessalonian synagogue "he reasoned with them from the Scriptures" (Acts 17:2), in Corinth he "reasoned in the synagogue, trying to persuade Jews and Greeks" (Acts 18:4), and he spent three months in Ephesus "arguing

---

1. Anne Lamott, *Bird by Bird: Some Instructions on Writing and Life* (New York: Anchor Books, 1994), 64.

persuasively about the kingdom of God" (Acts 19:8). Though Acts sometimes describes Paul as a herald proclaiming the message, it also portrays occasions when this proclamation took the form of dialogue.

How can these realities influence our preaching? How might a sermon, which by nature seems to require a one-way sharing of information, include dialogue?

INCLUDING DIALOGUE IN A SERMON

At least four ways exist to include dialogue in preaching.

- *Interview.* At an appropriate time in the sermon, a preacher might interview someone who has particular insight into the subject being discussed. The interview might include, for example, a cancer survivor for a message that deals with hardships, a couple who has celebrated their fiftieth anniversary for a marriage sermon, or a Bible scholar for a sermon that addresses a difficult doctrine. The preacher should provide a list of questions to the interviewee well ahead of time so that he or she can consider how to respond. As a variation of this idea, the preacher might serve as the interviewee. Some sermons naturally unfold around questions and answers ("Our text this morning answers five questions about prayer ..."). For such a sermon, the preacher might have someone else ask the questions, then answer them with the sermon's content.
- *Onstage Conversation.* A preacher might share the stage with another person—another minister, church leader, or a church member with teaching gifts—and divide the sermon into segments that each person delivers. The sermon proceeds like a conversation between the two people. Each segment could be brief—as in an actual conversation. Or, the segments might be larger, such that one person preaches one of the sermon's major points, the other person preaches the second major point, and so on. With this approach, both participants should give input into the sermon's preparation. Visit this website to view an example of such a sermon by Rubel Shelly and John York: http://www.rubelshelly.com/content.asp?CID=18718.

- *Onstage Panel.* A preacher can invite a small group of people—probably four to six—to serve as a panel that will discuss the sermon with the preacher on stage. The first part of the sermon might proceed like normal, offering teaching, illustration, and application about a biblical text. Then, the preacher could begin discussing the biblical text and topic with the panel, who sits on stage with him. The preacher might ask them questions, invite their insight, or encourage them to comment on the subject matter. And, the panel could ask the preacher questions to clarify, further explain, or to explore the implications of the message. The panel will function best if they have access to the teaching materials ahead of time, so that they can think through their responses and questions.
- *Question and Answer.* A preacher might invite the congregation to respond to a question, such as "With which biblical character do you most identify?" or, "Who has most influenced your faith, and in what ways did this person influence you?" Or, the preacher might invite listeners to ask questions about the sermon's content or application. In either case, listeners could offer their input verbally, on paper, or electronically (see Exercise 31 about using texting as a preaching tool). The preacher, then, can respond verbally during the sermon.

THE EXERCISE

1. Identify what upcoming sermon will best lend itself to dialogue, and how you can include this dialogue in the sermon. You might use one of the four methods described in this chapter or another method that comes to mind.
2. Choose the person(s) who are best equipped to participate in the message, and with whom you can work well.
3. Arrange a meeting with the person you will dialogue with in the sermon. Discuss how the sermon will proceed, what role the dialogue will play in the message, and how in particular each person needs to prepare. The person's competency, experience, and comfort level—and what type of dialogue you plan to include—will dictate how much you invite the other person to prepare and how much you provide them.

4. Continue to keep in touch with those involved.
5. Practice the dialogue sermon together at least once.
6. On the day of the sermon, meet briefly with the person(s) involved prior to the service to place final touches on the sermon and to pray together.

"I TRIED IT"

"I used this exercise over the course of a few sermons. For one sermon, I had a panel of people on stage with me to discuss the text. For another, a friend came on stage to do a sketch with me. And, for a few sermons, I have directly asked the audience for feedback. Each of these worked well, and I found that preaching in dialogue helped break the routine and brought a fresh focus on the text for my listeners and for me."

Caleb Gilmore, Bluff City, Tennessee

"This exercise was a positive experience, even though it wasn't easy for me. The preparation was different from any I had done. And, involving another person in the message delivery was a little strange. That said, it was worth it. I chose to use an interview method for my dialogue. I had the other person pose as a newspaper journalist who interviewed me as a witness to a biblical event. This process stretched me (in a good way), and the people really enjoyed it. I will definitely use it again."

Randy Overdorf, Elizabethton, Tennessee

RESOURCES FOR FURTHER STUDY

- *Interactive Preaching*, by D. Stephenson Bond (Chalice Press, 1991).
- *Dialogue Preaching: The Shared Sermon*, by William Thompson and Gordon Bennett (Judson Press, 1969).
- "Spreading the Word: How Team Teaching Helped Our Church and Saved My Ministry," by Dan Cooley. Access at http://www.christianitytoday.com/le/2011/summer/spreadingword.html.
- "Preaching as Dialogue: Moving Beyond 'Speaching' of the Word," by Kenton C. Anderson. Access at http://www.ehomiletics.com/papers/06/Anderson2006.pdf.

Pray Through Your Sermon

The late J. Vernon McGee told of a trip he took to South Africa. While traveling through a small town, he found a group of boys on the side of the road, crowded around a small circle drawn in the dust, playing a game of marbles. As McGee drew closer, he discovered that they did not use glass marbles like he had used as a boy. Instead, they played the game with diamonds. Completely unaware of their game pieces' value, the boys treated the precious stones like gravel.[1]

Too many preachers play marbles with diamonds. They fail to recognize the value of the sermons they prepare—the Word that God revealed through His Spirit, then empowered the preacher to interpret and proclaim. The sermons that lay on our desks—because they grow from the infinite power of God—hold potential to change lives and to change eternities. They deserve care, concern, concentration, and prayer.

Previous exercises in this book have addressed the role of prayer during the sermon's preparation. This week's exercise assumes, therefore, that you have sought the Spirit's guidance and insight from the moment you first considered the message, throughout your exegetical work, and during the formation of the sermon. With your manuscript or outline prepared and on paper, this exercise will lead you to lay it before God in an act of submission, humility, and prayer.

---

1. In J. Kent Edwards, *Deep Preaching: Creating Sermons That Go Beyond the Superficial* (Nashville: B & H Academic), 2.

PRAYING THROUGH YOUR SERMON

At least four ways exist to pray through your sermon. Often, multiple ways will naturally weave together as you pray.

1. Skim the sermon and pray for personal enlightenment and application. Ask God to transform the sermon into a mirror. Invite the Spirit to illumine your heart and mind as you skim through its paragraphs and points, to convict your heart with its applications, and to inspire awe in your spirit with its truths about the Father and Jesus Christ.

2. Pray the words of the sermon. Fred Craddock instructed his students to take their sermons into the chapel: "Start out, 'Gracious God ...,' then pray the sermon. My students say, 'But it's a sermon, not a prayer.' Well, pray it. It's amazing how that will bleed all the poison, and the desire to get back at people, and small-minded things. You're suddenly made to realize that the primary audience of this sermon is God."[2]

3. Pray for each segment of the sermon. Each section of a sermon intends to accomplish a particular purpose—to help listeners grasp a concept, to recognize how that concept should affect their lives, to encourage and equip them to obey, or perhaps to give them a sense of joy or hope. Therefore, read through each paragraph or point of the message and ask God to accomplish what He needs to accomplish through that segment. The example on page 267 demonstrates how I prayed through the first main point of a sermon on Acts 1:1–11.

4. Give God the editing pen. As you read through each sentence of the sermon, ask God if He would prefer you to say something differently, to edit a sentence or section entirely out of the sermon, or to add something you had not previously planned to say. We might assume His guidance as we form and polish our sermons, but do we ask for it? We cannot presume that God will guide and bless what we have not asked Him to guide and bless. "You do not have, because you do not ask God" (James 4:2).

---

2. Fred Craddock, "Taking P301 Again For the First Time," workshop presented at the North American Christian Convention in Indianapolis, Indiana, July 2003.

POINT: THE SPIRIT EMPOWERS OUR WITNESS.	PRAYER
EXPLANATION: When Jesus commissioned His disciples to proclaim His message, He also promised that the Spirit would empower them for this task. The Spirit appears prominently throughout Acts, empowering the vibrant ministry of the early church.	Lord, please use this portion of the sermon to ease our fears about witnessing about our faith. Allow the promises of the text to reassure us that we will not have to pursue ministries and spiritual conversations by our own strength and intellect, but that you will provide power and direction through the Spirit.
ILLUSTRATION: A. W. Tozer: "If the Holy Spirit was withdrawn from the church today, ninety-five percent of what we do would go on and no one would know the difference. If the Holy Spirit had been withdrawn from the New Testament church, ninety-five percent of what they did would stop, and everybody would know the difference."	I ask, Father, that this quote will force us to contemplate the differences in energy, vibrancy, and effectiveness of the early church as compared to our church. Convict us of our tendency to rely on our own strength, planning, and feeble human abilities to "do church."
APPLICATION: When the church recognizes that the Spirit empowers our witness, we will pursue ministries that stretch beyond our own logic and ability. Before, during, and after such ministries we will pray constantly—seeking the Spirit's empowerment and listening for His direction.	I pray that these applications will spur dreams and ideas within each of us of what our church might look like if we relied on the Spirit's empowerment. Please instill ideas in each listener, Lord, of how they individually and we corporately might witness for Christ as the Spirit empowers us.

THE EXERCISE

After you have prepared the content for your upcoming sermon—either an outline or a manuscript—continue your preparation by praying through your sermon.

1. Begin by meditating on a Scripture that teaches about the power of the Word and of preaching, such as Psalm 119 or 2 Timothy 3:10 – 4:8. Read the passage slowly—possibly even aloud—and contemplate its depth of meaning.
2. Choose one of the methods found in this chapter to pray through your sermon.

3. Make any adjustments in the sermon that you feel God led you to make during your prayer.
4. Enter the pulpit confident that you are proclaiming the words and the message that God wants you to proclaim.

"I TRIED IT"

"I prayed through each segment of my sermon. It gave me a sense of confidence that the words of the sermon truly expressed what the text was teaching. There was also a sense of God's peace that came over me as I stood to preach, because I had put in the time not only to write the sermon but also to surrender the sermon back over to God, with the desire to bring glory to Him and not to myself."

Mark Behr, Grand Rapids, Michigan

"I have discovered that prayer is the most important element in preparing myself to stand between God and His people. When I prayed through my sermon, in this conversation with God I sought His approval, His power, and His advice. As I did this for a few sermons, I sometimes received confirmation and confidence, sometimes I was led to make changes. There have even been times that I've scrapped the whole thing and started over. Either way my goal is to ensure that what I've prepared are truly the words of God."

Paul Viers, Abingdon, Virginia

RESOURCES FOR FURTHER STUDY

- *Deep Preaching: Creating Sermons That Go Beyond the Superficial*, by J. Kent Edwards (B & H Academic, 2009).
- *Spirit-Led Preaching: The Holy Spirit's Role in Sermon Preparation and Delivery*, by Greg Heisler (B & H Publishing, 2007).
- "Praying Through Your Sermon," by Kevin Meador. Access at http://www.prayerclosetministries.org/assets/PDF/Fire%20In%20The%20Pulpit.pdf.
- "Pray the Text," by Tom Rogers. Access at http://www.workingpreacher.org/sermondevelopment.aspx?article_id=429.

Make a Bee-Line to the Cross

One of my colleagues at Johnson University, Dr. Tommy Smith, tells about working at an A&P grocery store as a high schooler. Tommy grew up in a small town in East Tennessee. He knew the customers who came into the grocery store, and they knew him. During his last year at the A&P, he decided to attend Bible college to prepare for ministry. Some customers offered encouragement, others gave words of warning.

Tommy tells of one conversation that he wrote down in his Bible afterward. An elderly gentlemen who shopped at the A&P every Saturday learned of Tommy's plans. When Tommy carried his groceries to the car, the man shook his hand, slid a fifty-cent tip into his palm, and held his hand for a moment. "Son, preach Jesus," he said gently. "Because when you quit preaching Jesus, you quit preaching."

By this criteria, I'm afraid, too many of us have quit preaching. We have allowed Jesus and his cross to fade into the background, nudged from center stage by soap boxes, self-help advice, and speculation.

Charles Spurgeon offered profound insight when he described his own preaching, "I take my text and make a bee-line to the cross." Spurgeon, like the elderly man at the A&P, understood that the entire Bible, ultimately, tells the story of God redeeming His lost children through the death, burial, and resurrection of Jesus Christ. Jesus Himself viewed Scripture through this lens. After His resurrection, Jesus walked with two disciples on the road to Emmaus, "And beginning with Moses and all the Prophets, he explained to them what was said in all the Scriptures concerning himself" (Luke 24:27). Every verse in

Scripture contributes to the story of Jesus. A passage remains only partially understood, therefore, and partially preached, until it is connected with Christ.

RECOGNIZING CHRIST IN ALL OF SCRIPTURE

Every passage of Scripture either (1) prepares humankind for Christ, (2) proclaims Christ, or (3) equips humankind to live in response to Christ.

	Types of Passages	Preaching Considerations
Prepares for Christ	Most Old Testament texts, including laws, ceremonies, codes, narratives, poetry, and non-messianic prophecy.	What does this text reveal about God and/or humankind that finds its ultimate expression in the cross? Or, what needed lesson or experience did this text offer humankind to prepare them for Jesus' coming? Perhaps the passage reveals the holiness or judgment of God, the consequence of sin, or God's provision for His people. Maybe the text displays humankind's inability to live up to God's perfect standard and our need, therefore, of a Savior and grace.
Proclaims Christ	Messianic prophecy in the Old Testament, and Gospels or portions of other New Testament books that teach specifically about Christ.	How does this particular passage about Christ relate to the overall story of God's redemption of the world through Him? What element of Jesus' character and mission—which culminate in the cross—does this passage reveal? Why did God want us to understand the truth that this text presents about Jesus?
Equips for Response to Christ	Imperatives, vice/virtue lists, passages that address obedience and behavior issues.	The grace of God, offered through the cross of Jesus, is the root of Christian obedience. All calls for obedience, then, should begin with a reminder of the grace from which our obedience grows. Scripture often structures itself in this manner—imperatives (calls for behavior and obedience) generally follow indicatives (truths about God's redemption through Christ). Before preaching an imperative, therefore, look for the indicative that precedes it. For example, a call to "Put to death... whatever belongs to your earthly nature" (Col. 3:5; imperative) should grow out of "you have been raised with Christ ... your life is now hidden with Christ in God" (Col. 3:1, 3; indicative).

PREACHING CHRIST FROM ALL OF SCRIPTURE

If every text contributes to Jesus' story, every sermon can preach Christ. How, though, can we interpret each text with integrity in its own context, and connect it with the story of Jesus? Two suggestions should help.

1. *Interpret the text in its immediate context.* Every text occurs in a particular historical and biblical setting. Preaching Christ begins by carefully interpreting our sermon passages in their own contexts.
    *   If the sermon text overtly proclaims Christ, we can easily preach His story by simply preaching the text. Though this sounds obvious, it deserves mention because we sometimes take passages about Christ and make them about ourselves. If a text displays Christ's compassion, for example, allow the sermon to admire Jesus' compassion—ultimately displayed on the cross—before the sermon leaps to application about us showing compassion to others.
    *   If the sermon text does not overtly proclaim Christ (from the chart in this chapter, it "prepares" or "equips"), we still must interpret the text responsibly in its original context. What did Moses teach the Israelites? How did God intend this psalm to influence His people when David wrote it? What did the original author intend, and how would the original listeners have understood this text? Preaching Christ does not require us to twist passages and do hermeneutical gymnastics to allegorically squeeze Christ into our sermons. For example, when preaching about David and Goliath, we need not say, "And these five stones David gathered bring to mind the stones that lined the Via Dolorosa as Jesus carried His cross. And the blood that flowed from Goliath's forehead represents the blood that flowed down Jesus' face when the crown of thorns ..." Nothing in 1 Samuel 17 indicates such absurd symbolism. We must allow the narrative to teach what it actually teaches (see the example on page 272 for more discussion of this particular text).
2. *Connect the text with the larger story of Jesus.* A person could pull one scene from a novel or a movie and explain

that scene, describing the characters and action, and perhaps even drawing some truth or moral from it. That person will never fully understand the scene, however, until he or she recognizes how it connects with the entire story. In some way, that particular scene furthers the overall plot of the novel or movie. A similar principle holds true in Bible interpretation. Every narrative, teaching, law, prophecy, and poem in Scripture reveals a particular scene in the overall story of God's redemption through Christ. Therefore, after understanding a sermon text in its own context, we can identify what role our text plays in that overall story, and make that connection in our sermon.

AN EXAMPLE

The story of David and Goliath in 1 Samuel 17 is larger than David's courage or his deft use of a slingshot. David himself gave full credit to God: "I come against you in the name of the Lord Almighty, the God of the armies of Israel ... the whole world will know that there is a God in Israel" (1 Sam. 17:45–46). Just a chapter prior, God led Samuel to anoint David as the next king, and "the Spirit of the Lord came upon David in power" (1 Sam. 16:13). David stood before the Philistine giant confident in God's sovereignty, empowerment, and plan.

A thousand years before David, God promised Abraham, "All peoples of the earth will be blessed through you" (Gen. 12:3). A thousand years after David, God delivered a Messiah—notably through David's linage—who brought this blessing to all nations (2 Sam. 7:16; Gal. 3:6–9). Can a nine-foot-tall warrior stand in God's way? A vigorous Philistine army? God has a story to unfold—the story of redemption through Jesus Christ—and no giant, nation, nor any other obstacle will stand in the way.

We can interpret the David and Goliath narrative in its own context (first paragraph), then connect it with the story of Jesus (second paragraph).

THE EXERCISE

1. Review your last three to five sermons and evaluate how well you preached Christ. For those in which you fell short, consider how you could have connected your text and topic

to the larger story of God's redemption through Jesus.

2. For your upcoming sermon, consider where your primary sermon text fits in the chart on page 270, "Recognizing Christ in All of Scripture." Does your text prepare for Christ, proclaim Christ, or equip believers to respond to Christ? Review the appropriate Preaching Considerations for your text.

3. As described in this chapter, interpret your passage in its immediate context (you might review Exercise 14, "Exegete Before Sermonizing" for guidance). Then, identify what role your particular text plays in the overall story of God's redemption through Jesus Christ.

4. Include in the sermon how your text furthers God's story through Jesus.

"I TRIED IT"

"As I looked back over recent sermons, I noticed my tendency to get bogged down in the small details of a text and miss the bigger picture. I did this exercise while working through a series from Mark, preparing for Easter. The exercise challenged me to understand each story not just in its immediate context, but also to understand how each story connects with Jesus' overall purpose—the cross and the empty tomb."

Jason Warden, Knoxville, Tennessee

"A few years ago, I made it a goal to always connect the day's passage with its place in the bigger picture of God's Word and ultimately with Jesus. I found it helped people connect what had felt like loose excerpts. However, this exercise really challenged me to go beyond that and highlight a specific characteristic/application for their life today. It opened up a new way for me to add action statements and helped me reach a new level of sharing Jesus, even when preaching from the Old Testament."

Jonathan Absher, Follansbee, West Virginia

"When the time came for this exercise my text was James 1:27 regarding 'Pure Religion.' It was easy to make the connection between the teachings of Jesus and His half-brother. Jesus taught that we were to visit the least and help them in distress (Matt. 25:34–46). This surely includes the orphans and widows. Jesus also taught we should keep ourselves unstained from the world as He taught us to be 'pure in heart' (Matt. 5:8) and as He prayed that His disciples would be in the world but not of it (John 17:13–19). To preach James is indeed to preach Christ!"

Ken Overdorf, Beckley, West Virginia

RESOURCES FOR FURTHER STUDY

- *Christ-Centered Preaching: Redeeming the Expository Sermon*, 2nd Edition, by Bryan Chapell (Baker, 2005).
- *Preaching Christ from the Old Testament: A Contemporary Hermeneutical Method*, by Sidney Greidanus (Eerdmans, 1999).
- "The Amazing Disappearing and Reappearing Cross," by Bill Fleming. Access at http://www.preaching.com/resources/articles/11605340.
- "The Secrets of Spurgeon's Preaching," by Lewis Drummond. Access at http://www.christianhistorymagazine.org/index.php/past-pages/29spurgeon.

Illustrate Specifically

Life magazine recently celebrated its seventy-fifth year of publication by releasing collections of its most memorable photographs. The collections carry titles like "The 75 Best LIFE Covers of All Time," and "The 75 Best LIFE Photos." I stumbled across these collections online and remained glued to my computer screen for the next ninety minutes, browsing photographs of soldiers, celebrities, athletes, and events that have shaped culture.

The magazine has earned a stellar reputation in photojournalism for two reasons. First, its photographs typify the American experience. Though one might read facts and statistics about the Vietnam conflict, Joe DiMaggio's home-run swing, or Buzz Aldrin's walk on the moon, a photograph—a slice taken from time—transforms factual knowledge about such events into experiential knowledge. Second, *LIFE* photographs mesmerize observers because of their attention to detail—the mud and scar on the soldier's cheek as he stares out the open door of the helicopter, Joe DiMaggio's sinewy forearms and strained face as he launches a baseball into the bleachers, and the mirror image in Buzz Aldrin's space mask that reflects Neil Armstrong and the lunar module. The pictures take us there.

Effective sermon illustrations depend on the same two traits—they typify our listeners' experiences, and they include details that make listeners feel present in the stories. "An illustration is a snapshot from life," explains Bryan Chapell. "It captures a mood, a moment, or a memory in a narrative frame and displays that slice of life for the mind to see and the heart to know."[1]

---

1. Bryan Chapell, *Using Illustrations to Preach With Power*, Rev. Ed. (Wheaton, IL: Crossway Books, 2001), 85

DEVELOPING DETAILED ILLUSTRATIONS

How, though, can we translate what we observe in photojournalism into preaching? Three suggestions merit consideration.

- *Instead of "In other words," say, "For example."* Haddon Robinson said to a class of preaching students, "Poor communicators are always saying, 'In other words ...,' which really means 'I said it poorly the first time so let me take another run at it.' Effective communicators say, 'For example ...,' and provide listeners with concrete pictures of truth in life. In this way, good preachers are always turning the ear into an eye, helping people to see."

- *Move from general descriptions to specific instances.* Too often, in an attempt to illustrate a truth, we think only of general descriptions of people or experiences. The illustration grows more powerful, however, when we describe a particular day, time, and event that typifies that description. For example, a few years ago a student in one of my classes preached about prayer. "When I think of a person of prayer," he said, "I think of my dad. My dad prays constantly—it's as natural to him as breathing." I thought, *Good ... now take the next step, tell us a story about a particular incident.* He did. He continued, "I'll never forget when I was in middle school, and my father was offered a job in a new town. He and my mother agonized over the decision. Finally, one evening after supper—during which my father only picked at his food—he called the family into the living room. We all stood in a circle, held hands, and went around the circle until each one of us had prayed about the decision. He ended up taking the job, and we moved ahead as a family, with the peace and confidence that we were following God's direction." I almost stood and applauded! The general description ("My dad is a person of prayer") began the journey, but the illustration came full circle by telling of a specific instance.

- *Include helpful details.* Details invite the listener to experience the illustration—to see, hear, smell, taste, feel, and walk into the story. When Jesus told of the Prodigal Son's return home, He did not simply say, "And the father received him back and loved him." Instead, Jesus described the father seeing the son when "he was still a long way off," and being "filled with compassion ... he ran to his son, threw his arms around him and kissed him" (Luke 15:19–20). Jesus described the dialogue that occurred between the two, and the robe, ring, sandals, and fattened calf with which the father blessed the son. Details give the story texture, zest, and life.

THE EXERCISE

1. Identify the three or four most prominent truths, applications, or questions in your upcoming sermon. These probably relate to the major sections of the sermon—each point or movement typically focuses on a particular truth.
2. For each truth identified in step one, consider who or what often exemplifies it. If a truth relates to generosity, for example, what person do you know who exemplifies generosity?
3. For each example that came to mind in step two, isolate a specific instance—an event that took place on a particular day on the calendar—that typifies it. To spur your memory, think, "I'll never forget this one day when ..." If your grandmother is a generous person, to continue the example above, what particular event from your grandmother's life typifies her generosity? What do you remember her saying or doing on a particular day at a particular place that demonstrated her generosity?
4. Identify what details will bring each story to life for your listeners. Ask yourself: When did the event occur? Where did it occur? What might your listeners have seen, heard, felt, touched, or tasted if they had observed this event firsthand?
5. Write out each illustration and insert them into your sermon outline or manuscript.

AN EXAMPLE

My preacher recently presented a sermon from Luke 2:8–20. In one segment of the sermon, he described how the shepherds spread the message about baby Jesus, whom they visited in Bethlehem. For this segment of the sermon, he walked through the five steps described in this chapter to arrive at a specific illustration:

1. TRUTH: We should be so excited about Jesus that we want to tell others about Him.
2. EXAMPLE: When children are excited about something, they can't help but tell people about it.
3. SPECIFIC INSTANCE: A young mother in our church recently shared a story about her daughter taking her Bible to school and reading to her classmates.
4. DETAILS: (See the details provided in the illustration below.)
5. ILLUSTRATION:

Like the shepherds, we should be so excited about Jesus that we want to tell others about him. Children provide a great example of this—if they are excited about something, they can't help but tell others.

Brandi, a young mother in our church, told our small group about something that typifies this excitement. On Monday morning, Brandi's six-year-old daughter, Madison, asked if she could take her Bible to school. She explained, "I want to read a short story to my class." Her parents worried that taking a Bible to school might get her into trouble, but they didn't want to discourage Madison. So her dad, Nathan, went to the bookshelf and found an illustrated story Bible for her to take.

When Madison returned home from school, Brandi asked if her teacher let her read. "Yes," Madison responded. "And I read two stories—the Christmas story and the Easter story." Her mother asked why she chose those two. "That way my whole class could know about Jesus."

After telling this story, Brandi said, "Obviously this makes me so proud of her, but even more it challenges me as an adult to be bold just like she was!"

"I TRIED IT"

"Moving from general to specifics in illustrations truly makes them more powerful. I also found that the details evoke memories in listeners of similar situations they've experienced. I used this exercise for an illustration about something that happened in my childhood. Afterward, an elderly gentlemen told me about a similar event from his own childhood. He said that once he began to visualize the stories, the illustrations become more powerful, and they helped the Scripture text come more alive in his mind."

David Caffee, Englewood, Tennessee

"This exercise made my sermon preparation easier. After determining my Scripture and main points, I wrote the illustrations out. Since I manuscript my sermons, this let me know exactly where I stood in the preparation process. It also made the sermon more alive. Instead of being an afterthought, the illustrations became an integral part of the sermon. After I presented the message one of the church leaders remarked, 'I looked around and everyone, even the kids, were looking right at you and focusing on what you were saying.'"

Joseph Schmidt, Kewanee, Illinois

"Illustrations have consistently been one of the weak areas of my preaching. This exercise provides valuable help in improving this deficiency. It has been easy to recognize that my illustrations have lacked, but difficult to improve in that area—this chapter helped significantly. I now go step by step through my sermon and develop an illustrative photograph for my congregation of the important points I'm wishing to make. Thanks!"

Jeff Brunsman, Mount Gilead, Ohio

RESOURCES FOR FURTHER STUDY

- *Using Illustrations to Preach With Power*, by Bryan Chapell (Crossway Books, 2001).
- *Preaching with Freshness* (Preaching With Series), by Bruce Mawhinney (Kregel, 2008).
- "Making the Point With SHARP Illustrations," by

Hershael York. Access at http://www.preaching.com/resources/articles/11545675.
- "Preaching Moment 016: Mike Slaughter," view video discussion at http://www.workingpreacher.org/preachingmoments.aspx?video_id=15.

Land Smoothly in the Conclusion

I don't mind flying. As long as the airplane is big, the weather calm, and the flight smooth, I enjoy the experience. Subtract any one of these elements, however, and my face turns as green as a well watered spring lawn. Whether the flight remains silky or turns turbulent, however, its success depends on its landing. A poor landing ruins even the best of flights.

A similar principle holds true with sermon conclusions. A preacher might launch the message with a compelling introduction, soar for twenty minutes of homiletical genius, then crash and burn in the conclusion.

We want to land smoothly. Effective conclusions, however, prove elusive. Preachers who conclude well do so with an artistic intuition that even they find difficult to explain or teach others. This week's exercise may not provide the definitive word on conclusions, but it will give some helpful reminders and a concrete process that will help us grow in this aspect of our preaching.

EFFECTIVE SERMON CONCLUSIONS

Though the best way to conclude varies from sermon to sermon, most effective conclusions exhibit these four characteristics in varying degrees:

- *A Sense of Completion:* The conclusion helps listeners feel like they have reached the end of a journey, giving them a sense of finality, unity, and wholeness.
- *A Burning Focus on the Main Idea(s):* The conclusion usually includes a precise, word-for-word statement or restatement of the sermon's thesis. It may also include

a review of other important ideas that supported the
thesis.

- *A Final Picture of the Main Idea:* Often, the conclusion
  delivers the sermon's strongest illustration, one that reinforces the thesis. Some call this final illustration—usually a
  story—the "spear," because it brings the sermon to a sharp
  point.
- *Challenge and Encouragement:* The conclusion frequently includes a challenge to listeners to live out what
  the sermon taught, and encouragement that motivates
  them to do so.

THE EXERCISE

In addition to the characteristics described in this chapter, a conclusion provides a final opportunity for the sermon to accomplish its purpose. This characteristic holds such importance, in
fact, that the sermon's purpose may provide the best indication
of how the sermon can best conclude. Therefore, this week's exercise will help us design a conclusion for an upcoming sermon
that correlates with that sermon's purpose.

1. *Identify the Sermon's Purpose.* A sermon's purpose relates
   to—but should not be confused with—its thesis. The thesis
   states the primary truth that the sermon will proclaim. The
   purpose states what you hope that truth will accomplish
   in listeners. To define this purpose statement, complete this
   sentence about your upcoming sermon: "As a result of this
   sermon, listeners should …" Then, complete the sentence
   by defining what you hope listeners will think, feel, or
   do differently after the sermon. For example, if the thesis
   states, "God's grace is sufficient," the purpose might be,
   "As a result of this sermon, listeners should find peace in
   the grace that God provides."
2. *Give Particular Attention to the Verb.* A sermon's purpose
   statement revolves around its verb. Though the statement will
   fall into a broad category of thinking, feeling, or doing, the
   actual statement will include a verb that identifies more specifically what the listener will think, feel, or do. Perhaps, as
   a result of the sermon, listeners should seek, implement, recognize, appreciate, initiate, experience, grasp, begin, or apply.

3. *Formulate a Conclusion Based on the Sermon's Purpose.* If the sermon intends to help listeners comprehend a truth, how might the conclusion solidify that truth in their minds? If the sermon will lead listeners to appreciate something, how can the conclusion encourage this appreciation? If listeners should implement a particular behavior, how can the conclusion equip listeners for that behavior?

Sermon Purpose Category	Example Verbs for Purpose Statements	Ways to Conclude Sermon
Thinking	Understand, grasp, consider, comprehend, know, recognize, realize	Story or metaphor that reinforces the concept preached Quotation that reinforces the concept preached Summary of the teaching presented in the sermon Series of questions to stimulate further thinking
Feeling	Feel, sense, appreciate, value, experience, be grateful for, find hope in, find joy in	Story that touches on emotions Quotation that motivates or encourages Prayer that leads listeners to seek God's comfort, guidance, or grace Poetry or music that helps listeners express the desired emotion
Doing	Implement, apply, execute, perform, begin, initiate, accomplish, pursue, act, take steps to	Story that describes someone exemplifying the recommended behavior Quotation that influences the will Suggestions for tangible ways to apply the sermon An invitation or challenge to respond to the sermon immediately

ADDITIONAL SUGGESTIONS

- Save your best illustration for the conclusion.
- Do not say "in conclusion" or "finally." This will send listeners' eyes and attention to the clock on the wall.
- Do not let the conclusion drag on. As one of my professors used to say, "Don't circle the airport, just land the plane."
- Include only one illustration in the conclusion.
- Sketch out a rough draft of the conclusion before you write the introduction and body of the sermon. Before you make a trip, you decide on the destination, then map out how to get there. The same holds true of writing a sermon.
- The emotional intensity of the sermon should rise as you reach the conclusion.
- In most cases, sermons should end on a high note— encouraging and motivating.
- Choose your last words carefully. Often, a restatement of the thesis serves well as the final words that you speak.
- Consider ending by restating *part* or your thesis, and allowing listeners to complete the sentence in their minds. This works well if you have stated the thesis, word for word, enough times that listeners know it well. For example, after having repeated throughout the sermon, "When Jesus comes, everything changes," a preacher might end the sermon by saying, "When Jesus comes ..."
- In some traditions, every sermon ends with an invitation to receive salvation. If such an invitation does not flow naturally from the end of your sermon, end the sermon in a way appropriate to its subject matter and purpose, then allow some kind of break—perhaps just a few moments of silence, or step down from the stage—then offer this invitation.

"I TRIED IT"

"The best part of this exercise for me was the emphasis on the purpose of the sermon, how it differs from the thesis, and how it can guide the conclusion. As I reflected on the three purpose categories—thinking, feeling, and doing—it occurred to me that these three usually work together in a progression in my preaching. I want the text to change the way we *think*, which affects how we *feel*, which then leads us to *do* something about it. My conclusion must contain a clear call to action, otherwise I've only delivered a nice speech."

Brian Walton, Winchester, Kentucky

"Too often our messages take flight but never quite land. This exercise helped me to think through a more smooth landing— I have found it most helpful to give a final illustration, review my points (and have them on the screen), and make specific challenges at the end. I want to be sure that I clearly guide people toward the 'take-away' that I want them to have. This exercise forced me to pay closer attention to those final moments of the sermon."

Bob Emmert, Jefferson City, Tennessee

RESOURCES FOR FURTHER STUDY

- *Craddock on the Craft of Preaching*, by Fred Craddock (Chalice Press, 2011). See especially chapter 16, "Thirteen Ways to End a Sermon."
- "Tips for Concluding Your Sermons," by Rick Warren. Access at http://www.christiantoday.com/article/rick.warren.tips.for.concluding.your.sermons/15800.htm.
- "Sermon Conclusions" (3-part article), by W. Floyd Bresee. Access at:
  - » http://www.ministrymagazine.org/archive/1990/January/sermon-conclusions-1
  - » http://www.ministrymagazine.org/archive/1990/March/sermon-conclusions-2
  - » http://www.ministrymagazine.org/archive/1990/May/sermon-conclusions-3
- "How to Create Engaging Conclusions," by Ken Gosnell. Access at http://www.churchleaders.com/pastors/pastor-articles/145316-how-to-create-engaging-conclusions.html.

Interweave Preaching and Worship

A member of a church search committee recently called to check a reference on one of our university's graduates. This graduate had applied for the church's worship ministry opening. I had much good to say about the young man—he excelled academically, has solid people skills, and leads music proficiently. After my glowing review, the lady from the search committee asked, "In what areas will he need to grow?" I thought for a moment, then replied, "Well, like many young worship leaders, he does a fine job of leading music, but he hasn't yet grasped how music weaves together with other aspects of a worship service."

Later that day I reflected on the conversation and felt a twinge of guilt. I thought, "Yes, this can be said of many young worship leaders. Unfortunately, the same could be said of many preachers—and not just young ones—and their sermons." Many of us, I fear, fail to consider how our sermons relate with other elements of a worship service. "I preach," we assume, "and the worship leader leads worship. And never shall the twain meet."

This assumption reflects deficient perspectives of both worship and preaching. Worship is bigger than music and more expansive than the first twenty minutes of a church service. And preaching, when empowered by God's Spirit and pursuant of God's glory, demonstrates and instigates worship. Various elements of a worship gathering—elements that include preaching and music, the Lord's Supper, prayer, giving, and numerous other expressions—weave together to form a tapestry of worship.

PREACHING AS WORSHIP

Unfortunately, many—dare I say most?—preachers fail to recognize how their sermons influence, for better or worse, the larger tapestry of worship that listeners experience in church gatherings. This failure results from:

- *Insufficient Training.* Most seminaries and Christian colleges offer courses about preaching and courses about worship. Few, however, teach ministry students about the relationship between the two.
- *Faulty Separation.* Preachers and worship leaders often compartmentalize their ministries, and fail to see how their contributions to a worship gathering relate.
- *Self-Importance.* Preaching stands critical to the growth and maturity of God's church. Recognizing this importance, preachers sometimes push worship to the sidelines. Ironically, this mistake saps their preaching of power and impact. When viewed in the context of worship, and as a means to advance worship, preaching takes on a more substantial role. It becomes a part of the ongoing, worshipful, edifying, challenging conversation between God and His community.

When properly understood and weaved into the larger tapestry of worship, preaching advances a community's worship by:

- *Facilitating a Focus on Christ.* Christian preaching—like Christian worship—focuses on, celebrates, and responds to Jesus Christ. Such preaching praises His majesty, expresses awe at His mystery, and submits to His mastery. It exhibits a theocentric (God-centered) rather than anthropocentric (human-centered) focus, giving primary attention and time to God's character and acts.
- *Celebrating God's Overall Narrative.* In the Bible, both preaching and worship celebrated God's overall story. Consider, for example, the system of feasts and holy days presented in the Old Testament. Each holy day—from the Sabbath to the Passover to the Day of Atonement—celebrates an element of God's history and provision. Consider, likewise, preaching in the New Testament. In Acts, the sermons of Stephen, Peter, Paul and others traced God's overall narrative as it culminates in Jesus. Contemporary preaching, likewise, can inspire worship by celebrating God's story.

- *Advancing Scripture.* Scripture—God's unique, authoritative, revealed Word—drives both Christian preaching and Christian worship. When preachers and worship leaders allow Scripture to guide them, preaching and other elements of worship join seamlessly to celebrate and advance God's truth. This reality magnifies when preachers and worship leaders base their efforts on the same Scriptures.

THE EXERCISE

Michael Quicke explains, "Preachers can no longer consider their task apart from worship nor worship leaders see their role apart from preaching. Rather than both doing their own thing, reinforcing the tragic separation of preaching from worship, they belong *together* within the dynamics of the Triune God's gracious enabling. Preachers once shortsighted about worship now see that worship's big picture includes preaching."[1] The key to interweaving preaching with other elements of worship lies in collaboration. This week's exercise, therefore, will facilitate this collaboration.

1. Arrange a meeting to plan an upcoming worship service. Include four to six people, including you, those responsible to plan worship services, and others who could provide valuable insight into planning a worship gathering—perhaps some with teaching gifts and others who could bring creative, artistic expertise.
2. Prior to the meeting:
   - Complete a preliminary study on your preaching text(s). Research its historical and literary contexts and identify and define key words and phrases.
   - Invite those who will attend the meeting to read through and reflect on the Scripture text, emphasizing that the text will drive not only the sermon but also the overall worship experience. You might also invite them to read the two online articles listed on page 292 under "Resources for Further Study."

---

1. Michael Quicke, *Preaching as Worship: An Integrative Approach to Formation in Your Church* (Grand Rapids, MI: Baker, 2011), 90.

3. At the meeting:
   - Briefly explain the philosophy presented in this chapter—preaching should combine with other elements of worship to help participants focus on, celebrate, and respond to God.
   - Provide a succinct summary of your research of the Scripture text.
   - Brainstorm about what may occur in a worship service that grows from this Scripture text. Discuss questions such as these: What does this text reveal about God? How should we respond to what this text reveals about God? How does this particular revelation and this particular response relate to redemption through Jesus Christ? How can the elements of the worship gathering portray what God has revealed about Himself, challenge us to respond appropriately, and celebrate how these fit within God's overall narrative? How can the preaching event weave together with these elements?
   - Consider worship elements such as, but not limited to, these: congregational music, special music, sermon, prayers of praise, prayers of confession, prayers of petition, Scripture reading, responsive reading, the Lord's Supper, offering, drama, poetry, art, expressions of fellowship, testimony, and a benediction and/or charge.[2]
4. After the meeting, use the insights gained during the meeting to prepare your sermon and to work with your worship leader to prepare the remainder of the worship service.

ADDITIONAL SUGGESTIONS

- Depending on the flow of the service, you might break the sermon into segments, and include other elements of worship—perhaps music, prayer, drama, or testimony—between sermon segments.
- Give careful consideration to your sermon's introduction and conclusion. Because the sermon is a part of the overall worship experience, the sermon should grow from elements of the service that precede it, and prepare

---

2. Review Exercise 13, "Utilize the Five Senses" for additional ideas.

the congregation for elements of the service that follow it. The sermon's introduction and conclusion play a critical role in maintaining this flow.

- When you preach, consider your preaching as an act of worship before God.

"I TRIED IT"

"I completed this exercise while preparing a sermon and worship service on prayer. I worked with other leaders to weave together various elements of the service—the sermon, music, the Lord's Supper, and times of prayer. The impact was tremendous. Many of our church members said it was the best worship service they'd experienced. One man said, 'I wasn't ready for it to be over ... I wanted the service to go on all night!'"

Chad Broaddus, Cynthiana, Kentucky

"The practice of planning the entire worship service together, attempting to make the service flow as one 'big idea' as opposed to compartmentalizing the 'worship' from the 'sermon' has proved invaluable for us as a church. We have a group that meets two hours per week to attempt the interweaving of preaching and worship. It calls for ownership from all those involved, not just the preacher, but when done right, it has been a powerful component to our worship gatherings. It allows us to celebrate the whole story of God each and every week."

Mark Nelson, Knoxville, Tennessee

"The pleasure of working with a paid worship leader is a recent development in my ministry. We brainstorm to coordinate our themes, sermons, and music. This allows one aspect of worship to flow into the other. I have effectively divided some of my messages into segments. Each part led to a congregational song, a featured solo, or guided prayer. Quite often, it was worship that drove the point of the message home; it was worship that people remembered; it was worship that transformed an ordinary Sunday into a life-changing memory."

Tom Cash, Sault Ste. Marie, Michigan

RESOURCES FOR FURTHER STUDY

- *Preaching as Worship: An Integrative Approach to Formation in Your Church*, by Michael Quicke (Baker, 2011).
- *Worship Is a Verb: Eight Principles for Transforming Worship*, by Robert Webber (Hendrickson, 1992).
- "Beware Tuneless Preaching," by Michael Quicke. Access at http://www.preaching.com/resources/articles/11547624.
- "The Place of the Sermon Within the Worship Service," by Craig A. Satterlee. Access at http://www.workingpreacher.org/preachingworship.aspx?article_id=6.

Write for the Ear

I recently visited an author in his home. I sat with a few friends around the writer's kitchen table with coffee in hand and a Lazy Susan full of pastries and fruit spinning back and forth between us. My friends and I thoroughly enjoyed the conversation, and felt honored to spend time with this revered man in such a casual, welcoming environment. At one point during the conversation, however, one of my friends asked a question, and the author responded, "I've just written something about that." He left the kitchen and rummaged through his office until he found the piece he'd written. He brought the article back to the table and read it to us. It was not a brief piece. Our eyes glazed as he read. The pastries grew stale. The sun set. Crickets chirped. Then he finished.

Had we come across the article in a magazine, I'm confident we would have enjoyed reading it. What pleases the eye, however—long, flowing sentences filled with adjectives, adverbs, dependant clauses, and parenthesis—bores the ear.

Preaching is an oral event. We prepare sermons not for our congregations to read, but for them to hear. Most college and seminary training prepares us only to write for the eye. Our listeners will better hear our sermons if we learn to write for the ear.

HOW TO WRITE FOR THE EAR

The following ten suggestions will help us write sermons for our listeners' ears.

- *Imagine your hearers.* As you prepare your sermon, visualize particular people from your congregation sitting around your desk. If you looked into their eyes and speak with them about your sermon text and topic, what would you say? How would you say it? Allow the rhythms of conversation to guide what you type.

- *Prepare orally.* Speak your sentences aloud before you commit them to paper. Then, record on paper what you speak. With this approach, the sermon begins where it will end—in the audible realm.
- *Use simple words.* In most cases, a short, simple word works best. Around seventy-five percent of words used by Sinclair Lewis, Robert Lewis Stevenson, and Charles Dickens have only one syllable. The same holds true of Psalm 23 and the Lord's Prayer. "All the big things in life have little names," says Haddon Robinson, "such as *life, death, peace, war, dawn, day, night, hope, love,* and *home.* Learn to use small words in a big way."[1]
- *Use simple sentences.* In most cases, the simple structure of noun – verb – direct object communicates best orally. "Paul visited Ephesus" reaches the ear better than "Ephesus is the city that Paul visited." Furthermore, simple sentences contain only one idea—if you wish to communicate two ideas, use two sentences.
- *Be direct.* An old story describes a novice copywriter who produced this new advertisement for a bar of soap: "The alkaline element and fats in this product are blended in such a way as to secure the highest quality of saponification, along with the specific gravity that keeps it on top of the water, relieving the bather of the trouble and annoyance of fishing around for it at the bottom of the tub during ablution." Thankfully a more experienced colleague reduced it to two words, "It floats." We preachers, who tend toward wordiness, should learn to speak so directly.
- *Speak personally.* In formal writing courses, students learn to avoid personal pronouns like "I," "we," or "you." Such terms have an appropriate place in conversation, however, and in preaching.
- *Speak casually.* Oral communication, unlike formal

---

1. Haddon Robinson, *Biblical Preaching: The Development and Delivery of Expository Messages,* 2nd ed. (Grand Rapids, MI: Baker, 2005), 191.

written communication, sometimes breaks rules of grammar. It uses contractions, sentence fragments, and can begin sentences with "And" or "But." In *Just Say the Word*, Robert Jacks explains,

> We were carefully taught. No sentence fragments. None. Run-on sentences are an abomination and you should never use them because you'll get marked down when the teacher grades your paper. Don't use contractions. It's not a good idea to ever split infinitives. A preposition is something you should never end a sentence with. And don't begin sentences with "And." Never, never, never repeat yourself.
>
> The problem is: that's the way we're supposed to write, but it's not the way we talk to each other. And when we *write* that way for *speaking* we too easily come up with some awful-sounding stuff.[2]

- *Repeat yourself.* Readers can review significant paragraphs or reread confusing sentences. Listeners do not have this luxury. Listeners appreciate, therefore, when preachers repeat their main ideas. Anything underlined, highlighted, or typed in bold print in a sermon deserves repeating. And, listeners appreciate a review of the sermon's major ideas during transitions and in the conclusion.
- *Label sermon segments.* If the main segments of the sermon are a list (maybe three aspects of grace, or four characteristics of a forgiving person), number them and make the outline verbally clear: "The first aspect of grace is ....The second aspect of grace is ..." If the sermon's segments do not fit neatly into such a list, label each segment with a concise summary sentence: "We discussed, first, that forgiveness is difficult. Next, we learned that forgiveness is necessary. Finally, we will discover how God empowers us to forgive." Though such efforts may feel trivial to us, remember that our listeners have not lived with the sermon all week like we have, nor do they have the message on paper in front of them. They need

---

2. Robert Jacks, *Just Say the Word: Writing for the Ear* (Grand Rapids, MI: Eerdman's, 1981), 2.

guidance, therefore, to understand the movement of the sermon. Like visitors to a new city, listeners appreciate signposts.

- *Plan for pauses.* When you introduce a new idea or something that listeners will need to contemplate, include a reminder in your outline or manuscript to pause.

THE EXERCISE

1. While you prepare your upcoming sermon, read through the suggestions discussed in this chapter once a day.
2. After you complete your sermon outline or manuscript, invite two or three people to meet with you in a casual environment—perhaps over lunch or coffee. During this meeting, talk through your sermon with them. You may bring your notes with you, but do not read them. Instead, share the sermon's content conversationally. You might consider recording the conversation so that you can refer to it later.
3. As soon as possible after the conversation described in step two (preferably immediately afterward), do a final edit of your sermon. Consider how you related the sermon's concepts in conversation. How can you reword what you have on paper to more effectively "write for the ear?"

"I TRIED IT"

"Before I preached my sermon, I talked through it with both my youth minister and my wife. I found that what I said was significantly different from the written manuscript. I was able, then, to edit the sermon and make it more conversational before I preached it. Afterward, those in my church said the sermon was easier to understand and that I came across more personable. Also, I found that I could more easily preach the message without notes."

Joe Heins, Auburn, Indiana

"This exercise is a must-try! We have to remind ourselves each week that our sermons will be heard, not read. So, we have to get out from behind the computer! When you talk through your sermon with someone before you preach it, you get immediate feedback through their facial expressions and responses. You will see if those parts you thought were clear, or particularly impactful, really are. It helped me to discover what resonates with a listener before I preached my sermon to the church."

Paul Wingfield, St. Louis, Missouri

"Each week I try to share the content of my sermon with my wife, who always offers helpful feedback. Still, I found it extra-helpful to bring a few additional people into this week's conversation. By now my wife knows me well enough to interpret the basic idea of my message, whether I've communicated it clearly or not. Involving others gave me additional perspective on how well (or poorly) I had written for the ear. I found that using people with different thinking styles (analytical, creative) also helped."

Scott Kenworthy, Indianapolis, Indiana

RESOURCES FOR FURTHER STUDY

- *Just Say the Word: Writing for the Ear*, by Robert Jacks (Eerdman's, 1981).
- "Writing for (Not by) the Ear," by Donnell King. Access at http://www.writing-world.com/grammar/ear.shtml.
- "Writing for the Ear," three-part series by Shauna Hannan. Access part one at http://www.workingpreacher.org/sermondevelopment.aspx?article_id=229. (See links to parts two and three on the menu on the left side of the page.)
- "Five Ways to Write for the Ear, Not for the Eye," by Brad Phillips. Access at http://www.mrmediatraining.com/index.php/2011/04/13/5-ways-to-write-for-the-ear-not-for-the-eye.

Preach with Men in Mind

One morning I read a review of David Murrow's intriguing book, *Why Men Hate Going to Church*. That afternoon I drove past a church building and its sign caught my eye: "Friendships are the flowers in the bouquet of life."

"That," I said aloud to myself, "is why men hate going to church!" Friendships are the flowers in the bouquet of life? What man, driving past such a sign on his way to work, or to a meeting, or to watch a game with his buddies, would read such a sign and think, "I planned to go fishing Sunday morning, but that sign changed my mind. I want to go to that church, instead, and learn how friendships are like flowers"?

Exercise 21 of this book, "Preach With Women in Mind," noted that women comprise a majority of church attenders in a typical American congregation. We should respond to this revelation in two ways. First, we should make certain that some elements of our sermons connect with women; male preachers, especially, need reminders about communicating effectively with women. Second, we should consider how we might preach in a way that draws more men into the fold. In addition to those elements that connect with women, what elements can we include in our sermons that will particularly connect with men?

CONNECTING WITH MEN

God created every person—male or female—uniquely. Not everything discussed in this chapter, therefore, will apply to every man. Typically, however, sermons that connect well with men exhibit some or all of the following seven characteristics.

- *Challenge.* God wired men with a competitive nature. Their hearts race and their spines tingle when larger-than-life challenges rise before them. They want to stand in David's shoes before Goliath, beside Moses when he confronts Pharaoh, and with the early Christians boldly proclaiming Christ in the face of persecution and mar-tyrdom. They seek adventure, risk, and the battle for good. On Sunday mornings, therefore, men sit back in their pews, cross their arms, and glare toward the pulpit: "Challenge me, preacher, to do something significant, to be someone who matters."

- *Mission.* Movies that target men—think *Braveheart*, the *Rocky* series, or *Saving Private Ryan*—portray men caught up in missions larger than themselves, causes for which they make great sacrifices and to which they devote themselves entirely. Men rally around such mis-sions. The cause of Christ surpasses all other causes in scope and significance. Rather than rallying believers to rise up, however, we too often downplay our mission: "Following Jesus is easy—just say this simple prayer ....If you will just volunteer for one hour every-other month, we can get this ministry staffed .... I know you're busy, but maybe you could squeeze in this one church activity? I promise I won't ask you to do anything else." At such anemic challenges, men yawn. Their ears perk, though, and their minds begin formulating plans when we lay before them the mammoth mission of Christ: "Following Jesus requires *everything* of you—His cause and calling demands nothing less. What are you holding back? What do you need to sacrifice? What can you do to further the only cause with eternal significance?"

- *Encouragement.* A friend made this observation, "Moth-er's Day sermons make women feel like queens. Father's Day sermons make men feel like dirt." His comment gave me pause because, sadly, my own sermon files evidence its truth. While we glorify and encourage mothers, we induce guilt among fathers (cue "Cat's in the Cradle"). Men, like women, thrive on encouragement. Rather than drowning men in criticism, therefore, why not take the approach of a good coach at halftime, and give a pep talk? "You can do this! It won't be easy, the enemy won't just lie down and surrender, but by the strength God provides, you can win this battle!"

- *Doctrine.* Men need reasons to act. Belief precedes behavior. Christian behavior—even Christian mission—grows from biblical doctrine. Because God exists, because humankind sinned, because of sin's consequences, because of Jesus' incarnation, because of the cross and the empty tomb, because of the Holy Spirit, because of heaven and hell, we believe, repent, obey, journey, reach out, and proclaim. We must not assume that men don't like doctrine. Men need doctrine, and even appreciate doctrine because it provides reasons to embark on the mission of Christ.

- *Authenticity.* Few things repel men more than a speaker who puts on a false front. Ironically, a speaker who tries to appear more "macho" than he really is, attempting to better connect with men, causes the men in the congregation to roll their eyes and start checking their smartphones for the score to the ballgame. Be yourself.

- *Clarity.* Men appreciate clarity. They don't want to read between the lines, or to infer meaning from a fuzzy sermon. They prefer direct communication. They connect best, therefore, with sermons that teach clearly, logically, and directly.

- *Practicality.* Men want to know what to do with the information we give them. A sermon that offers only information will leave them wanting. They appreciate applications—specific ideas, steps, and suggestions to act on the truths we preach. How will Sunday's message influence how they live in the office, on the jobsite, in the classroom, or around the dinner table on Monday? If we cannot answer this question—and if we do not answer the question in our sermons—we will not connect with men.

THE EXERCISE

1. Ask five men who hear you preach regularly for feedback about how well your preaching relates to them. You might seek their input face to face, over the telephone, via email, or through whatever means will work best in your circumstances. Consider asking questions such as these:

- During my sermons, when do you feel most engaged?
- When does your mind begin to wander?
- If you could stand before a room full of preachers to advise them about connecting their sermons with men, what advice would you give?
- If you were to give me a letter grade (A – F) to evaluate how well my sermons relate to the men in our church, what grade would you assign?

Ask these gentlemen if you can contact them again after your upcoming sermon (if they will be in attendance to hear it).

- Review your last three to five sermons. Circle or highlight each time you used these (or similar) terms: challenge, battle, victory, risk, adventure, journey, mission, and cause. If you use Microsoft Word or similar software, the search feature will help you find these terms quickly.
- Assign yourself a letter grade (A – F) regarding each of the following elements:
    » Encouragement: Would men have felt torn down or built up by this sermon?
    » Doctrine: Did the sermon contain significant truths about God and His Kingdom?
    » Authenticity: Did I resist the temptation to put on a false front, and instead present myself authentically?
    » Clarity: Did I clearly, logically, and directly state my main ideas?
    » Practicality: Did the sermon offer concrete ideas, steps, and/or suggestions to act on what it taught?

2. Prepare your upcoming sermon with men in mind. Do not pretend your audience consists entirely of men—recognize that women will sit before you, also (as we discussed in Exercise 21)—but intentionally design some parts of the sermon to connect with men.

3. After you preach, get back in touch with the men you contacted in step one. Ask them questions similar to those listed in step one, but ask them about the specific sermon you just preached. Then, invite them to assign you a letter grade (A – F) representing how well the sermon related to men. Compare these evaluations with the grades they assigned you in step one and the grade you assigned yourself in step two.

"I TRIED IT"

"I have tried for some time to target men in my sermons, without excluding the rest of the audience, because if men are fully engaged in church the rest of the family often follows. This exercise helped me stay on target. When I asked a few men about my preaching, their feedback was incredibly helpful—I realized I wasn't coming across like I thought I was. Specifically, they encouraged me to be even more practical in my sermons."

Jonathan Goss, Bluefield, West Virginia

"In the sermon I prepared for this exercise, my intent was to challenge and encourage men to rise up at work, home, church, and in their social lives, to be exemplary Christ followers. I attempted to make this sermon direct and fun. Some men joined me on stage to share some funny life experiences. This experience was a good reminder to me that men and women don't always approach things alike, and often see the same things quite differently. The sermon was well received—our men appreciated the sermon and its intent."

Steve Fair, Noblesville, Indiana

"When completing this exercise, I had already planned a sermon about men being good husbands. I started the sermon by saying that wives should submit to their husbands. This really got the men's attention (not to mention the women's). When I was sure the men were 'hooked,' I switched the emphasis, and told them that if they want wives who love and trust them, they first have to be godly husbands, worthy of respect. I challenged them to sacrifice themselves for their wives. Men later told me that the sermon made an impact."

Steven Johnson, Clarks Hill, Indiana

RESOURCES FOR FURTHER STUDY

- *Why Men Hate Going to Church*, rev. and updated ed., by David Murrow (Thomas Nelson, 2011).
- *Wild at Heart: Discovering the Secret of a Man's Soul*, rev. and expanded ed., by John Eldridge (Thomas Nelson, 2011).

- "Why Men Hate Going To Church: An Interview With David Murrow," by Michael Duduit. Access at http://www.preaching.com/resources/articles/11550735.
- "Preaching to Men: An Interview with Tony Evans," by Michael Duduit. Access at http://www.preaching.com/resources/articles/11563928.

Read Fiction

On a recent weekend, my wife took our children to visit her parents. A prior commitment kept me at home. In keeping with my tradition for such weekends, I treated myself to an evening by myself. I ate at my favorite restaurant, then spent the remainder of the evening at Barnes & Noble.

I browsed the bookstore while sipping a way-too-expensive decaf latte. I paused next to a shelf of early twentieth-century American classics. One looked short enough to read in one setting. I pulled it from the shelf, found a soft leather chair, and reclined with my coffee and Ernest Hemingway's *The Old Man and the Sea*.

Hemingway's novel describes an aged fisherman, Santiago, who hooks a marlin off the coast of Cuba, then battles the enormous fish for three days and nights. The struggle takes a great toll on the old fisherman, both physically and mentally (most of the book focuses on this battle). Finally, Santiago draws the marlin close enough to thrust a harpoon through its body. He ties the dead fish to the side of his boat and sets sail for home. Before he reaches home, however, sharks feast on the marlin's corpse, so that Santiago arrives back at his village with only a bare skeleton tied to the side of his boat.

With that, essentially, the book ends. The battle—meaningless. The struggle—fruitless. All of life, the reader senses—hollow.

I rose from the leather chair, dropped my empty coffee cup into a trash can, moped to the shelf, and returned the book. With a sigh, I turned to leave the store.

When I turned, however, I almost knocked over a rack of *SparkNotes*—booklets that offer overviews and evaluations of great works of literature. The booklet about *The Old Man and the Sea* sat at eye level. I lifted it from the rack and skimmed its pages. More so than Hemingway's other novels, the booklet made clear, *The Old Man and the Sea* reflected his own perspective of life. He lived to the extremes—battling, drinking, and dancing his way around the globe until, in a state of despair, he ended his life with a shotgun blast at age sixty-one. In the end Hemingway found life—even after experiencing its greatest luxuries and adventures—hollow. *The Old Man and the Sea* was the last novel published in his lifetime.

I recalled my plans for an upcoming sermon. In a couple weeks I would preach a message on Ecclesiastes. "'Meaningless! Meaningless!' says the Teacher. 'Utterly meaningless! Everything is meaningless'" (Eccl. 1:2). Hemingway and Santiago could certainly identify.

I turned to replace the *SparkNotes* on its rack, but while I closed the booklet the heading of a particular page caught my eye: "Crucifixion Imagery." Crucifixion imagery? In *The Old Man and the Sea*? I saw nothing in the book but battle and despair. The Harvard literary scholar who penned this booklet, however—and I later learned numerous other scholars—point to particular images they believe Hemingway embedded in the book to send readers' minds toward Jesus. The way blood flowed from Santiago's palms, his cries of anguish that sounded like a man "feeling the nail go through his hands and into the wood," and even the manner in which Santiago carried his mast across his shoulders point to the cross.[1]

Now the sermon, like Ecclesiastes, had a hopeful conclusion.

WHY PREACHERS SHOULD READ FICTION

I've read numerous novels that did not fit as neatly into upcoming sermons as did *The Old Man and the Sea*. Even so, preachers will benefit from a regular diet of fiction for at least four reasons.

- *Communication Techniques:* Writers know that readers can easily close a book and return it to its shelf. They use language and plot, therefore, to keep readers engaged.

---

1. Read more about this crucifixion imagery at http://www.sparknotes.com/lit/oldman/themes.html.

Preachers can learn from fiction writers about imagery, nuance, dialogue, movement, suspense, and climax.

- *Cultural Understanding:* Culture communicates its values and worldviews through various means, including its literature. By reading fiction—the stories of our culture—we gain insight into how those in our pews perceive life's major issues, such as love, relationships, morality, and death.
- *Cultural Relevance:* Paul quoted Greek poets when he preached in Athens. Likewise, when today's preachers speak intelligently about the culture—whether regarding film, literature, or current events—this helps them gain a respected hearing. Such relevance includes an awareness of classic and popular fiction.
- *Illustrations:* Preachers who read fiction sometimes find illustrations that help relate biblical truths to contemporary listeners. A particular plot line, a scene, or a quote from a book might illuminate a point in a sermon.

THE EXERCISE

1. Read a brief novel or a short story. If possible, find a work short enough to read in one sitting, so that you can immerse yourself entirely in its plot and characters. You might consider one of the suggested classic novels listed below, each between 100 and 150 pages (though do not feel limited to these suggestions or this genre):
   - *Of Mice and Men,* by John Steinbeck
   - *The Death of Ivan Ilyich,* by Leo Tolstoy
   - *The Red Badge of Courage,* by Stephen Crane
   - *The Prince,* by Niccolo Machiavelli
   - *The Strange Case of Dr. Jekyll and Mr. Hyde,* by Robert Louis Stevenson
   - *The Time Machine,* by H. G. Wells
   - *Twenty Thousand Leagues Under the Sea,* by Jules Verne
   - *Animal Farm,* by George Orwell

   Or, feel free to choose a short story. Libraries and bookstores offer numerous collections of short stories, including collections by respected authors like Mark Twain, F. Scott Fitzgerald, William Faulkner, and J. R. R. Tolkien. This website also contains the full text of several classic short stories: http://www.classicshorts.com/author.html.

2. After you read the novel or short story, visit www.sparknotes.com and/or www.cliffsnotes.com and search for a discussion of the story you read. If either offers such a discussion, browse through it and note particularly what it says about the story's themes and motifs.

3. Reflect on the following questions:
   • What can you learn about communication from the author? Consider especially the story's movement, plot, images, characters, and dialogue.
   • What did you observe in the story about human nature, cultural values, or cultural worldviews?
   • Did the book contain any spiritual elements? If so, how do these compare with biblical truth and your own experiences?
   • How did you feel during and after you read the book? What emotions and ideas did it evoke in you?
   • If you could ask the author any question about the book, what would you ask? How do you think the author would respond?

4. State the message of the book in a sentence. Though various themes may appear in the book, typically these various themes all contribute to a larger message. The message may or may not compare favorably with Christian truth. At this point, however, simply identify the message, not evaluate it. For example, perhaps the story conveys one of the following messages:
   • Life passes too quickly.
   • Our decisions steer our destiny.
   • Secrets destroy relationships.
   • Life's highest achievement is romantic love.
   • Misunderstanding creates prejudice.
   • Relationships require forgiveness to survive.

   Stories seldom state their themes outright—usually they lead readers through the life experiences of a protagonist who learns a significant truth through those experiences. For this reason, do not discount your own experience with the book—if it leads you to anger, passion, or intrigue, these may hint toward the message the author attempted to convey.

5. Consider what biblical themes or texts relate to the message of the book—either in agreement or in opposition.

6. Consider how your experience with the book can influence your upcoming sermons. Perhaps it will help you better understand your listeners and the culture in which they live, maybe the message of the book demonstrates (either positively or negatively) the message of a sermon, or the story might have included a particular scene or quote that can serve as an illustration.

"I TRIED IT"

"This exercise invited me into a story where the characters wrestled with tragedy and hope. The story encouraged me to approach the week's sermon with a keen awareness that the people shuffling through the doors on Sunday morning are deep in the midst of their own nuanced narratives. I was mindful not just of the depth of emotion and plot in the biblical narrative, but also in the lives of those sitting in the pew. I was reminded that reading fiction often helps us to discover the reality before us."

Jared Wortman, Durham, North Carolina

"This exercise reminded me of the power of communication that we see in good stories. I read a memorable novel that captured my attention; maintained my interest with plot twists, engaging dialogue, colorful characters, and mounting suspense; and concluded with a resolution that surprised and satisfied. This caused me to deliberately include these aspects—or at least some of them—in my upcoming sermon. Also, it reminded me to lay aside the commentaries from time to time to read good fiction. I know this practice will make me a better communicator."

Greg Robbins, Heath, Ohio

RESOURCES FOR FURTHER STUDY

- *Novel Preaching: Tips From Top Writers on Crafting Creative Sermons*, by Alyce McKenzie (Westminster John Knox, 2010).
- *Lit!: A Christian Guide to Reading Books*, by Tony Reinke (Crossway, 2011).
- *The Homiletical Plot: The Sermon as Narrative Art Form*, exp. ed., by Eugene Lowry (Westminster John Knox, 2000).

- "Do the Tasks of Preaching and Writing Intersect?" by Arlyn Norris. Access at http://awakeatsunrise.com/?p=1070& utm_source=feedburner&utm_medium=feed&utm_cam paign=Feed%3A+AwakeAtSunrise+%28Awake+At+Su nrise%29.
- "Why Preachers Should Read Fiction," by A. Craig Troxel. Access at http://www.opc.org/os.html?article_id=37.

Critique a Video of Yourself

Each autumn weekend, football teams crash helmets, pop pads, throw blocks, and celebrate touchdowns. Then, just hours after their stadiums empty, coaches plant themselves in front of screens to pore over game film. By afternoon of the next day, they bring their players into the screening rooms, as well. Frame by frame, they analyze their teams' performances. Who missed that block? What play would have better exploited the defense's weakness? How did the opponent's wide receiver elude our cornerbacks, and why was our safety out of position? What did we do well? Which blocks freed our running back to score the touchdown? Which defensive scheme best stopped our opponent's passing game? What tactics created success in our punt returns?

The film tells the story. Athletes who block for tailbacks, shoot jump shots, swim the backstroke, swing the bat, and flip around the parallel bars all analyze videos of their performances for the same reason—they want to improve. The video screen reveals their strengths and weaknesses and helps set an agenda for practice.

Likewise, preachers can improve their craft by watching videos of their sermons. Such videos reveal our strengths and weaknesses and provide a basis for our plans for improvement.

THE EXERCISE

1. Arrange for someone with a video camera to record your upcoming sermon.
2. Design a Self-Evaluation Form that will help you evaluate the sermon video. While developing the form, reflect on what previous exercises in this book revealed about your preaching—what particular aspects of your sermon content and delivery need improvement. See a suggested form on the next page.
3. View your sermon video, using your Self-Evaluation Form to analyze the message's content and delivery.
4. Based on your evaluation, choose three aspects of your preaching that need improvement. Consider how you can improve in these areas (previous chapters in this book may help). Often, we can improve an area of weakness by focusing on its opposite. For example, if the video reveals that you mumble, focus on enunciation. Or, if the video reveals a tendency to pace, focus on remaining in one spot for two minutes before you move.
5. After you preach your next sermon, evaluate it with particular regard for the three areas you worked to improve. You might video record this second sermon, also, or you might just ask a few trusted friends to provide feedback about your three areas of focus.

ADDITIONAL SUGGESTIONS

- Complete this exercise once a month for a few months and track your progress.
- Wait a couple weeks after the video is recorded to watch it. After a couple weeks have passed, you will not be as intimately involved with the sermon and can evaluate it more objectively.
- Ask a preaching friend or two to watch your sermon. You might give them the same evaluation form you used. Then, buy them lunch and let them share their thoughts about the sermon.
- Video yourself preaching the sermon before you present it to your congregation. This will help you make adjustments in the content and delivery prior to the preaching event.

EXAMPLE SELF-EVALUATION FORM

CONTENT

1. The introduction captured listeners' attention.	1 2 3 4 5
2. The introduction raised a compelling need or question.	1 2 3 4 5
3. The introduction flowed smoothly into the body of the sermon.	1 2 3 4 5
4. The sermon gave adequate explanation of biblical truth.	1 2 3 4 5
5. The sermon focused on a single, dominant idea ("thesis").	1 2 3 4 5
6. The major segments of the sermon related to the thesis.	1 2 3 4 5
7. Listeners understood the logic and flow of the sermon.	1 2 3 4 5
8. The sermon transitioned smoothly between main segments.	1 2 3 4 5
9. The conclusion brought the sermon to a challenging climax.	1 2 3 4 5

RELEVANCE

10. The sermon included an illustration for each major truth.	1 2 3 4 5
11. The sermon adequately answered the "so what?".	1 2 3 4 5
12. The sermon exposed listeners to God's glory.	1 2 3 4 5
13. The sermon helped listeners to learn biblical truth.	1 2 3 4 5
14. The sermon challenged listeners to live more faithfully.	1 2 3 4 5
15. The sermon equipped listeners to live more faithfully.	1 2 3 4 5
16. The sermon encouraged listeners to live more faithfully.	1 2 3 4 5

DELIVERY: VERBAL

17. My voice had appropriate variety in pitch.	1 2 3 4 5
18. My voice had appropriate variety in volume.	1 2 3 4 5
19. My voice had appropriate variety in pace.	1 2 3 4 5
20. I paused between main ideas and to let listeners contemplate points.	1 2 3 4 5
21. I enunciated clearly.	1 2 3 4 5
22. My volume remained strong at the ends of words and sentences.	1 2 3 4 5
23. I spoke with the same manner with which I converse with friends.	1 2 3 4 5

DELIVERY: NONVERBAL

24. I looked at my listeners more than I looked at my notes.	1 2 3 4 5
25. My gestures appeared natural.	1 2 3 4 5
26. My movements helped and did not distract from the message.	1 2 3 4 5
27. I appeared believable.	1 2 3 4 5
28. I appeared passionate.	1 2 3 4 5
29. I appeared humble.	1 2 3 4 5
30. I appeared authentic.	1 2 3 4 5

31. What verbal "ticks" do I need to watch for ("um," "you know," "like," or other words or phrases that I tend to overuse)?

32. What nonverbal "ticks" to do I need to watch for (pacing, rocking, scratching behind an ear, or other gestures that I overuse)? HINT: Watch video in fast-forward.

33. Was this sermon more or less effective than usual? Why?

34. If I could preach this sermon again, what would I do differently?

"I TRIED IT"

"I completed this exercise in three steps. First, I watched myself on video only, with the sound turned off. Then, I closed my eyes and listened to my sermon. Third, I watched the video along with sound. This three-step approach allows for a more insightful, concentrated analysis—especially when comparing two sermons. In addition to noting areas that need improvement, be sure to document all that you are doing well and build from those strengths. This exercise should produce positive results. It did for me!"

Steve Page, Bristol, Tennessee

"The biggest lesson I learned from this exercise is that the best place to evaluate my sermon is not from behind the pulpit. When you are preaching, you focus on the message. It is not the best time to evaluate yourself because you simply can't hear and see what your audience does. Watching the video puts you in the place of your audience. If you never do this exercise, you will never know how you come across from the stage."

Kraig Bishop, Winchester, Virginia

"The first time I watched my sermon video, I saw many areas that needed improvement. When I watched it a second time, though, several days later, I saw many things I had done well. My church lacks a great deal in the way of sound technology, so I have to remain behind a large wooden pulpit—though I'd like to move more, it's impossible in my circumstances. I will continue to work on other aspects of my content and delivery, however, and I will certainly repeat this worthwhile exercise."

Jim Lawler, Rushville, Indiana

RESOURCES FOR FURTHER STUDY

- *Delivering the Sermon: Voice, Body, and Animation in Proclamation* (Elements of Preaching), by Teresa Fry Brown (Fortress Press, 2008).
- "How to Evaluate Your Sermons," by Joel Beeke. Access at http://katekomen.gpts.edu/2011/07/how-to-evaluate-your-sermons.html.

- "Practice Makes ...?", by Peter Mead. Access at http://biblicalpreaching.net/2009/12/10/practice-makes.
- "Sermon Evaluation Sample." Access at http://www.bettersermons.org/article.php?id=267.

Bonus Exercises

- *Incorporate Testimony:* People connect well with other people's stories. While various types of sermon illustrations work—such as analogies, metaphors, statistics, or quotes—the story of a living and breathing person usually makes the most impact. This impact magnifies when a person tells his or her own story. In an upcoming sermon, either insert some testimony of your own, describing an experience from your life when God worked, or invite a church member to share something from his or her experience that relates to your sermon. If the person is nervous to give the testimony live, you might video the testimony, allowing for a few "takes" and minimizing the nervousness connected with public speaking.

- *Fashion Compelling Titles:* Publishers, film producers, and magazine editors give careful attention to titles. The right title will grab the attention of a potential audience, and compel them to buy the book, watch the film, or pick up the magazine. Conversely, a bland title will cause even the most entertaining of productions to flounder because of a lack of an audience. Particularly if you publish your sermon titles in a newsletter or on a website, they merit careful attention. For your upcoming five to ten sermons, therefore, develop titles that capture interest by touching on needs people feel or questions that trouble them. For ideas, you might visit a website like www.sermoncentral.com, browse through sermon titles, and ask yourself, "If I was not a preacher or Bible scholar, which of these titles would most piqué my interest?

- *Think Apologetically:* We often assume our listeners believe in God, and that they believe in the God of the Bible. We assume they view the Bible as true and authoritative. What if someone wanders into your worship center who does not share these convictions? What statements in your sermon will cause these listeners to shake their heads, or make them want to raise their hands and say, "Prove it, Preacher, because I'm just not buying it"? To identify these elements of your sermon, print it with a wide right margin, then read through it with a pen in hand. Play the devil's advocate, writing questions in the margin that a skeptic might ask. After you write questions throughout the sermon, go back and consider how you would respond to each. Choose at least two or three of these questions and answers to incorporate into the sermon.

- *Seek Illustrations Outside:* I recall hearing this sermon illustration several years ago, during a sermon on perseverance: "As I walked across the church yard this morning, I couldn't help but notice the tree next to the drive. As autumn has progressed, all the leaves have fallen from this tree—all the leaves, that is, except one. As I watched that one leaf clutching to a branch in this morning's breeze, I couldn't help but wonder, what makes one leaf hang on when all the others fall away? What makes one persevere when all the others give up?" A simple walk outside can reveal numerous, similar illustrations. During preparations for an upcoming sermon, walk away from the computer screen or the legal pad and see what truths of God are illustrated in the world outside your office. What do you see in flowers, trees, and shadows? Perhaps you'll see children playing, adults jogging, or a hummingbird darting to and fro. Observe colors, listen for nature's orchestration, and consider the Creator. What do you see, hear, or smell that might illustrate a point in your upcoming sermon?

- *Show Websites:* We hope that our sermons will equip listeners to respond to the truths we preach. With only thirty minutes to preach, however, time for such equipping can prove elusive. We can maximize our time by pointing our listeners toward resources they can utilize during the week that will equip them to apply what they've learned. We can find many such resources online. And, if we have the technology available, we can show our listeners helpful websites during the sermon. If an upcoming sermon addresses financial stewardship, for example, you might show listeners websites that provide biblical financial advice and tools. Similar websites exist about prayer, evangelism, Bible reading, worship, and family issues. For an upcoming sermon, show listeners two or three websites that will equip them to apply what they have learned.

- *Read Classic Preachers:* Preachers of past generations gave greater attention to the craft of writing sermons than many preachers give today. Their sermons, therefore, provide marvelous examples of wordsmithing, sermon construction and flow, illustrations, applications, and an awareness of context. Set aside an hour to read sermons by classic preachers. If you have books on your shelf of such sermons, feel free to use them. Or, simple Internet searches will reveal numerous sermons by such masters as Charles Spurgeon, A. W. Tozer, James S. Stewart, George Whitefield, Phillips Brooks, and John Henry Jowett. As you read, note what you feel made these preachers effective.

- *Peruse the Newspaper:* Many of our listeners view the church worship center as a refuge from the world in which they live the other six days of the week. They need preachers who can connect the worship and instruction of the worship center with the realities of life in the outside world. To stay aware of the world in which your listeners live, spend at least one hour reading the local newspaper. Pay particular attention to stories about matters that will affect those who hear your sermons, such as the local economy, politics, schools, tragedies, and celebrations. Then, consider how your upcoming sermon should connect with your listeners as they live in the community described in the newspaper.